That Men May Understand

That Men May Understand

AN AMERICAN IN THE LONG ARMISTICE

BY

Harold Rugg

DOUBLEDAY, DORAN AND CO., INC.

NEW YORK   1941

PRINTED AT THE *Country Life Press*, GARDEN CITY, N. Y., U. S. A.

To
LOUISE RUGG
and
HARALD RUGG

ACKNOWLEDGMENTS

AS I SEND THIS BOOK TO PRESS a word of indebtedness to persons who have helped to make it possible. In the truest sense nothing short of the total book, from the page inscribed to my wife to the enumeration of the other creative Americans who helped me to understand, can record even approximately my deep sense of obligation to others. In addition to these many personal references, however, I should like to express my gratitude to my research and editorial assistants, Ruth LaVoy and Marvin Krueger, who have contributed so much in the way of ideas and form to the actual construction of the book; to Burdette R. Buckingham and Henry Hilton for reading the manuscript and making many helpful suggestions for its improvement; to Ginn and Company for permission to reprint Chapter XXIV of *Citizenship and Civic Affairs* and the inscription page of *American Life and the School Curriculum*, and to The John Day Company for permission to reprint the inscription page of *The Great Technology*; to Dr T. H. P. Sailer of Englewood and his neighbors, who supplied me with the data for Chapter II and read and criticized the chapter in manuscript form; to Dr J. M. Gambrill, who made available his elaborate file of materials on the period of witch-hunting from 1921 to 1926; to Maurice R. Robinson, founder and editor of *Scholastic*, and his editorial associates, particularly Kenneth M. Gould, for data and critical suggestions with special reference to the merchants of conflict, and to my publishers, Messrs Malcolm Johnson and John M. McK. Woodburn particularly, who made it possible for me to present my statement to the American people at this time.

Contents

BEFORE YOU READ THIS BOOK

THE FUNCTION of this book and the events which brought it into being are stated explicitly in the book itself, especially in the first few chapters. Friendly critics who have read the manuscript and noted its necessary absorption in matters of controversy have urged that I make clear at the very beginning where I stand on several insistent issues of our times. A statement of position shall, therefore, be my foreword.

I BELIEVE

I subscribe with profound admiration and deep loyalty to the historic American version of the democratic way of life, our greatest resource and possession. In essence it is sovereign personalities binding themselves together in that confederation known as society. Because in America it is a union which our people have created themselves, it gives greatest promise of guaranteeing personal sovereignty.

The American democratic outlook, I hold, is man-centered—it respects the dignity and worth of each personality, prizes human life above all things, values integrity, respect, tolerance and fair play, and it seeks to guarantee equal justice to all men. In these respects it differs sharply from the totalitarian—Communist, Nazi or Fascist—concept that the human being is a mere instrument of the state.

I believe that within the limits of Nature's bounty man is also master of his destiny. He is not poured into a rigid social matrix. Given the sculptural materials of social history, man as master craftsman carves out his own fortune. The day-by-day events which compound themselves into slow-moving glaciers of social trend and then precipitately become speeding avalanches are *human* events, and I believe, therefore, that men can give them intelligent direction.

It follows that I am a devotee of "progress." I believe that by taking thought man can build a better world in which to live. He has already done so in many areas—witness the doubling of the length of life, the drastic reduction of pain and fatigue, the flowering of literacy, the lengthening of the radius of intellectual communication and human sympathy, the maturing of the creative act and the spread of esthetic appreciation. I believe, then, that the American way of progress is the way of unrestricted play of intelligence upon all of the problems and difficulties of our people. Moreover, I believe that the social-economic changes and reforms necessary in this country can be accomplished and should be accomplished under the American Constitution and the present framework of our government. But solutions will come, I believe also, only through thorough and long-time study and design by competent experts in economic, political and social affairs; our truly grave problems will not be solved by makeshift panaceas.

Twenty years of study of American life have made me

an optimist with respect to its potentialities; an optimist, however, by documentation and not by faith alone. I am convinced that our people stand today at the verge of a great culture, the first on the time line of history capable of bringing forth a civilization of abundance, of tolerance and of beauty. I see the American problem as that of realizing this great civilization. We have, I am convinced, all the makings—the indispensable natural resources, the democratic tradition, the scientist-engineers, to design a fine material civilization, the capable technicians to operate it and the artists to guarantee its beauty. Our culture, I say, is potentially a great one because, having invented efficient prime movers, man need no longer be a cringing slave of nature; because the successful union of democracy and technology is possible, and because the scientific method can at last be applied to the man-man relationships as well as to the man-thing relationships.

I believe, on the other hand, that our historic American way of life is in grave danger: first, because of the conquering lust of the mad dictators of Eurasia; second, because of growing skepticism concerning the validity of democracy in the minds of our more credulous citizens, and third, because of a few false patriots in our midst who, while mouthing the slogans of Americanism, stamp on the Bill of Rights, destroy tolerant discussion of issues, bear false witness and defame the characters and reputations of other Americans who are sincerely striving to honor and protect the democratic process. I believe that the menace of the Eurasian dictatorships compels our people to marshal all of their resources to defend American democracy, even if that leads to involvement in war.

I am convinced that the supreme problem that torments men's souls today is the redefinition of the concept of freedom to fit the changing conditions of our times. (In this book I name it the "crux.") The present nationwide attack on education makes clear that our people must decide how they wish the application of freedom to economic enterprise interpreted in the schools. Confronted as we are by a social impasse in which the baffled supporters of private and social enterprise stand at loggerheads, the reconciliation of the conflict between the "I" traits and the "We" traits in human beings must be fouund. Briefly, my own position is this:

I believe in private enterprise. But I believe in social enterprise too. I believe we should leave the play of individual initiative as free as possible and in as many areas of life as human ingenuity can contrive. The spirit of free enterprise was, I think, the chief psychological factor in the successful building of the world's highest standard of living, and I am confident that it can still play an important part in the solution of the difficult social-economic problems ahead. But in a democratic society each man's freedoms stop where his neighbors' begin, and in one as interdependent as ours there are many possibilities of encroachment. Our people found, as their simple agrarian civilization transformed into a complex industrial one, that they had to institute various kinds of regulative controls on individuals' freedoms. Moreover, they were compelled to parallel private enterprise with an increasing amount of social enterprise. In doing so they were really redefining freedom in economic and social life. The need for clarification of the proper bounds of freedom, I believe, poses the creative ordeal of the Americans in the twentieth century. It is to maintain their Bill of Rights but also to formulate a Bill of Duties—both of which will give energy to our people and guide them in a strange new world. I repeat, I believe in social enterprise as well as in private enterprise and hold that the one true test to distinguish which shall be private and which social is the public good, the general social welfare, not the aggrandizement of individuals.

There is no royal road into the new epoch, at the crossroads before which we now stand; there is only the hard way of education and especially of the building of consent among the people. In this process the school can and must provide real leadership. Through the study of society and its problems the school must devote itself to the development of sensitive, clearheaded, fearless and confident young men and women who understand American life as it is actually lived and are determined to make it a magnificent civilization for themselves and their children. To this end the life and program of the school must be designed directly from the culture of the people, not from a classics-intrenched curriculum. Now is the time to build not a subject-centered school but a truly society-centered as well as a child-centered one.

I believe one sure psychological foundation of government by the consent of the governed is understanding. *That men may understand* has been a guiding purpose in all of my work, for I recognized that the only hope of solving the American problem lies in the education of a large body of citizens who understand its factors and who are concerned to do something about them by building a program of action.

I believe, moreover, that to guarantee maximum understanding, the very foundation of education must be the study of the actual problems and controversial issues of our people. There is no way by which the democratic principle of consent can be carried on other than that of the parliamentary discussion of issues. But consent based upon knowledge of only one aspect or side of a problem, upon the avoidance of controversy, is a travesty of both knowledge and democracy. To keep issues out of the school, therefore, is to keep thought out of it; it is to keep life out of it. Moreover, democracy cannot be understood except as it is lived. Our young people and their elders must practice it in the family, in school, in community organizations—everywhere. To study government effectively they must take part in governing. Obviously they can do this most realistically in the government of their own group life.

I believe that the task of solving the problems of the economic-political system, insistent though those are, should not monopolize all of our energies. I think we should work vigorously at the job of creating a society in which each individual can live as a person, in which each can state himself for his own soul's sake. I am confident that the struggle of men to understand and describe the creative process and their success in fusing technological efficiency with the subtle principles of esthetics indicate that both tasks will be accomplished. Not only has man succeeded in designing and building nations of communities and operated economic systems of complexity and power; in addition he has made a portrait of himself and his culture in a wealth of materials and media—in community design, architecture, literature, music, painting, dance and the theater. Thus he has worked both as scientist-engineer and as artist and, working as such, has brought into play two methods of thought and work —the method of science or experimental inquiry and the method of organic awareness, traditionally but inadequately named "intuition." It is important to recognize that both methods, while different and serving unique functions in the creative process, are indispensable in solving our present problems.

Of supreme importance is it that we explore and cultivate the creative act. Because of the creative ordeal which man has endured during modern times, we already know much of the constituents of the creative process—expression, in-

digenousness, organic form, functionality, technical competence. In our short three-hundred-year culture history our
people have been struggling through the three great stages
of that ordeal: (1) a two-century-long period during which
cultural norms were largely imported from Britain and
Europe, (2) a confused transitional period of rebellion
against the alien norms, with the emergence of partially
indigenous improvisations of new forms of expression,
(3) a third and more profound stage of development—a
mature regime of original design and competence of statement. This third stage will have arrived for America when
a large body of our people are truly living creative lives,
when a psychological climate is hospitable to creative effort
and appreciation and when our creative workers on the
social frontier will have succeeded in producing that abundant life for all which is now potentially possible.

HAROLD RUGG

Teachers College
Columbia University
February 7, 1941

AMERICA IN MINIATURE

Chapter I

"I HAVEN'T READ THE BOOKS, BUT——!"

FIERY CROSS FAILS TO SCARE
PASTOR IN BOOK DISPUTE

MINISTER DENOUNCES RED HUNT IN WHICH
SCHOOLBOOKS WENT INTO FURNACE

Books on civics and social science . . . have split
this little western Ohio town wide open in a row
over the "teaching of Communism." The rural Red
hunt . . . has resulted in: explosion of a dynamite
charge and the burning of a fiery cross in front of
the home of ————, school board president. . . .
Dramatic burning of a dozen library schoolbooks in
the school furnace. . . . The books . . . seized at a
board meeting the other night and shoved in the furnace were mostly those in the social-science series
by Harold Rugg. . . .[1]

NINETEEN-FORTY seems to me now to have been the most
clarifying year in my long search for understanding. It was
a year of book burnings and book bannings. A year of nationwide attacks on American teachers and behind-the-
scene attempts by minorities to defeat liberal education. A
year of replies and denials by eminent American educators.
A year of public hearings of charges and countercharges
and of dramatic town meetings in which citizens, teachers
and youth speak out in righteous indignation against self-
appointed censors of the schools.

★   ★   ★

[1]The Cleveland *Press*, April 9, 1940, reporting the burning of the Rugg
social-science books in Bradner, O.

Book burnings in 1940? Yes! And not merely in little towns like Bradner, O.; in bustling cities as well they have been proposed, even by members of boards of education:

A member of the Board of Education's teacher committee proposed today that "a bonfire be made" of the 180 Rugg social-science textbooks, formerly used in local schools, and said she would recommend such motion at the board's next meeting.[2]

From the country's third largest city came the most drastic denial of the very basis of democracy—namely tolerant understanding. A national officer of a patriotic organization announced her opposition to books that educated young people to think:

Mrs Ellwood J. Turner, corresponding secretary of the Daughters of Colonial Wars, yesterday urged that a social-science textbook be banned from Philadelphia schools because it "is very, very un-American." The book . . . was written by Dr Harold Rugg, professor of education at Columbia University. The book, she said, "tried to give the child an unbiased viewpoint instead of teaching him real Americanism. . . . All the old histories taught my country, right or wrong. That's the point of view we want our children to adopt. We can't afford to teach them to be unbiased and let them make up their minds."[3]

A Hearst newspaper in an Eastern city, reporting a public hearing of charges against Harold Rugg and his books, announced this hysterical outburst:

"There sits the ringmaster of the fifth columnists in America, financed by the Russian government," shouted the captain, pointing his finger at Dr Rugg. "I want you people to look at him."

[2]Binghamton (New York) *Press*, April 18, 1940.
[3]Philadelphia *Record*, February 20, 1940.

And in Texas an editor, accepting the truth of unproved charges of un-Americanism, joined in the witch-hunt:

The interest aroused in school textbooks which belittle and malign America is bearing fruit. A writer in the Pampa [Texas] *News*, after quoting statements made by the editor of *Forbes*, says: "Certainly the man who advocates the Rugg books being taught in the American schools does not believe in the American system; he does not believe in free enterprise; he believes in a form of bureaucratic control. The most important thing in our land is the proper education of our children. If there is anything that miseducates them as to American principles, it is the Harold Rugg textbooks."[4]

The most outstanding thing about it all is the suddenness of the reversal in the public mood. A year and a half ago I returned from a six months' nationwide survey of creative work and public opinion. Twenty thousand miles I traveled from coast to coast and from Canada to Mexico. I was in scores of communities—yet not a whisper of such opposition did I encounter. There was no witch-hunting of liberals; there were no attacks upon "the books."

On the contrary, I came home happy and encouraged over the vast amount of creative work I saw and with citizens' approval of the work my associates and I were doing. I felt that twenty years of my own work were coming to a rich fruition.

That was a year and a half ago. But in the year 1940 "the Rugg books" (or just "Rugg") were the topic of serious discussion at fashionable dinner parties, Rotary, Kiwanis and other luncheon clubs, parent-teacher and other public meetings. Eight to ten million Americans talked about them over the breakfast, luncheon or dinner table, heard about them over the radio, read about them in the newspapers. Hundreds of editorials took sides pro and con. They were the subject of magazine articles. Patriotic societies and various social organizations resolved against them; liberal organizations broadcast resolutions supporting them.

On the one hand, the books were denounced as "subversive" . . . "un-American." It was said that they "undermine patriotism" . . . "twit the Founding Fathers" . . . "have an alien ideology" . . . "plan to substitute a new social order for our American government" . . . "would regiment private enterprise" . . . "debunk our great heroes of the past."

On the other hand, they were defended by teachers and citizens because they "teach American life as it is actually lived" . . . because "an unprejudiced reader can read the books with a great deal of profit and pleasure" . . . because "Rugg is a practical visionary and hopes to bring about a better United States by making this generation of children, the leaders of our nation tomorrow, more analytical and better informed citizens than we are" . . . because "one who has studied under Rugg cannot fail to be impressed by his sincerity and vision of an ever greater and happier United States."

★   ★   ★

For many months all my writing of new materials for young people has been interrupted. Most of my energy has been spent writing denials of false charges, preparing statements of what I do and do not believe, riding trains to meet attacks in every section of the country, appearing at "heresy" trials, debating patrioteers in community meetings, speaking at civic clubs. Each of these meetings has been a revelation in understanding; each is America in miniature.

Take the recent public hearings. The American people, a true cross section, are always there and they speak—their moods if not their minds. Three hundred, four hundred, five hundred citizens or more, old and young, men and women, lawyers and housewives, bankers and farmers, farm wives and clubwomen, teachers and professors, ministers and social workers, D.A.R.s, the Klan, war veterans and their "Auxiliaries." The national press is sure to be there—AP and UP—and the local press.

The hearings open according to formula. A representative for a patriotic organization brings the charges—often an ex-captain, an ex-major or even a retired major general. According to formula also are the charges. For example: I am unfitted "to write textbooks for our children" because I was "at one time of the opinion that a little group of Communists in Moscow . . . was setting the world's greatest example of social reform." One such person charged that I was engaged in the "League of Independent Political Action . . . Communist front. . . . All of its officers are Socialists . . . calling for a repeal of any law that would control subversive groups in America . . . membership in that group would not fit a man to write textbooks for our children."

Some feel sure that they can document their case. "This man," said one of them, pointing to me sitting at one side, watched and watching while the curious meeting went on, "is listed in *The Red Network. The Daily Worker,* the Communist paper, quotes him favorably." To prove it he held up the book, "published" he said, "by Mrs Elizabeth Dilling, a very rich woman who spent a fortune and her life in getting together information on people whom she considered to be in a trend to the left." He quoted nine lines about the Communist Youth Association of Russia which I had included in a five-page speech on "World Youth Movements" given at the new York *Herald Tribune's* 1933 conference. I had spoken with Mrs Eleanor Roosevelt and Colonel Henry Breckenridge. My brief reference to Russia had followed an elaborate description of "the original youth movements [which were] a world-wide expression among awakening youth of the idea that only by inner self-education can a society of fine, co-operating individuals be produced."[5] Time after time since 1934 Mrs Dilling's book has been quoted against me.

But a rebuttal always follows. A supporter rises and reminds the audience of the true nature of *The Red Network* and its author. In the case of one such meeting a local citizen had prepared a mimeographed analysis of Mrs Dilling, her book and her activities. He rose and spoke: "It is true that Doctor Rugg is mentioned in *The Red Network*, but," he added, "that should be considered a compliment, because hundreds of the most distinguished and loyal Americans included are also charged by Mrs Dilling with being 'red,' or at least 'pink.' "

At another meeting a patrioteer jumped up, holding high a copy of *The Daily Worker.* "You write for this paper!"

"I have never written one line for *The Daily Worker* in my life or authorized anyone else to do so in my name."

"*Friday* magazine is one of your organs!" He was now holding up two copies of *Friday.*

"I have never written a line for it, in fact, must confess that I have never even read an issue clear through."

"Well, they like you! They say good things about you!" At that several in that audience laughed *with* me.

[5]New York *Herald Tribune. This Crisis in History,* p. 54. Third Annual Women's Conference on Current Problems. 1933.

At the same meeting a man who had known me twenty years rose to the defense. "Is Doctor Rugg a Socialist or a Communist?" Neither, he said emphatically. Then he went on to recite my nine-generation-long ancestry in New England, telling of my great-great-grandfather Asa's fighting at Lexington and Concord in 1775 and of the participation of other ancestors and relatives in every war since. He mentioned my cousin—the eminent chief justice of the Massachusetts Supreme Court. Simply and directly he told how when still a youth I had been a weaver in a New England textile mill, getting firsthand an understanding of industrialism and building an interest in "the underdog." He spoke of my later engineering training and experience which, he said, helped prepare me especially for the task of describing industrial civilization for young people. He sketched briefly the twenty-year story of the books, the research involved in making them, how they came to be written and used and how ten thousand teachers had taught them for eleven years without opposition from a single one.

But the real animus back of the charges is generally against anything "progressive," particularly, in my case, the Progressive Education Association. One vehement patrioteer violently attacked the association, saying that its purpose is "to prevent patriotic exercises in school—you might become Americanized . . . to prevent the flag from flying on school grounds . . . and to take chapel exercises out of school. That's the background of philosophy that doesn't T up with anything I know of Americanism."

One sits aghast at such ridiculous statements concerning the aims of the Progressive Education Association—the outcome of a half century of hard and intelligent work at the improvement of education by scientists as well as artist-teachers. But the applause that frequently greets denunciations of this kind is sufficient warning of the long road yet to be traveled before the people generally will come to understand what we are doing for democracy and the youth of America.

★   ★   ★

Some of these meetings are revealing adventures into the state of the American mind under the stress and strain of social hysteria. One day last year I sat for five hours with the principals in such a drama. Throughout much of the time the audience room was a combination of Billy Sunday tabernacle of evangelism and political rally.

A huge middle-aged woman stood up, eyes staring from one side to another, her shrill voice almost shrieking:[6]

"I am here, not thinking that I was going to be at all, but I am and I want to say just a few words. Righteousness, good government, good homes and God—God most of all—Christ is on trial today."

Higher and higher her voice rose; round her arms waved; she turned from side to side. The books must be bad. She hadn't read them, but—she was worried about the irreligion of the times, especially about our homes. "You can't take the youth of our land and give them this awful stuff and have them come out safe and sound for God and righteousness. Are our homes falling down? Where are the altars in the homes?"

Leaning forward and swaying from left to right, she continued, "I'm saying that this is a banner day for righteousness if the people would turn back to God. . . . Wake

[6]In this instance and in a few others we had a stenographer make a verbatim record of what was said.

up America and turn back to God! And you will see things go forward."

As she sat down hands were clapping all over the room. "Half of them?" I thought. "Yes—three quarters." That prosperous, scholarly looking man across the room applauded her too. I noticed that he always applauded the evangelists and patrioteers alike. He looked like a college professor or a judge, but in spite of his prosperous appearance there was something sinister about him. He came alone, sat alone, never smiled or spoke to anyone. I caught him looking at me from time to time with a kind of cold appraisal. Who . . . what . . . was he? I should like to have found out, but he left quickly and alone at the close of the afternoon.

At the same meeting a quiet, sensitive woman on the opposite side of the room sat listening through it all, rarely smiling, never applauding, writing occasionally. Who . . . what . . . was she? I should like to have talked with her, too, but hours later, when it was over, she disappeared. Too bad.

At one of the meetings a round-faced, slick-haired youngster of twenty, who had been walking restlessly up and down the aisle, got the floor. He bent down, knees almost touching the floor; he jumped up, waving his arms and shouting:

"If you let these books go in and if what I've heard is true, it 'll damn the souls of the men, women and children of our state. I'm urging you not to let any book go in that is questionable as to whether that book is holding up God or not. . . . And I thank God that I don't have Communism taught to me, and I don't want it taught to any innocent child in this state."

He, too, got a big hand. He seemed almost beside himself—
yet I suspected he was putting on an act. He ran up and
down the aisle again.

"America and Communism are as far apart as the North and
South poles, and if you let some man or some group bring a
book in that will knock God completely out of the picture you
have made an error you will never get over."

The experiences and scenes at many of these meetings
seem incredible. Many times I wondered whether I was
attending forums of discussion or Wednesday-evening tes-
timony meetings of Holy Rollers. My colleagues in education and I would look at each other and shake our heads.
"We've got a job on our hands." And this kind of thing
was happening all over America.

★   ★   ★

The most astounding fact revealed in most of the meetings was that almost nobody had read the Rugg books.
Person after person started out with the same phrase: "I
haven't read the books, but——"

"I haven't read the books, but—I have heard of the author, and no good about him."

"I haven't read the books, but—he's from Columbia, and
that's enough." . . . "I hear that chapel isn't required any
more in the universities like Columbia."

"I haven't read the books, but—my brother says the
schools and colleges are filled with Communists."

Over and over again it came: "I haven't read the books,
but," in essence, "they are bad!" from young and old, men
and women alike.

★   ★   ★

Time after time, sitting on the side lines, I commented
to myself: Just what is back of all this? There is always a

dangerous tension in the room . . . not of violence—not the least suggestion of that; yet tension is there. I am convinced it is strain born of fear. The people are afraid—afraid of Communism . . . afraid of fifth columnists . . . afraid of Hitler . . . afraid of the "parasites across the ocean" . . . afraid of the breakdown of their old loyalties.

But in these meetings the central note of the American way has always been sounded by the chairmen: "All shall be heard." These were real hearings attended by garden-variety Americans, a true cross section of American society, revealing an accurate measure of our national temper.

After the charges, as I have said, the rebuttal always comes. People rise in support of the democratic method, tolerance and the discussion of all sides of all issues in the schools. Parents, teachers and administrators, who have not only read the books but actually used them with young people, stand to speak in their defense. I remember well the recent town meeting in Manhasset, New York, where at the behest of a patriotic organization the books had been summarily banned by a board member. I asked how long the books had been used there.

"Ten years," came the emphatic answer.

"No objection from parents, teachers or other citizens?"

"Not one!" was the laconic reply.

"No objection from the students?"

"Not one!"

High-school students, filling the front row as usual, and nearly bursting with indignation, rose and turned on their elders in the large audience. "We protest against this business! Why didn't you come to us? We've studied these books. Look at us! Do we talk or act like Communists? Has studying the Rugg books harmed us? Not a bit! We've been taught to understand our country, to love it and to respect its leaders, not to pour slime on it!"

Time after time young America has made itself heard.

A young student who studied the Rugg books when he was in the Englewood Junior High School wrote:

I have watched with interest the development in the anti-Rugg campaign which has raged in Englewood and elsewhere for the last several months. It has been my conviction that one who has actually studied from Mr Rugg's textbooks should voice his opinions on the matter. It is with this purpose that I write, having used the Rugg books for two years in the junior high school.

In those two years I have found nothing in the books that smacked of un-American tendencies. If anything, I acquired a greater understanding and respect for the principles for which our country stands. I learned much which has given me the ability to see behind the fanfare and superficiality of certain political practices and other issues for which American youth must be educated. I am certain that my views are shared by the great majority of my fellow students who have studied from the books.[7]

College professors of history and the other social sciences have risen at meetings and defended my thesis that we must build understanding of social change, that we dare not keep any important part of American life out of the schools. Shall controversial issues be discussed? Of course! they answer. There is no other channel by which education in thinking can be carried on. At one such meeting a young

[7]Eric A. Jensen, in "Statements Regarding the Use of the Rugg Series of Social-Science Texts in the Englewood School System." Englewood, N.J., May, 1940.

social-science instructor said the startling changes of today were

"going to continue. There is not anything in the world that can stop them. The question is: Can we make the change patiently, intelligently and peacefully; can we be tolerant and sympathetic? Can we look at our worst enemies and find out what they think? Can we pick out those things which are good and eliminate those things which are bad?"

Another said:

"Minority and majority groups alike are on trial in this thing today. The very right of our citizens to bring charges of this sort represents the right to free speech. But it's our citizenry that is on trial; Doctor Rugg is not on trial. We're fighting for free and tolerant education in our state. I'm fighting for a chance for my child to be taught freely and honestly."

At the meetings I have attended I have always been asked to speak. I have seen a changing mood developing among the people. Hostility slowly gives way to a mild interest, even to tolerance and some new understanding. The people get so much out of their systems. They become used to seeing me there. They are ready to listen to my side. I try to clear up their doubts and questions, taking up, one by one, the charges that have been made against me and my books there and in other places. I remind them that I heartily approve the very kind of free and open discussion that they have been conducting. It's what I advocate, write and teach, I tell them. It is the American way in action. It is the way of "town meeting," which at the age of eight I attended in my ancestral Massachusetts village. The proceedings reveal the same elements of democratic action: face-to-face discussion . . . talking it out . . . all questions and problems in the open.

Bring controversial issues into the school? Of course, I say: "To keep issues out of the school is to keep life out of it." Some heads always shake a little at that—"Young minds shouldn't be tainted with problems"—I can almost read in their thoughts. Of course, I add, the problems must be within the understanding of the students.

My thesis, I always explain, is that all of American life must be brought into the school—not merely the magnificent achievements and gains; those, yes, but the deficiencies and losses as well. I point out that most of those who attack the Rugg books are people who, for one reason or another, do not want young people to understand all of American life as it is actually lived.

★   ★   ★

"That men may understand," I tell them, has been the drive back of all my work for twenty years. For two decades I have been trying in my books to blaze a clear path toward understanding for young people—understanding of the tremendous agelong changes and of the rapid changes in industrial society during our own times. We dare not, I insist, keep children in ignorance of these changes and of their hidden significance.

But the People Do Not Understand!

One night on the train, returning to New York after the most strenuous of these defense meetings, I lay wakeful in my berth. The whole drama of conflict kept passing in review—the many tense scenes of increasing censorship on the nationwide stage. I could see the present period of social hysteria and witch-hunting in the schools as the fifth of a series since the beginning of the Long Armistice in 1918. I could see two good and sufficient reasons for the present attacks: (1) the artificial creation of an incredible wave of suspicion and name calling which has swept across the entire country and (2) the soil of social unrest prepared for this by the coincidence of the eleventh and twelfth years of the Great Depression, with the coming of a critically important and bitter presidential campaign, and the frightening menace of war from conquering dictators. The consequence of this unprecedented coincidence is that "total crisis" looms just over our social horizon. The people generally have become jittery and credulous. Merchants of conflict prosper.

But, more important, I could see clearer than ever before that *the people generally do not understand;* they have not the slightest notion of what is back of it all. They must be informed, I kept thinking; they must be brought to understand the whole problem, for there is no other way to save democracy. But how could they be reached?

Perhaps by nothing short of years of adult education. Someone must bring out the charges—the twofold charges: first, those made against me and others who have been striving to bring American life into the schools and then, straight out, the charges we make against the perpetrators of these conflicts.

I turned on the light in my berth and took from my brief case O. K. Armstrong's "Treason in the Textbooks" article.[8] I studied the cartoons carefully—drawings showing teachers pouring slime on the Constitution and on religion! Here was the worst attack of all—and made against a million American teachers! Here was the work of a few persons using the instrumentality of a national organization—probably without the knowledge or approval of the membership—to destroy the fine creative things of education. And they call *me* subversive!

[8] See Chapter V, pp. 73-75.

I took out the analysis of the country-wide attacks on liberalism and progressiveness in American life that I had made in June 1940 and reread it. Now, six months later, I could see the destructive effects of the attacks being magnified by the more recent ones. What could be done about it? How could the people become informed?

More and more I became convinced that somebody, many somebodies, simply had to speak out, promptly and vigorously. I thought of John Philpot Curran's 1790 "Speech upon the Right of Election" from which the quotation has come: "Eternal vigilance is the price of liberty!" Never has vigilance been needed more than at this very moment!

I thought of William Lloyd Garrison and the Salutatory of Volume I, No. 1, of his *Liberator*, January 1, 1831:

I am in earnest. I will not equivocate; I will not excuse; I will not retreat a single inch, and I will be heard.

★   ★   ★

And then the picture rose before me of the great three-year battle for liberty that had raged around the schools in Englewood, N.J. Here was a real case study in democracy. Here were wide-awake citizens successfully beating off an un-American raid on their schools under the leadership of true American patriots—Dr T. H. P. Sailer, board members led by Mrs G. Kingsley Noble, several ministers, junior-high-school teachers, a tolerant and public-spirited newspaper editor and others. These citizens, several hundred of them, had lifted themselves by their own emotional and intellectual bootstraps and had gone into action against Bertie C. Forbes and his silent partner.

And they had won! Their counterattack is a new thrilling story in the annals of American democracy. They had preserved their liberties and the American democratic way in that fine community. And their method was the only possible one under the American tradition—public study and discussion!

To the story of Englewood, then:

Chapter II

ENGLEWOOD: A CASE STUDY IN DEMOCRACY

It is the common fate of the indolent to see their rights become a prey to the active. The condition upon which God hath given liberty to man is eternal vigilance; which condition if he break, servitude is at once the consequence of his crime and the punishment of his guilt.

(JOHN PHILPOT CURRAN, 1750–1817, *in his speech upon the right of election, 1790*)

RUGG, I am going to put you out of the Englewood schools, and after I do that I am going to start out through the country to put you and your crowd out of all American schools. That's the mission of my declining days."

This was Forbes's silent partner on the Englewood, N.J., Board of Education speaking. It was near the close of a four-hour luncheon at the Yale Club in March 1940 to which he had invited me with Roy Weed and Winton J. White, the superintendent of schools. And it was near the end of an interminable "collective monologue" on his part, to use my wife's phrase for such conversation.

The Rugg books had been used in Englewood for six years with approval by teachers, parents and children. But for three of these years this board member had been trying to put them out. His colleague, Bertie C. Forbes, was under public criticism for having refused to meet me[1] to talk out

[1]On the occasion of Forbes's first attack a mutual friend invited us at my request to have lunch and talk over our difficulties. He refused.

20

our problems face to face in the true American way. But this man[2] had finally decided to talk to me. I say *"to me"* deliberately. Our meeting was certainly no adventure in understanding for him. He made it perfectly clear that he had studied my work and had unearthed my whole nefarious plot. To prove it he opened the suitcaseful of my books which he had brought—my texts, the Workbooks of Directed Study, The Teacher's Guides and other material, including *The Great Technology*, which I said had nothing to do with the schoolbooks but which he insisted was the root of all the evil in them. He gloated over the "research" to which he had turned in his old age of retirement and leisure and for which he found he was admirably fitted.

His hatred toward what I believe and teach must have run very deep for him to spend the hundreds of hours he must have spent in clipping out and classifying newspaper, pamphlet and magazine items and articles and writing interlineations on hundreds of pages of my textbooks, cross-referencing this, commenting on that. Research, it was, with a vengeance—the great mission of his declining days!

He told us how his first reading of Rugg three years before had launched him on a broader research into things radical in American colleges and schools. He was aghast, he exclaimed, at the radicalism, the un-Americanism he uncovered on every side. He was shocked at the widespread "subversive" utterances and the questioning of American civilization that he found.

His crusade was not limited to the textbooks; it took him to Union Theological Seminary and to Teachers College. I remember him one day in 1938, nervously moving about among the student body of our large course in educational

[2]For three years he has worked without seeking publicity. For three years he has desired not to be interviewed by the press, to speak openly or even vote against the books in board meeting. In this account also, therefore, I shall respect his desire for anonymity.

foundations in the Horace Mann auditorium. At one moment off to the right, at another to the left, he listened restlessly to the remarks made from the platform by the four professors who were conducting a panel discussion on some problem of American or world affairs. He stayed only a few minutes, leaving in the same tense, nervous way. Later some of my colleagues told me that he had visited them and attacked me and other members of the faculty, urging our elimination from the college.

So much for the man I am told by Englewood friends has been the power behind the attack. I deal with him at some length because it was he who initiated the attempt to ease my books out of the schools quietly.

1937–38: The "Hush-Hush" Period

Authoritarians have several ways of working: moral persuasion, loud talk and violence. The first two methods were used in Englewood.[3] The story lays bare all the steps: first, a "hush-hush" period, during which efforts were made to put the books out of the schools quietly; second, months of direct attempts to censor the schools; third, more months of counterattack on the part of citizens who demanded public study and discussion, publication of community views and the making of community decisions. I know of no example of an American community battling for the preservation of its liberties which illustrates the American way in action better than that of Englewood.

The "hush-hush" period lasted through 1937 and 1938.

[3]A few necessary community facts about Englewood: a suburban town bordering on the Hudson River, directly opposite Manhattan, New York City. Population in 1930, eighteen thousand. One of the wealthiest suburban communities in the United States. Board of education of five members appointed by the mayor for five-year terms. Politics traditionally Republican. Nineteen-forty census showed few of the people of less than second-generation nativity in the United States.

Warning came: "Tell the teachers for their own good to get rid of the Rugg books." Here was deliberate censorship throttling the schools. Secret pressure was the method. In blunter phraseology, it was quiet persuasion "for your own good" . . . "toe the line" . . . "line up."

This pressure is the favorite instrument of those who have been trying to censor the schools. A citizen tells the superintendent "to get rid of the books." Not wishing to lose prestige and perhaps even his position,[4] the superintendent passes the word on to the principal or supervisor, and from him it goes to the teachers. It is a behind-the-scene pressure process by which a tiny minority of the adult community coerces the administration and the faculty and finally the children's education. This method is not new in American educational history; in my thirty years of work I have encountered it many times in many places. Far too many superintendents, principals and teachers have been dismissed because of heroic refusal to be "co-ordinated" by pressure groups. Only when there have been fair-minded board presidents, vigorous, democratic board majorities or unrelenting vocal activity by determined citizens of prestige have the raiders and censors of the schools met defeat. Lacking these, fear pervades the life of the school. Teachers and children are regimented. The lock step is produced. Democracy in education is "subverted."

Authoritarians within the Schools Also

Frequently the quietly-ease-'em-out regimentarians receive reinforcement within the schools themselves. This was true for a part of the Englewood faculty. At least the community whispering campaign against the books was

[4]Records in my files prove that in seven of the known local fights to put the Rugg books out of the schools since 1939 the real issue was not "the books," but some local political or personal issue.

not resisted by certain teachers of the "disciplines" in the senior high school. Thousands of senior-high-school teachers in America are strict disciplinarians at heart; many of them are complete authoritarians in political and social life as well. Within the school they still cling tenaciously to the *memoriter* study of demonstrational geometry and to the rigorous mastery of the structure and form of language and literatures as the most effective way to "train the mind." Theirs is the way of authority: "learn it" . . . "memorize it" . . . "recite it" . . . "I command and you obey." They also prefer the easy way of "manage things behind the scenes quietly." They deny the democratic way, which is the hard way of tolerance, of opening the mind to all sides of a question, of searching for data and determining their validity, of undergoing the ordeal of group discussion and decision.

All of these groups took part in the authoritarian-democratic struggle over the Rugg books in Englewood. But in the spearhead of the attack was still another force.

1939–40: Open Attack

In the spring of 1939 Bertie C. Forbes[5] was appointed to the Englewood Board of Education, and since the summer

[5]For his history I rely on his record as he prepared it for Who's Who in America: He was born in Scotland in 1880, lived there until 1901, went to the Union of South Africa where he worked as a newspaperman for three years. He came to the United States in 1904 and became a naturalized citizen of our country in 1917. He worked as a financial reporter and editor for various Wall Street and Hearst organs. He became nationally known as writer of a daily Hearst-syndicated financial column and as owner and editor of his own financial magazine *Forbes*. For most of a quarter century then his reputation has been that of a Hearst newspaperman and owner of the business magazine *Forbes*. Although these are announced as financial organs, he uses both to publicize his interest in many subjects and to get a hearing for his personal brand of philosophy which he calls "The American System."

of 1939 he has led the public attack on "un-Americanism in the schools." Up to the time of his appointment he had been regarded in the community, and so far as his name was known outside it, as a man concerned primarily with publicity. It is important to bear in mind then that it has been a Hearst newspaperman of foreign birth who since 1939 has led the attempt to exclude "un-American" teachings from the schools, both in Englewood and throughout the country. Every such utterance by Forbes as the following (and there are many in his columns and magazine) must be interpreted in that light. In *Forbes* for August 15, 1939, he described my books under the heading "Treacherous Teachings," stating that one was

. . . viciously un-American, that its author is in love with the way things are done in Russia, that he distorts facts to convince the oncoming generation that America's private-enterprise system is wholly inferior and nefarious.[6]

He went on to say what he was going to do about it:

I plan to insist that this anti-American educator's textbooks be cast out. Moreover, I find this same fellow's outpourings included in a list recommended for inclusion in a school library. I am protesting. I would not want my own children contaminated by conversion to Communism.[6]

Forbes was to use his every effort to root out my "anti-Americanism" everywhere in the land:

In my humble opinion it is time for members of boards of education all over the continent to inquire more closely into what is being fed our offspring and to consider seriously what steps should be taken against teachers who have no use for Americanism, who want to see America ape Russia or other lands under dictatorships.[6]

[6]*Forbes.* August 15, 1939.

The public attack began in Englewood on July 22, 1939, when Forbes announced to the board of education and the press that he was conducting an investigation of the textbook situation and that already he had found what he considered "subversive" and "poisonous" teaching in the Rugg social-science materials:

Mr Forbes, learning that the disputed Rugg history textbooks are in use in the Englewood school system has raised the question of whether or not they should be withdrawn.[7]

". . . he [Forbes] is utterly out of sympathy with their contents and believes the children of Englewood should not be permitted to use them."[7]

This pronouncement marked the beginning of a vigorous campaign of publicity which has had almost constant public reverberations ever since. Almost immediately (July 23, 1939) the New York *Herald Tribune* carried an item that my books "have long been the subject of similar controversies" (which was not true at that moment!) . . . that the Advertising Federation of America had assailed one of my books as being "extremely biased and misleading" in its presentation of American business . . . and that A. G. Rudd of Garden City, Long Island, had described one of my texts as "an attempt to sell collectivism to the younger generation of America."[8]

The Citizens Demand Public Study and Discussion

Forbes's attack brought results, not only in the newspapers' publicity, but in increased community discussion. Rumors began to spread in Englewood that the Rugg books were going to be quietly removed from the schools. Public-

[7]Englewood *Press*, week of July 22, 1939.
[8]New York *Herald Tribune*, July 23, 1939.

spirited citizens, led by Dr T. H. P. Sailer,[9] hearing these rumors, formed a Committee of Parents and Taxpayers to look into the situation.

Some of the citizens began to ask bluntly: "Wasn't this a problem for community study and discussion? Shouldn't an attack based upon charges of 'subversiveness' and 'un-Americanism' be examined openly? Which of these two—the Rugg group or the Forbes group—is subversive and un-American?"

Dr Sailer, throwing himself into the fight for free and open community discussion, wrote as chairman of the committee:

Poisonous is what poisons, and subversive is what subverts. . . . Mr Forbes presents no evidence to show that any pupils have been poisoned or subverted. On the other hand, we can name many fine young Englewood boys who have studied the books and swear by them—loyal young men who love their country and believe in its destiny and greatness.

As to the charge of "un-Americanism," it is our opinion that a majority of our fellow citizens hold political and economic views nearer those of Mr Rugg than those of Mr Forbes. It is un-American either to seek to override the opinions of the majority or to suppress the views of any considerable minority.[10]

Forbes carried on his own research into the soundness of the Rugg books and reported his findings in his Hearst column during November and December of 1939. But most of his "investigations" were concentrated on *a single page of the seven thousand printed pages of my twenty books.*

[9] Dr T. H. P. Sailer, many years a resident of Englewood, distinguished retired religious leader with lifelong activity in foreign missions, saw the Rugg Social-Science Pamphlets in their initial process of construction nearly twenty years ago in the Lincoln School.

[10] The Bergen *Evening Record*, May 24, 1940.

He took this one page out of the context of its chapter
and book and thereby tended to destroy its meaning. Several times in a newspaper barrage against me he has used
this single excerpt.

★   ★   ★

By October 1939 the Rugg books or just "the books"
or even just "Rugg" had become the chief topic of dinner,
luncheon and tea conversation in Englewood and up and
down the valley. Near-by communities heard, read, began
to wonder, question and discuss; in one instance a political
election was fought on the issue of the Rugg books, with,
I am happy to record, Rugg winning out at the time.

By late November parents and teachers of the Englewood Junior High School students who were studying
"Rugg" decided to bring the problem into the limelight of
public discussion. On November 20, I spoke at a parent-
teacher meeting[11] before some four hundred citizens of
Englewood and the surrounding towns on the subject of
modern education. Efforts had been made to get Forbes to
attend, but he stayed away. (From that day to this he has
never attended a single gathering at which I have been
present.)

It was clear that the public wanted to talk about the
books. It was clear also that Mr E. H. West[12] of Haworth,
a neighboring New Jersey town, was eager to get into the
fray. Because of the behavior of E. H. West and his associates (since duplicated in other New Jersey and New York
suburban towns) it was a harsh meeting, but from it I
learned one lesson. I learned that the die is cast, that we cannot appease the authoritarians who are trying to censor

[11]See Englewood *Press*, November 23, 1939.

[12]Since that time West has been one of the chief agitators against
Rugg and the Rugg books, especially through the American Legion.

American schools. If we do, freedom of thought and discussion in our educational institutions will be made impotent. And I learned that night the hate and ruthless determination which motivate the tiny minority who would rule our schools.

★   ★   ★

By early winter of 1939 scores of the leading citizens of Englewood, imbued with the democratic view, had aroused themselves to meet the challenge. On December 14 the Bergen *Evening Record* reported:

Forty-eight prominent Englewood residents today petitioned the board of education in a public letter demanding that no change be made in the social-science textbooks of the city's schools without full inquiry by the board of education.

The list of signers included the pastors of six churches, active church workers, the head of the Parent-Teacher Association, several teachers, an ex-mayor, a judge and the officers of such organizations as the American Association of University Women and the Women's Club.

Blast after blast then came from Forbes in the Philadelphia *Inquirer* and in the New York *Journal-American* and other Hearst papers throughout the United States. Finally, after long refusal to do so, I replied to his absurd "charges" in the Englewood *Press* of January 11, 1940, asking that in the proper American tradition he reprint my answer in his Hearst column and in his magazine. The request has never been honored or even acknowledged.

Week after week Forbes's column continued its name-calling bombardment. Over and over he repeated the question: "Are too many educators poisoning the minds of the young generation with prejudiced, distorted, unfair teachings regarding the American system of economy and dazzling them with overly-rosy pictures of conditions in totalitarian countries?"

Englewood seethed in agitation. In December I spoke at the annual congregational dinner at St Paul's (Episcopal) Church before an audience of five hundred on the theme "Education for a Changing Civilization." The rector had invited me in the interests of fair play and freedom of speech, believing that his people should have an opportunity to judge my opinions firsthand. Several board members and other distinguished citizens gave their approval. But rumors were in the air. One: "Your books are slated to go out at the next meeting. The anti-Rugg group has three votes. Only two members are for you." Another: "The board now stands two to two. No one knows how the fifth member will vote. Most people think he will go with Forbes." But in spite of Forbes's constant hammering away in the papers the books stayed in—undoubtedly because of the vigorous work of the Citizens Committee.

More months passed, with Forbes continuing his attack. Finally in May he filed a statement with the board, calling me and my books "un-American, unpatriotic and unfit for the young minds for whom we are educationally responsible," and presenting, as he said, "a mass of information concerning the Rugg textbooks. . . ."[13]

At the same meeting Mrs G. Kingsley Noble, another board member, fought Forbes openly. She presented a systematic statement showing the fairness of my books to industry, their pro-Americanism and their anti-Communism. She said that

she has read the Rugg books from cover to cover, has interviewed parents, teachers and children and has watched her own two sons use the books to great advantage and can come to the single conclusion that they are excellent.[13]

[13]Englewood *Press*, May 16, 1940.

Throughout the spring the controversy continued to be the center of conversation. A headline in the Englewood *Press* reported that "an avalanche of letters upholding Rugg books" had been received. The New York City newspapers played up the Englewood events as news. The American Committee for Democracy and Intellectual Freedom entered the fight on "Rugg's" side, sending throughout the country a defense statement signed by one hundred and fifty distinguished citizens, among them businessmen, scientists, publishers, educators, writers and publicists.

There was no doubt that Englewood was aroused. In May 1940 the Committee of Parents and Taxpayers published on its own initiative and at its own expense an eighteen-page pamphlet entitled *Statements Regarding the Use of the Rugg Series of Social-Science Texts in the Englewood School System.*[14] Over a thousand copies were distributed without cost to Englewood taxpayers. The pamphlet, assembled largely by Dr Sailer, summed up the controversy to date. It provided information concerning myself, my background and the background of the books. It included a statement by the teachers of the social-studies department of the Englewood Junior High School, showing how the Rugg books were being taught and refuting various adverse criticisms. A series of quotations taken from five of the books and dealing with the points of controversy were given to show the fairness of the books to industry, their anti-Communism and pro-Americanism; also a letter from a taxpayer, a statement from a student who had used the books, a statement from a parent of a child in the Englewood schools and a carefully prepared paper supporting the historical reliability of the books by Dr Theodore Skinner, professor of political science, New York University.

[14] The author and publishers of the Rugg books had nothing to do with its initiation, design, construction or dissemination.

Matters hung more or less in the balance for some time, although open hostility and opposition did seem to be on the wane. On May 23, 1940, the Englewood *Press* said:

. . . The number and tone of letters published in today's Englewood *Press* show that there is keen interest, chiefly in favor of the books. The fact of the matter probably is simply that the people of Englewood are not alarmed over the effect of books that have been used in their schools since 1934 without having given rise to any criticism, without having done an apparent harm.

On May 25, 1940 the *Press* announced that the board would delay decision on the Rugg books until June 11. On June 6 the Englewood *Press* carried in large headlines "a Compromise Plan," put forward by the clergy of the town in the interests of peace. This proposed keeping the Rugg Reading Books and the Workbooks but dropping the Teachers' Guides.

In June the date of "decision" arrived, but no action. Dates for new meetings and "the vote" were set; citizens supporting the books were present. So the matter dragged on.

Was the Controversy Harmful to the Community and the Schools?

As the first full year of open controversy was ending an editorial in the *Press* (June 6, 1940) reported that a feeling of uneasiness was spreading through the community, that little good had been accomplished by the Forbes attack and that people were questioning seriously whether the work of the schools was not being impaired.

. . . The very thing we feared is coming to pass. Statements and counterstatements are being made that reflect on personalities. Name calling is in the air, and bitterness is showing itself. The public denunciations have been bad enough; those uttered at breakfast and dinner tables before the children who should have respect for teachers and for their subjects must be worse. Neighboring little Haworth went through exactly the same thing; so did several other communities; and more because of the internal harm than because of the charges against the books, they ousted the Rugg texts.[15]

The sad part, it went on to say, was that "all on both sides are true Americans, abhor Communism and Fascism alike, want their children indoctrinated with Americanism and the American way." Whether all in this controversy were "true Americans" I am not now convinced. When I think of the extent to which Forbes went with his destructive publicity and his unseemly name calling—I wonder.

At the end of June 1940, three years after the first efforts to "get rid of Rugg" were made, several hundred taxpaying citizens who had children in the Englewood public schools were actively keeping the books there. This was shown by a published analysis of the signers of two petitions—one signed by citizens who favored the retention of the books, the other by citizens who wanted their elimination. (Remember that Englewood is what may be called a "private-school town." It is one of the three wealthiest small communities in America, and many of its young people go away to private schools.) Here are two revealing sets of figures:

Of 265 pro-Rugg signers 78 per cent had children in Englewood public schools.

Of 138 anti-Rugg signers 23 per cent had children in Englewood public schools.

Of 265 pro-Rugg signers 51 per cent had children who had studied "Rugg."

Of 138 anti-Rugg signers 7 per cent had children who had studied "Rugg."

[15]The Englewood *Press*, June 6, 1940.

In publishing this analysis the Englewood *Press* of June 20 said:

Should not the decision for or against the Rugg books rest with the majority opinion of those taxpayers who not only pay taxes but also support our most democratic of all institutions, the public schools, by sending their children to them?

★   ★   ★

In June the press reported the death of one board member and the resignation because of failing health of the silent Mr X. It expressed the opinion that "the Rugg textbook controversy would undoubtedly quiet down for some time to come."

★   ★   ★

Summer passed, and the schools were ready to open. Forbes returned to the publicity fray with new tactics. He began assailing the teachers of the social studies, reporting at a board meeting and to the press that Miss Agnes B. Deans was breaking down the children's faith in America. He stated that a twelve-year-old boy (some said it was his own son) had told him that Miss Deans had made the statement that "there are several countries in Europe which have as good, if not better, forms of government than ours."

Instead of taking this attack lying down, the teachers struck back at Forbes. The Englewood *News* for September 9, 1940, reported in large headlines, "Teachers Indignant over Charges Faculty Member Spoke Un-American"; the long article which followed explained what the teachers' ideals and methods were. Miss Deans emphatically denied Forbes's charge, and citizens under Mrs Noble's leadership rose to the defense of the teachers. Newspaper items indicated that the community was turning against Forbes. On September 16 the Bergen *Evening Record* reported in headlines, "Over His Attack on Teacher of Rugg

Books Englewood's Anger against Forbes Grows"; on October 9, "Forbes, Rugg-Texts Critic, Is Dropped from Committee" (of Teachers and Textbooks of the Englewood Board of Education).

Englewood, a Case Study in Democracy

This brings the Englewood story to the winter of 1940–41, and here I shall stop. As I send this book to press the social-science books are still in use in the Englewood schools. Will they stay? Who can predict? In any event the episode provides an excellent case study in democracy. For three years the people have stubbornly defended their right to carry on their own affairs. An attack was made upon their schools; the attack was beaten off. That is the American way in action.

If there is a lesson for America in this story it is that "eternal vigilance *is* the price of liberty." Someone must be vocal; someone must speak out, if the democratic process is to survive. Someone must say, with William Lloyd Garrison, "I shall not compromise, and I shall be heard." Englewood had its vigilant and vocal believers in democracy. It also had those who would censor the schools, and the radius of their influence extends far beyond the region of Bergen County, N.J., or the metropolitan community of New York City.

> On November 26, 1940, the Englewood Board of Education voted four to one, Mr Forbes dissenting, to retain the Rugg books in the schools.

> On January 14, 1941 the Mayor of Englewood declining to reappoint Mr Forbes on the Board of Education named Mr A. H. Springer in his place.

Chapter III

TWENTY YEARS WITH A BLANK
SHEET OF PAPER

HAD I HAD the slightest prevision of the scope of the enterprise that was to develop out of the three-page mimeographed letter sent to my schoolmaster friends in the winter of 1921–22, I am confident that I would never have undertaken it. Had I known that on not less than four thousand mornings in the next twenty years I would go to my desk to fill several blank sheets of paper before night with words descriptive . . . words episodic . . . words generalizing . . . words analytic . . . words interpretive . . . of man and his changing society, I am sure I would have turned away and chosen another kind of task. As Buck said to me fifteen years later[1] when the junior-high-school series had been completed and we were making plans for the extension of Man and His Changing Society upward and downward in the schools: "Harold, you've got a life sentence." That's what it is proving to be—a life sentence at hard labor, with a continuous stream of blank sheets of paper.

[1]Burdette R. Buckingham, former director of educational research in several universities, pioneer leader in educational measurement, partner and general elementary editor of Ginn and Company, close friend and special sponsor and editorial guide in developing Man and His Changing Society. Many are the times I've said: "Praise be, Buck's on the job!"

Be that as it may, from the morning I set out my writing table in the Yonkers house in the summer of 1922 to today, some kind of "dead line" has enslaved me. First it was "The pamphlets must arrive on time." Then when the pamphlets gave way to Man and His Changing Society after 1929, there were always Buck and Mildred Galloway in Ginn's Boston office demanding copy or proof or decisions . . . or Edmund Stevens calling for illustration lists and photographs . . . or Mrs McGinnis asking for map specifications.

And yet I suppose I've really loved putting a hundred publications "to bed" one by one.

★   ★   ★

I came back to New York in September 1940 to find that the discussion of the "heresy" trials of the books had spread across the entire country. At that moment my friends began to say again: "Tell your story . . . tell it now. You're obligated to speak out in defense. Remember this attack is an attempt to censor all modern education; indeed it is really a part of the general retreat to orthodoxy. You're merely a symbol—a good target to hit. You must speak!"

For years people had been saying it: "You've got a real story. Why don't you write it down? Make a book about the books, about America in our times, about the American problem as you have seen it develop."

One of the most emphatic in urging was Henry Hilton:[2]

"Tell how you started all this social-studies business twenty years ago . . . how you borrowed money and

[2]Long one of the senior partners and a chief force in Ginn and Company; under their new organization, its president. For many years since we were neighbors at Chicago he has been not only a kind of elder brother and counselor to me but my ardent sponsor on many occasions. In 1938 he was honored by our alma mater, Dartmouth, with an honorary degree.

hired assistants to help you write the Social-Science Pamphlets . . . how you printed them yourself and got teachers and superintendents to experiment with them. Tell about the three experimental editions and how you destroyed thousands of pages of type and began again and again. Tell how you lectured all over the country and made two yearbooks for the National Society and prodded the geographers and historians to bring the full story of America into the schools. Tell how publishers' agents—including our own—encountered your pamphlets in hundreds of school systems in thirty-eight states, until finally nothing could be done but try to get them and publish them in commercial form. Tell how they became a whole library, reaching from the third grade to the high school, with millions of young Americans and their parents reading and approving them."

Ten years ago, on the completion of the first commercial edition, I did begin to write the story of the books. I planned it to be a record of the preceding decade of research and experimentation in trying to bring a realistic picture of American life into the schools. I designed the proposed volume, wrote several chapters but finally gave it up.[3] There were several reasons, but the chief one, I think, was that I was not yet ready to make definitive appraisals, generalizations and interpretations either of our own infant enterprise in the social sciences or of the rapidly changing social scene in general.

Then followed the harassing years of the Great World Depression and the tightening tension of the interregnum of dictatorship. Finally the renewal of open warfare in Eu-

[3]I did succeed in making a formal thirty-two-page report called *Building a Science of Society for the Schools*. Ginn and Company, 1932.

rope in 1939 brought the twenty-year Long Armistice sharply to a close; the subsequent collapse of France and eight other European countries launched a new stage of social hysteria and witch-hunting and awakened our people generally to a clearer conception of the nature of our society and our times. For me personally and, I believe, for my liberal colleagues and friends, the recent developments validate our earlier tentative appraisals; but, more important, for the first time we have been jolted into an awareness that the structure of all democratic life and the new education which could serve as the true implementation of democracy are gravely menaced. And not only have our reputations been smeared; the constructive educational building of two decades and the very foundations of our personal lives are being destroyed.

For me the publication of the Armstrong "Treason" article and the sensational censoring of the schools in September 1940 brought the gravity of the whole situation to a focus. I listened carefully to Mr Malcolm Johnson and his associates in Doubleday, Doran as they urged: "You've got a story. Millions of children are reading your books. Because of these attacks millions of Americans are asking: 'What is it all about? Why is there so much fuss about Harold Rugg and his books?' Tell your story now and we'll publish it." So the reams of blank paper came out again.

"And don't forget," some said as I started to write, "begin with your own story; tell first what the books are and how you made them."

All right then; here, in brief compass, are "the facts" of the making of the books. Their bare recital may be dull, but I assure my readers that the events back of them have been anything but that. Perhaps the human story that follows[4] will serve as compensation.

★   ★   ★

No doubt many of my readers know the books; their children indeed may have studied them, for they have been in use in more than five thousand school places, in many instances for more than ten years. For those who do not know, they are now (in the winter of 1940–41) a twenty-book series called Man and His Changing Society,[5] designed for use in the various school grades from the third to the senior high school.

They are the outcome of twenty-one years of work (1920–41) in the experimental development of new reading and study materials for young Americans. During the first nine years the work was carried on in the Lincoln School of Teachers College, Columbia University; after that, while I have been professor of education in the college.

1920–22

I went to Lincoln on January 1, 1920, and soon after began to design, write and publish for experimentation in public schools the Social-Science Pamphlets. A thousand pages of mimeographed materials were written for young people, dealing with immigration, town and city life, indus-

[4]Chapter IX gives the early background, Chapters X and XI the life history of the ideas around which the enterprise was built, the first years at Lincoln, social, psychological and aesthetic frontiers which we explored—especially that of the psychology of consent, the very foundation of the building of democratic government.

[5]Published since 1929 by Ginn and Company, Boston, New York, Chicago, San Francisco, Columbus, Dallas and Atlanta. Six volumes constitute the original junior-high-school series; six more the revisions of those or volumes which supplant them for use today; eight are for the elementary school and were prepared in collaboration with Louise Krueger (Rugg), founder and director of the Walt Whitman School, New York City.

tries and trade, geographic factors in American life, conservation of natural resources, and the like. These were studied for two years by the Lincoln School children under experimental conditions. By the close of the second year it was clear that further progress could be made only with printed materials.

1922–23

With the aid of two assistants, whom I paid myself from borrowed funds, I wrote and published privately the first printed edition of the pamphlets, ten booklets ranging from 118 to 289 pages each.[6] From 1922–29 the research, publication and distribution of the pamphlets were largely financed[7] by the splendid co-operation of hundreds of public-school administrators and teachers who bought one hundred thousand copies a year to use in "experimental classes" during the eight years. The first edition was used in about one hundred school places.

1923–27

I expanded the enterprise, raised more money, brought in sixteen research assistants and with their help wrote and published the second edition of the pamphlets, twelve three-hundred-page books.[8] These were used co-operatively

[6]The titles will give the best indication of their content and organization: *America and Her Immigrants, The City and Key Industries in Modern Nations, Town and City Life in America, The Westward Movement and the Growth of Transportation, The Mechanical Conquest of America, America's March Toward Democracy, Americanizing Our Foreign-Born, Resources and Industries in a Machine World, Waste and Conservation of America's Resources, How Nations Live Together.*

[7]The Lincoln School and Teachers College paid my salary as educational psychologist and as professor of education; also the salary of a secretary and one part-time assistant. The remaining expenses, $378,000 in seven years' time, I financed from the sale of the pamphlets.

[8]There are the titles: *Town and City Life in America, Resources, Industries and Cities of America, Industries and Trade Which Bind Na-*

under experimental conditions in 375 school systems in thirty-eight states by several thousand school administrators and teachers with fine enthusiasm and progressive methods. From them came a vast body of suggestions for improving the "teaching" arrangement of the material.[9] Many of them met with us in round-table meetings in different parts of the country. My hat is off to them! They are the stuff of which American democracy is made and by which it will be defended against its maligners.

1927–31

With the aid of several associates I completed the researches, scrapped all the old pamphlet editions and made the first commercial edition of six six-hundred-page junior-high-school volumes,[10] together with six Workbooks of Directed Study and six Teacher's Guides. Their preparation was made possible partly by the sale of the pamphlets, which totaled three quarters of a million copies and provided ninety thousand dollars for research, and partly by the very generous support of the publishing house whose co-operation in such experimental developments of the

tions Together: Part I, The Great Industrial Nations; Part II, The Changing Agricultural Nations, The Westward Movement and the Growth of Transportation, The Mechanical Conquest of America, America's March Toward Democracy, Part I, America's March Toward Democracy, Part II, America and Her Immigrants, Problems of American Industry and Business, Problems of American Government, How Nations Live Together and *A Book of Practice Exercises in Map Location for Supplementary Use.*

[9]As an interesting commentary on this assistance I can report that in the autumn of 1940 I sold four tons of discarded paper, the bulk of it reports, annotated copies of pamphlets, tests, question blanks, and the like, returned by our co-operating teachers.

[10]The titles: *An Introduction to American Civilization, Changing Civilizations in the Modern World, A History of American Civilization, A History of American Government and Culture, An Introduction to Problems of American Culture, Changing Governments and Changing Cultures.*

school program I regard as unexampled in the history of
textbook publishing—Ginn and Company.

1933–36

Louise Krueger (Rugg) and I designed and wrote eight
books for grades III to VI inclusive.[11] To build the needed
foundation for the later understanding to be developed by
the work of the junior high school these went in very large
numbers into the elementary schools.

1936–40

The junior-high-school series was systematically reconstructed to fit the drastic world changes of the 1930s. New
material dealing with the emergence of the dictatorships of
Stalin, Hitler, Mussolini and the Japanese War party had to
be added. The series was brought up to date, practically rebuilt. Two new volumes—*Citizenship and Civic Affairs* and
America Rebuilds—were prepared.

1940–41

In preparation now is *World History* and *World Problems: The Struggle of Dictatorship and Democracy*, the
first of a senior-high-school library of some half-dozen social-science volumes.

★   ★   ★

About midway in the twenty-year enterprise fourteen of
the Little Reading Books for the primary grades were prepared by collaborators who for several years constituted a
part of my total group. In 1931 ten of the books, written

---

[11]The titles: *The First Book of the Earth, Nature Peoples, Communi-
ties of Men, Peoples and Countries, The Building of America, Man at
Work: His Industries, Man at Work; His Arts and Crafts, Mankind
Throughout the Ages.*

by Louise Krueger (Rugg) and Arensa Sondergaard, were published and distributed by Books for Children, Inc.,[12] which was organized for that purpose.[13]

THE TWENTY-YEAR OUTPUT

This is the chronological and factual record,[14] and here is the output for twenty years, succinctly summed up:

Twenty-five thousand printed pages of materials prepared for children and youths from ages eight to eighteen, used by several million young people[15] in over five thousand school places; in some places only one or a few of the books have been studied, in some the elementary books only, in others the junior-high-school books only, in still others all of both courses.

A program of research including (1) "the biography of ideas" which is sketched in Chapters X and XI of this present book, (2) twenty-five studies of various phases of modern civilization and of the psychological organization of materials for the school, their grade placement and teach-

[12]They are still distributed from the office of Harold Rugg, Teachers College, Columbia University, New York City.

[13]The ten Little Reading Books: *The Story of a Pumpkin, Hallowe'en Fun, The Snow Man, The Little Fir Tree, A First Grade Bunny, Sending in the Alarm, Bobby and Jane at the Park, A Day with Old Joe, A Valentine Surprise, Three Guesses.*

[14]An elaborate outline of the entire body of reading and study materials is given in the Appendix. I hope that my readers will study it, forbidding in appearance though it may be. It gives a fairly comprehensive view of the kind of description of society the books contain and the major changes in content and organization which have come through the years.

[15]It is impossible to state with even approximate accuracy how many young people have studied or even read the books, because there is great diversity in the methods of using them. In a large number of cases the books are owned by the school or school system, and each copy is used each year by more than one child; in fact, in hundreds of systems the same copies have been used continually from six to eleven years. It is my confident estimate, however, that not less than five million young Americans have studied one or more of them.

ing methods,[16] (3) the co-operative trial of the experimental editions of the Social-Science Pamphlets for seven years by several thousand teachers and administrators . . . tests and appraisals made of the pamphlets as teaching materials . . . prolonged conferences with co-operating teachers . . . evaluations of the materials obtained through thousands of objective tests.

Eyewitness studies of geographic, economic, social, political and educational conditions were made in the Philippine Islands and Puerto Rica (1925), in China and Japan (1931–32), in the Union of South Africa (1934), in New Zealand and Australia (1937) and in practically all European countries at varying intervals from 1923 to 1932 inclusive. Many of the personal observations made on these trips have been recorded in the volumes of Man and His Changing Society and in *Scholastic* magazine.

More than one hundred articles were published in *Scholastic* magazine[17] (senior-high-school level) from 1931 to 1941, all dealing with the problems of our changing social scene and the trends and factors which precipitated them.

Three yearbooks for national societies[18] organized and edited.

[16]Objective research was the keynote of the whole enterprise. Being without precedent and extensive beyond example, it required the collaboration of many minds, especially in technical studies. The technical investigations included twenty-five studies: three studies of existing curricula in history, geography and civics, of the procedure of national committees from 1892 to 1921 and of pupils' abilities and attainments; thirteen studies of what problems of contemporary life to teach, of the chief trends of civilization and of the central concepts and principles which educated minds use in thinking about them; three studies of the grade placement of curriculum materials and of the development of pupils' abilities; six studies of learning and of the organization of curricula.

[17]See pp. 156 and 160.

[18]Two of these I made as chairman of committees of the National Society for the Study of Education: (1) "The Social Studies," *The Twenty-Second Yearbook*, Part II (1922); (2) "The Foundations of

"THE RUGG BOOKS"

MAN AND HIS CHANGING SOCIETY

VOLUMES IN THE SECOND COURSE

NEW AND REVISED VOLUMES IN THE SECOND COURSE

Community and National Life

WORKBOOKS AND TEACHERS' GUIDES

Pupil's Workbook of Directed Study and a Teachers' Guide accompany each of the above volumes

VOLUMES IN THE FIRST COURSE

Curriculum-Making," Parts I and II, *The Twenty-Sixth Yearbook* (1926), the third as chairman of the Committee on Curriculum of the John Dewey Society: The Third Yearbook, *Democracy and the Curriculum*. Appleton-Century, New York, 1939.

WORKBOOKS AND TEACHERS' GUIDES

A Workbook accompanies each of the above volumes. Teachers' Guides are available

FOR TEACHERS

★   ★   ★

So much for the bare statistical record. As I believe this book will show, back of the whole enterprise and driving it forward has been my conviction that the only hope of preserving American democracy is to educate a large body of Americans to understand American life and to foster in them an energetic fighting spirit to make it an abundant life. "That men may understand" has been my theme from the very beginning. "Tolerant understanding" has been set up—in articles and pamphlets, essays and books, during the entire history of the enterprise—as one of the great goals. The American people must come to understand the American problem and, I have believed, there is no other way to bring that about except through education—adult education, and the education of youth and children. The American problem is the task, I say, of building in North America the fine way of life that is potentially possible.

Throughout the twenty years I have kept before my mind the picture of millions of young Americans learning to confront courageously life as it has been and is actually lived in America. I have seen them building a great belief in and enthusiasm for the potential economic and spiritual abundance which lies across the threshold of the new epoch of modern history now being ushered in. By giving our young people an honest and intelligible account of advancing civilization, I hoped to develop that spirit. Although other countries and peoples, past and present, are dealt with, I worked always from the American orientation.

The task was a huge one: nothing less than preparing a total word portrait of contemporary society, one dealing with all phases of the culture—social-economic system, government and other institutions, the arts and the psychology of the people. And the vast panorama is the result of careful and costly research and study of the works of the most profound scholars of the world and domestic scene.[19]

Painting the portrait has been a tremendous ordeal, but I look upon it with pride and satisfaction, despite the attacks of those who would destroy it.

★   ★   ★

Most satisfying of all perhaps is the knowledge that millions of the parents and teachers who have studied and used the pamphlets and books have understood and appreciated them and their aims. Throughout it all they have known what I was doing and have given me emphatic expressions of approval. The daily mail received during the past ten years has rarely failed to bring at least one such expression from a parent, a teacher or a child. Personal greetings at educational meetings have confirmed the spirit of the letters. One of the most thrilling sights at the many meetings of citizens and teachers in which I participated in the past twenty years has been the front row filled with junior-high-school boys and girls sitting absorbed through hours-long discussions of "education and changing civilization."

[19]See Chapters X and XI for the study of the life history of the ideas upon which it is based.

After each such meeting excited requests to autograph copies of my books are almost sure to be made.

Many amusing conversations could be reproduced of children complaining that they had a hard time to get the books away from a parent who insisted on reading them when they wanted to study. There was the especially exciting one of a Prime Minister who laughingly described to me that his constant preoccupation with my textbooks— *The Building of America, Changing Civilizations in the Modern World* and others—nearly caused a drastic dislocation of his domestic life. His "Imagine a textbook doing that!" was encouraging as well as amusing.

★   ★   ★

There were of course a few exceptions,[20] a few instances of actual opposition, but until the past two years the Rugg books enjoyed a nationwide vogue. To every school administrator and teacher and to the ninety and nine among the parents who used the Rugg books they meant a fine and proud Americanism.

I say the *parents and educators understood.* They knew that we were working to build admiration and loyalty to our democratic American way of life. They did not find the great American heroes "debunked." The achievements of these men—Washington, Jefferson, Madison and all the others—are described at great length and in many places. Indeed a vast company of great men unsung or treated

---

[20]Two examples come to mind: a zealot on the West Coast who tried for years to oust the books from California schools and finally succeeded in getting them out of her own home town . . . the case of Verne Marshall (in 1940–41 associated with O. K. Armstrong, Robert Lancaster and others in the No Foreign War Committee), editor of the Cedar Rapids (Iowa) *Gazette,* who failed in a similar agitation from 1934–38, only to succeed in the nationwide hysteria period of 1939–40. And there were a few others who fought me and the books on the ground of "un-Americanism."

casually in other materials find recognition in Man and His Changing Society—the heroes of health, of housing, of social engineering, of soil conservation, of industrial invention, of the arts, of every creative area in which Americans are working and trying to solve the American problem.

When M. K. Hart accuses—"The Rugg books are materialistic. There is little in them about the spiritual or intellectual development of the American people"—I want to throw up my hands! Literally thousands of pages have come from my fountain pen on the cultural development of our own people and others around the world. The whole of one book, *Man at Work: His Arts and Crafts*, and large sections of others are devoted to the historical and contemporary story of architecture, drama, music, the dance, the development of alphabets and language, of number and measurement. I say without hesitation that not less than fifteen hundred pages of my series discuss the spiritual and intellectual development of our people. Actually my books were the first of any school materials which gave conspicuous space to the arts and the esthetic developments of man.

The parents are not worried about their children getting all sides of a problem, no matter what the problem is, provided it can be understood by the young people. They know and approve the procedure. For example: "Why not study about unemployment?" they say. "This young generation is going to have to help devise ways of eliminating unemployment and solving just such problems. Why keep them in ignorance of the facts? The facts and conditions are all around them anyway!"

The parents and teachers do not read into my materials that I am trying to "sell the children the idea of a new collective society," as those who attack us say. Instead they agree that young people cannot thoroughly understand the dangerous enemies of democracy, whether of the Communist or Fascist type, unless the story of Communism and Fascism is read and the principles of these forms of government studied and contrasted with our own. How else, I have heard them exclaim, can our children put up a fighting loyal defense, unless they know what they are fighting against!

In the ten years from the publication of the first volume of Man and His Changing Society until the summer of 1938 there was never any fear that I was "advocating Communism," preaching the socialization of all property. On the contrary, the parents liked my conception of the "American Way of Progress"[21] which I had built up carefully in the books, especially in *Our Country and Our People*, *The Conquest of America* and *America's March Toward Democracy*, and now the central theme of the new volume *America Rebuilds*.

Alone among the schoolbook authors of America, I had refused to dodge the problem of public and private ownership.[22] From the beginning I took the position that school histories of America were obligated to tell what the American people had actually done about regulating free enterprise, how they decided to carry on some of their enterprises through public ownership and operation—for example, the national defense (army and navy), local and state protection of life and property, the postal service, community water supply, and the like—and some on the private enterprise basis; that they believed in both private and public schools, public and private hospitals and health services, public and private power enterprises, and the like.

[21]I wrote an article for *Scholastic* in 1934 under that title; it was later reprinted in various magazines and was widely distributed by Ginn and Company.

[22]Chapter XII, "The Crux: I and We" describes in detail how I "teach" it.

Our telling the young people the historical facts about
public and private ownership, operation, control and regulation did not mean to the parents that we were subtly indoctrinating the young people with our own conception of
a new social order in which—to use the Communists' terms
—all the means of production were socialized! On the contrary, they understood that we interpreted the American
way of free enterprise in the schools by showing how the
American people had actually been redefining freedom for
seventy-five years through new social legislation and
through the development of other new governmental social
controls and agencies that would keep the aggressive tendencies of the too-active and too-free enterprisers within
reasonable bounds.

At this point I can't resist offering you a sample.

Chapter IV

THE AMERICAN SPIRIT: A SAMPLE CHAPTER[1]

IN MANY PLACES where patrioteers criticized the books the people hadn't read them. Perhaps the reader hasn't either, so I reprint here a single chapter from one of them in order that he may read it. It's only one, but I've chosen the one that deals with the crux—the problem that torments the minds and souls of Western men. It's my brief summary of the American spirit which conquered the vast American continent, built the world's richest civilization and brought our people to the verge of physical abundance, practical-working democracy and integrity of expression.

Several facts should be kept in mind as it is read: It is only a summing up, the next to the last chapter in the fifth junior-high-school volume *Citizenship and Civic Affairs*. It is used generally by fifteen-year-olds in the ninth grade, who, it is presumed, have already studied several of the twelve books for grades III–VIII inclusive.

[1]This is Chapter XXIV of *Citizenship and Civic Affairs*, one of the volumes in the Rugg series: Man and His Changing Society.

Chapter XXIV · The American Spirit

Before we close our study of citizenship and civic affairs one important task remains to be done. We have studied about American family, neighborhood, and community life. We know a good deal about how the American built up a government and how he runs that government today. We have seen how he becomes educated, how he spends his leisure time. But as yet we have said little about the American himself—his personal characteristics or traits, his deep-seated desires, what he wants most, how he looks at the world, what he thinks and feels deep down inside himself. In other words, we must still try to understand the unique American character . . . the American way of life . . . the American outlook . . . the American point of view . . . the American mind. We shall call it the "American Spirit."

In taking up this task we shall really be studying the "psychology" of the American people. We cannot of course make a thorough study in a single chapter. We cannot do that even in a few years. To know the American mind thoroughly would require a lifetime of study, and even then the analysis would not be complete; for the "American" is forever changing—slowly, it is true, but surely.

Nevertheless, in this chapter we shall make at least a beginning in the investigation of what we call the "American Spirit."

I. THE FRONTIER HELPED DEVELOP THE AMERICAN SPIRIT

Of course the "American Spirit" takes in a great many ideas, but perhaps the outstanding one is the idea that the American people feel that "each individual man or woman should be left as free as possible to work out his own problems." And the development of this feeling was to be expected because of the very history of America during the first 250 years. From your own knowledge of this history you know that people were living on American frontiers

591

from the time of the first settlements in the 1620's to as recently as the 1880's and 1890's. In fact, if the settling of Oklahoma is included, there was a frontier right up to 1900. Throughout all this time there was opportunity for any courageous independent young American to stake out a farm of 160 acres (later successively 320 and 640 acres), build a house on it, and claim it as his own. For the land, he had to pay only a very small sum, throughout most of the time not more than $1.25 an acre. In other words, until the turn of the century there was "free" land for those who had initiative enough to develop it.

Let us now search into the meaning of the expression the "American Spirit" a bit more carefully. What characteristics did our pioneering fathers develop in these years of struggling to meet their problems?

1. Resourcefulness

You know that the people on the frontier lived a hard and lonely life. Farms were miles apart in mountain clearings and scattered over the great open spaces on prairies and plains. Neighbors, therefore, were scarce, most of the time miles away. Nearly everything a man and his family had to have they raised or made for themselves. There was no "corner store" where they could buy food or clothing. Cabins and barns had to be made from trees chopped down by hand. There were no police or militia to keep order, to protect people's lives and property. The pioneers themselves had to drive off the wild animals and Indians, to provide security against storms, floods, and drought.

Every person, including little children, had to "stand on his own feet," to take care of himself. He had to be his own aid or support. He had only his own abilities and energy to draw upon, and his only hope of surviving was in using them to his very best advantage. All these taken together mean "resourcefulness." It is easy to see, then, that under the difficult conditions of pioneer days men and women of great resourcefulness had to be developed and were developed.

2. Intense spirit of freedom

Naturally men and women on the frontier felt *free*! They had space. Daniel Boone, the famous trail blazer of the Appalachian wilderness in the years after 1760, used to say: "I can hear my neighbor's gun. He's too near. I'll move on farther west! Got to have elbowroom! With people building farms over there, I can't breathe!" So Daniel Boone kept moving west until finally he settled in the real wilderness of Missouri across the Mississippi River. Millions of Americans of every generation felt the same way—they wanted space so that they could move about.

On the real frontier, where there wasn't another family for miles and miles, they felt free! "Free as a bird," they said. Here was unlimited opportunity, they felt, to build a home, to make a place of their own. Free! For centuries they and their ancestors in Europe had tried in many ways to secure freedom, but they had not been successful. But here, on the vast untouched continent of North America, they really *were* free! Never before in any civilization were the conditions better for developing in people the idea of freedom.

3. A new sense of equality: lack of social classes

The frontier and the new villages and towns made man feel *equal* also. In European communities there was never a feeling of equality among the people. In every European country the population had always been divided into "classes." At the top, living in stone castles on hills, were the great titled landlords—"the Duke of This" and "the Count of That" . . . "Sir This" and "Lady That." Lower in the scale, and huddled in thatched-hut villages around the castles, were the "lower classes"—the farmers and the craftsmen. Lowest of all were the serfs; near-slaves they were, bound to the land and to the landlord in the castle. It was this European "class" life that the brave men and women who left England and other countries wanted to get away from; and they chose to settle in America. Once here, they decided that they would *not* permit people to have titles; at least such class distinction between citizens would not be tolerated. This was one factor which helped to create among the American people a sense of equality.

But another, and perhaps the chief, factor was the frontier itself. As long as there was free and open land, the spirit of equality remained strong among the people. You can see how that would be. Conquering a wilderness put men and women of all stations in life on the same level. All had to use their muscles to help build a way of living. Money, stocks, bonds, fine laces and silks, jewels, and so forth were scarcely even thought of. It was personal strength, courage, and skill that determined whether a man lived or died.

Under such conditions a man's work, no matter what it was, gave him a position of dignity in the region or community. Laborers were scarce and a worker was respected. The "hired man," like his employer, felt independent! Could the hired man not eat at his employer's table, even marry his daughter? He not only could—he frequently did!

You can see, then, how this peculiarly American sense of equality developed among the people a widespread *spirit of classlessness*. The old German or British idea that a child was born into a class and would probably always stay in it was entirely lacking on the American frontier and, to a large extent, in the villages and towns that developed behind it. "I'm as good as you," felt most men as they looked one another in the eye and measured their strength.

4. Belief in the ladder of opportunity

Of course, we must not forget that some people did get rich, while others stayed poor; that some had greater ability than others. Some—for example, those elected to office in government—were given greater power. On every frontier, differences in wealth and power did develop within a few years after settlement started. In this one sense, therefore, classes—the rich and the poor . . . the strong and the weak . . . the leaders and the followers—did develop.

But the idea of the ladder of opportunity was always present in every community. If a man had ability he could climb to riches or to social prominence. "Strive to get to the top," fathers told their children. "Be prompt and honest! Save your money and invest it wisely! Earn the respect and keep the good will of your neighbors! Look out for yourself, but get along with your fellow men and serve your community! You'll go far if you try! In fact, the ladder of opportunity stands before you, and you can get what you want if you 'have it in you.' You can be mayor . . . you can be governor . . . yes, you can even be President!"

5. The competitive spirit regarded as the driving force

But notice carefully that running through all this discussion is the idea of competition. Throughout American history fathers and mothers have been telling their children that life is a struggle. They have said:

"As you climb the rungs of the ladder of opportunity you will find others pitted against you. You will have competitors; you will have rivals. Others will be seeking the jobs that you want, the offices in school or community government that you would like to hold, the honors that you are striving to get. You'll have to compete with these people. From the beginning you'll have to fight for whatever you get, for others will be after the same things. And remember, the one who will win the fight will be the one who is strongest. The first to finish the race will be the one who runs the swiftest."

So spoke millions of parents to millions of children, and thousands of teachers to thousands upon thousands of pupils. Thus, the competitive spirit has been built up in our people from the very start of our history. The drive for "success" is an unending one.

Many Americans today question the wisdom of building up such a high degree of competitive spirit. And it must be admitted that they have many good arguments. Competition does develop widespread conflicts among people. It gives the strong and shrewd people great advantages over the weak and less clever ones. And it has been found that competition must be curbed to some extent.

Other Americans, on the contrary, assert that the competitive spirit helps to keep people at their jobs, striving for a better standard of living, for better jobs, for success. It keeps them "on their toes," they say. Take it away and you destroy the most important motive for work.

So we see that there is a very difficult problem here which must be studied and solved in the coming years by our people, namely, how far shall we continue to cultivate the competitive spirit in America?

6. Belief in private ownership

Having cut down a forest of trees and stumped it, having built a house in the clearing, having plowed the land and cultivated crops, the pioneer tended to say: "That's mine! I made it, so it's mine! Keep off it! You keep off me and I'll keep off you!" In one of Robert Frost's poems a farmer expresses this feeling exactly: "Keep off each other and keep each other off."

Similarly, in the frontier villages and towns the storekeepers, the lawyers, the doctors, and others built up their businesses by their own efforts. Craftsmen invented new tools and crude machines, and scraped together enough money to build a small shop, a mill, even a factory. Because each of these people had built up his enterprise himself, it was to be expected that he should feel the pride of the "selfmade" man, that he should feel that what he had made and owned was "private." Each one said of his business, as the farmer had of his farm—"That's mine! I made it! I invented it! I developed it! The profit it brings belongs to me!"

Never forget, then, that throughout most of American history every single American—on the frontier farm, in the crossroad hamlet, and in the growing village and town—had a deep sense of, and respect for, private ownership.

7. Hard work! Thrift!

But for most people the ladder of opportunity was not a "power escalator"! A person could not rise without effort; he had to climb, rung by rung, pulling up his own weight by hard work. Both on the frontier and in the villages and towns behind it, people knew what it was to work hard. Hours of labor were long—twelve to fourteen a day; six, even seven, days a week. Fathers, mothers, and children alike rose with the dawn and worked all day. Eighty hours a week was not uncommon—twice as many as people work in most industries now. In fact, today the new Federal hours-wages law requires that no more than 40 hours a week shall be worked in certain industries. But on the frontier industriousness was prized; idleness was regarded as an evil.

Not only was industriousness the style, but "thrift" was preached and practiced by the grownups. "Save your pennies and the dollars will take care of themselves," parents told their children. "Save and invest your money!" . . . "Lay by something for a 'rainy day'!" . . . "Save the extra grain you grow in the 'fat year'; next year may be a 'lean' one!"

8. Producers can't get something for nothing!

In the frontier days people knew they had to work for everything they got, and, as we have said, they had to work hard. To grow crops, one had to plow and plant, cultivate and harvest. To get a new dress or suit, one had to raise a sheep, shear its wool, clean and card the wool, spin yarn and weave it into cloth, cut and sew the garment. So it was with almost all the things people had. A person paid, and in full, for what he got. He paid by good headwork in planning, by hard handwork in producing. Throughout the whole history of the frontier, people were producers; they produced things and ideas, all by hard work—headwork and muscle work.

9. Discipline yourself!

Through every stage of life the idea of "discipline" was drilled into people. Our frontier ancestors came by the idea honestly enough, for that matter. The Puritans who first settled our Eastern seaboard lands in the early 1600's had been taught by their fathers in England to regard discipline as a supreme virtue. They passed the idea on to their children, generation by generation. Although life in the growing towns became easier, on every new frontier, as people moved westward across the continent, they learned the idea of self-discipline all over again.

"School yourself! To get a living is a struggle!" Indeed it was to the frontiersmen of America. To get up early in the morning and to work hard all day, year in and year out, required a strong will. To farm in the dangerous wilderness with a rifle near by required courage. To live alone, miles from the nearest neighbor, required fortitude. To withstand blizzards of snow and storms of hail, to live through river floods and burning droughts, took courage. To stick to the farm, to see the job through, took persistence— "stick-to-itiveness," they called it. All these together mean discipline. And for nearly 300 years discipline was the watchword on every frontier and in most of the little villages and towns.

10. Integrity of craftsmen

Finally, the early American developed integrity of craftsmanship. What does this mean? As you know, in the frontier homes as well as in the little towns behind the frontier, people had to make most of the things they needed. They had to have houses, furniture, barns, wagons, harnesses, gates, fences, locks, lanterns—an endless number of things. They had to fashion them out of wood, out of metal, out of whatever appropriate materials were at hand. Ready-made things either were not available or, most often, were too expensive to buy. And these things had to be made well, for they had to last a long time.

So it was that fathers and mothers lived by these rules, and taught them to their children: "Do it well. Do it as well as you can. Don't be content with merely a 'good' job; be satisfied with nothing less than the very best you have in you. Work so that you may be proud of whatever you finish. If you are making a house, make as fine a house as you can with the materials that you have. If you are making a table, let it be a *good* table, one that will stand firm, one that will look well, one that will serve the purposes to which it will be put, one that you'll be proud to have made. Be as good a house-builder, as good a furniture-maker, as good a locksmith, as good a harness-maker, as it is within your power to be."

What these fathers and mothers were teaching their children was, in short, "Be a good craftsman." Thus the spirit of integrity of craftsmanship was developed in early America, and it still exists today in some of our small villages and towns.

If you scan the foregoing paragraphs, you will see, in one series, the *individualistic* characteristics of the American—the "I" or "Me" traits; resourcefulness ... the feeling of being a free man ... of being equal to others ... of not belonging to a social class ... of having ownership ... of needing to work hard and to be thrifty ... of being a producer who pays for what he gets, not an exploiter or a speculator ... of being a self-disciplined person. These "I" or "Me" traits help to show why the American became an individualist, looking out for himself.

But the man on the frontier was not alone in everything he did. Let us see.

11. Some necessity for co-operation

Even on the frontier there were times when these hard-working, independent Americans had to work with others. There were some things they just could not do by themselves. For example, a man had to have help in "raising a barn" or "raising a house." He could put the frames of the walls together alone, perhaps, but to lift them up into place he had to have the help of several men. Also when there was fear of an attack by Indians many neighbors gathered at a single house, the strongest one, to defend themselves. A cloudburst or the sudden flooding of a river also brought the farmers over a large region together, and all set to work to build a levee or whatever else was needed to check the damage being done. Illness or an accident was a magnet which drew neighbors on all sides to help the individual or family in trouble.

These people also depended on one another in spiritual as well as in material ways. "Just to talk to another woman!" the frontiersman's wife so often thought and exclaimed. "If someone would only come!" Sheer loneliness, then, was enough to draw neighbors together at frequent intervals. Even the stranger who stopped at the cabin was welcome to a bed and a meal—if only for "company's sake" and the news that he brought. Also, great social occasions were made of barn-raisings, corn-huskings, quilting parties, and the like. At such times, men, women, and children, neighbors from far and wide, met at a man's house and helped with the task to be done. The day was climaxed by a community dinner and dance.

So while the pioneer wanted generally "to keep off his neighbor and keep his neighbor off"—to have elbowroom—he wanted also to be close to him on many occasions—for protection, for help in work, and for play. Never did he forget that he "had to get along with his neighbor"—especially after farms were built closer together and hamlets and villages and even towns grew up.

Are you beginning to understand now how the "American" came to be the kind of man he is; how, because of the special conditions of living on the frontier, he came to have certain traits? On the one hand, he was "individualistic"—with "I" traits, "It's mine!" traits, "I can manage alone!" traits. And, on the other hand, he became a co-operative man in many ways—developing "We" traits, "Let's do it together!" traits. We bring these ideas together in a kind of outline:

I. The Individualistic, or "I," traits:

Resourcefulness. Looking out for myself.

Freedom. To make of myself what I will.

Equality, absence of class lines. I'm as good as you!

The ladder of opportunity and the desire for success. I can climb to the top if I wish to. I want and shall strive for a better living, a better social position. I want to be approved by my fellows and to be given positions of public responsibility and power.

The competitive spirit. I must fight for whatever I get!

Private ownership. I found it! ... I made it! ... It's mine to do with as I please!

Hard work and thrift. The only way I'll get anywhere.

Producers of things, not middlemen or speculators. I, myself, produce or make what I use and consume. And I don't get anything for nothing.

Discipline. Because life is a struggle I must. have courage, persistence, fortitude.

II. The Co-operative, or "We," traits:

Desire for security in material matters. Physical danger is threatening, so let us work together for our own protection. Alone we are helpless to deal with nature. The weaker ones must be helped by the stronger ones.

Desire for companionship. Let us gather together for company's sake.

Willingness to give up some kinds of freedom. Yes, I want to be free, but my freedom stops where my neighbor's begins.

II. AS VILLAGES AND TOWNS AND CITIES AROSE DID THE AMERICAN SPIRIT CHANGE?

For a long, long time, perhaps until nearly our own times, the American spirit continued to be about the same. The American changed a little, but really not much. Certainly fathers and mothers continued to preach to their children the American doctrine of success: to stand on their own feet, to work hard and do their jobs well, to pay their debts, to save and invest wisely. They taught them that they were "as good as their neighbors," and that they had equal opportunities to succeed in whatever they set out to accomplish.

Now let us go on with the story of what happened in America.
Year after year restless and more adventurous men and women kept
moving westward. Their desire for "the better land over yonder"
pushed them on and on to new frontiers. They reached the Pacific
coast by 1850; by the 1870's and 1880's farms and ranches and
mines had been established on all the high plains and mountain
plateaus. The last frontier had finally been reached; soon it also
disappeared.

As the crest of this great Western movement advanced, huge
numbers of homesteaders stayed behind and developed fine farms.
Some of their children did too, and their grandchildren and great-
grandchildren. But not all remained on the land. The villages and
towns that had been springing up everywhere behind the frontier
drew greater numbers away from the land. And each year new-
comers from the East increased the village populations. Some of
these people were doctors and lawyers who opened offices. Some.
were men who invested money in stores and banks; some built
factories and opened mines. A great many others worked for money
wages or salaries in the new businesses and industries.

More and more emphasis on "social co-operation"

As these villages and towns grew up the people in them had to
learn to live close together. For example, instead of owning several
thousand or 640 or even 160 acres of land, most of the people had
to be content to live on small 50-foot or 30-foot lots. Even estates
of the richest townspeople were never more than a few acres.

This building of houses close together caused serious community
problems. People and their property had to be protected against
fire. At first neighbors helped neighbors whenever a house caught
fire. Later volunteer fire departments were formed; at the sound
of a bell or whistle citizens dropped whatever they were doing to
"run to the fire" to help put it out. Finally public-supported fire
departments had to be provided.

There was the problem of a sufficient supply of clean water.
Individual pumps and wells gave way to community reservoirs and
costly purification plants. Water was sent through pipes into every
house and building in the town. And all this came to be paid for
by public taxation.

There was the problem of crime. People needed protection from lawbreakers. In the end it was necessary for every community to have a police and court system. This too was supported by public funds.

There was the problem of protecting the health of the people, who now were living so close together. Not only impure water but impure foods of every kind had to be carefully guarded against so that disease and ill health should not spread on account of them. A vast system of medical inspection was built up. People sick with dangerous contagious diseases were quarantined. Vaccination and other treatments were used to prevent disease.

We review these facts of history briefly to show you that slowly one important change came about in the American outlook. People learned that they could not live entirely to themselves. For their own protection or advantage they had to work together. Fire in the community was a dangerous thing, and could be prevented and stopped only if all the people acted jointly to prevent it and check it. In other words, they had to *co-operate,* to work together toward a common end. The only way they could be sure of clean water and plenty of it was to join hands and finance the development of a pure-water system. That too meant co-operation. Criminals and lawbreakers could not be dealt with unless the people acted together to provide a police system. Again co-operation! An unchecked disease, they knew, would spread from house to house, from neighborhood to neighborhood, until the whole community was in danger of being wiped out. So all the people became partners in the business of health protection. Co-operation over and over again.

Now all these problems of the village, town, and growing city reached into the home of every family in the community. They were the concern of all the people. There is a word to describe these problems that touch the public as a whole. They are called "social" problems. So we can say too, that in trying to solve them by the joint efforts of all, "social" co-operation was being used.

So the Americans came to say "We" more and "I" somewhat less

Thus we find that in many ways the people became less *individualistic and more socially co-operative.* There had to be more "give and take," more willingness to compromise.

Not in all ways, of course. In business and industry and farming each man continued to compete with his neighbor to get as good a living, to make as much money, as he could. And each was still free to own many things—his own business, his own land, his own house and furnishings, his own automobiles, clothes, and the like. He was free to move about on the streets and roads. He was free to get a public-supported education, to use public libraries, museums, and the like. He was free to assemble with other citizens in public auditoriums. He was free to speak or write his own mind about the government and its officials, about problems and people.

But some of his freedom had to be curtailed for his own welfare and the welfare of all other people. The American way says that *the citizen must earn his freedom by accepting obligations.*

As our long, careful study of government showed us, the people passed laws which controlled to a certain extent what people were allowed to do. Motorists had to obey certain regulations. For example, they had to drive on the right side of the road, stop and go according to the red and green traffic signals, travel no faster than the speed limit, and the like. People could not make loud noises, block the streets, leave garbage or rubbish in public places, spread disease, and the like. They could not keep their children out of schools. They could not refuse to pay taxes. They could not put up houses or other buildings anywhere they pleased. The law of the community set down certain "nuisance" and danger restrictions. Libel and slander laws restricted to a degree what people could say and write against their neighbors or others. Thus, one by one, many individual liberties had to be given up or curtailed so that all could live safely.

Moreover, the community as a whole took over the management of many of its affairs. There was a change from private to public ownership. Many things that had formerly been owned privately were taken over by the community. For example, 100 years ago main roads and bridges were built by single owners or private companies, which collected charges, or tolls, from the people who used them. As the years went on, towns, counties, states, and even the national government discovered that it was better for such things to be operated publicly. So they took over the ownership of some of them, built other new ones, and kept them all in good condition —all of which was paid for by public taxes.

The same thing was done, as you have just seen, in the case of education. Schools were made public, were tax-supported. They were run *co-operatively* by all the people. Similarly, with water supplies, with parks and playgrounds, with enormous forest reserves and state parks, with most libraries, and some hospitals. Step by step, most of these were made public, financed by taxes, and run co-operatively in the interest of all.

These changes from the extreme private, or individualistic, attitude to the co-operative one came about very slowly, of course, and always peacefully, without violence. In the case of schools, as you have seen, many citizens were opposed to making them public. But today, certainly 90-odd per cent of the people believe that they can be operated best if they are free and public. The same is true of roads and streets, parks and playgrounds, water supplies, and protection of life and property. All these have become "publicly" owned or operated, and the people generally approve of the idea.

Do you see now how the American spirit came to be *both individualistic and co-operative*? In many ways the individual man and woman were left free to work out their own lives, but in certain others they had to do as the community, the state, and the nation as a whole decided. Thus increasingly the Americans came to say "We" more and "I" somewhat less.

A difficult problem: Are the great cities changing the American character?

What the American character will become in the future cannot be predicted. Much depends upon how conditions of community life change. We know that the growth of great cities during recent years has created some grave problems. You have already read about how large cities have altered the way people live. Family and neighborhood life has changed sharply. Either people do not even know their neighbors or, if they do, they display little interest in them. Cities have become so big and impersonal that few understand the problems or know the officials personally. Public interest in elections and in problems of government has decreased; many citizens do not bother to vote.

Take the question of equality and classes in America. Has the attitude of the American people toward the idea of equality, of having no sharply divided classes, changed? Perhaps the answer is both "yes" and "no." Certainly, to some extent the ladder of opportunity still stands before the people. But the fact cannot be denied that it is harder today than ever before to get a job. Competition is keener. It is hard to be sure that one's merit will be recognized and rewarded. In general it seems to be true that making a place for oneself in industry, business, and the professions is becoming ever more difficult.

Yet, against that view, one must remember that never has the individual American had greater opportunity than now to serve his community and nation in some kind of public work. In the next volume of this series—*America Rebuilds*—we shall take up the discussion of this problem in great detail.

The ways of earning a living in the great cities have changed American life sharply. Practically all city people work for wages or salaries. Most factories, power companies, great stores, and such businesses are owned and operated by large corporations, and each has thousands of employees. The heads of these corporations know few of the workmen on their pay rolls. Men and women tend to become "cogs" in a machine rather than the personal friends of the employer. There still are many small stores, offices, shops, and the like which are run by their owners, who hire their assistants, clerks, mechanics, and other workers; in them a certain degree of personal friendship does bind all together. But increasingly the corporation is absorbing small businesses. At work as well as at home, then, life has become impersonal.

And more recently it has become difficult for people to get work at all. In 1933 more than 15,000,000 workers—one third of the nation's employable workers—were without jobs! Even when the factories, mills, farms, mines, and businesses of all kinds were running busily in 1940, nearly 9,000,000 people were out of work.

Do you think these many changes in ways of living could take place without corresponding changes in the personal characteristics of the individual American—in the way he looks at life? Look back at the list of the characteristics we gave earlier (page 600). Some of them, of course, are the same today. Desire for success, for example, is still ingrained in the people. Many still feel independent, saying "I'm as good as you." But take the remaining items on that list—for example, resourcefulness, looking out for oneself. Do most of the people living in cities surrounded by stores, markets, doctors, hospitals, and the like, have to do everything for themselves as the frontiersmen did? Take private ownership. Do most farmers own their farms? Do city-dwellers own their houses? Do shop and factory workers own the plants they work in? Is there free land to find and develop? Are there still good opportunities to invent a new machine and get it built and sold? How is the American character affected by changed conditions?

Consider the problem of producers. On the frontier all men could say, "We are producers; we make the things we use and consume." Do most people do that today? Indeed not. An enormous, complicated, world-wide scheme of buying and selling things has come in its place. Small farmers may have a truck garden, a few hens, a pig, and a cow or two, but, for the most part, they do not consume the things they raise. They produce things to sell.

Take the changes brought about by industry. In most cases the workers in factories do not even see the finished product on which they have worked. Each does only one step in the process of making it. They are denied the thrill of making a complete article. But, most important of all, the actual number of people needed to produce a manufactured thing has seriously declined, whereas the number who buy and sell things has greatly increased.

What about integrity of craftsmanship or workmanship? There is no doubt that the fine spirit of craftsmanship is disappearing. This is partly due to the increasing dependence upon machines to do man's work. In recent years, as power-machine factories have supplanted the hand craftsman, there has been much less demand for craft skill. Work has become more specialized—each person doing one separate special job over and over again. Also the spirit of "do it well enough to get by," not "do the best job you can," has unfortunately grown among the workers in many industries and businesses of the great cities.

We have merely hinted at the kinds of changes that have come in the American spirit. As our study of American life continues throughout the high school we shall learn much more about the American character. But perhaps the beginning we have made in this study has at least given us a glimpse of what the real "American way" is.

Chapter V

MERCHANTS OF CONFLICT[1]

A Four-Foot Shelf of Conflict

As I write there stands behind me a four-foot shelf of conflict about "un-Americanism" in the schools. It is a twenty-year documentary record—newspaper clippings, articles and cartoons from national magazines, scrapbooks and folders, pamphlets, bulletins and official reports, chapters clipped from books, transcriptions of records of hearings, stenographic records of Hearst newspaper interviews, what not.

More than three of the four feet cover the current years from the spring of 1939 through the autumn of 1940.

[1] Throughout this book I use the term "merchants of conflict" and its variants for literary purposes. The attacks on the schools are dramatic affairs and can be described adequately only in dramatic and commonly understood words. I am describing the effects of the attacks and stating merely my own personal interpretations of them. I use the term "merchant" in that special connotation of "to sell," which in recent years has become common parlance; for example, "I sell you that idea" . . . "he sold the people his proposition." I do not imply that the persons named in any such connection engage in the described attacks for purposes of pecuniary gain. I use the term "conflict" in its standard dictionary connotation: "a prolonged struggle," a "clashing or variance of opposed principles, statements, arguments." Later in this chapter I define the term "unrest" by means of an elaborate discussion of its "build-up." That conflict and unrest, so defined, have developed as a direct consequence of the attacks is clearly established in this book.

Nearly a foot deals with the period 1921–26, half an inch with 1927. A few inches record events in 1934–35, and occasional items refer to controversies in scattered communities at odd moments since the close of the World War. Altogether there are thousands of items covering five recurring waves of social hysteria since 1918. It is, of course, but a meager sample of the national literature of conflict, but it is a representative sample and contains the key items. In this chapter we shall work with the three feet of current conflict materials; in Chapter VI we shall examine the data of "This has happened before!"

Popular Protest or Stimulated Hysteria?

Does this file indicate nationwide popular protest? It does not. Although six to eight million Americans have buzzed with questions about Rugg and his books since 1939, the entire phenomenon is a record of controversies initiated by a few persons standing in strategic places. With few exceptions these episodes of strife have been created and kept alive by men who have access to powerful national means of communication and community action.

Here is the personnel of the general staff:

1. Merwin K. Hart, of Utica, N.Y., and New York City; called by conservative leaders of education in New York State, "Public Education Enemy No. 1," executive of his personally organized New York State Economic Council.
2. Bertie C. Forbes, of Englewood, N.J., and New York City; for many years a columnist for the Hearst newspapers and publisher of his own magazine *Forbes*.
3. Major Augustin G. Rudd, of Garden City, Long Island, N.Y.; former U.S. army man, business executive and active in the American Legion.
4. E. H. West, of Haworth, N.J., and New York City; business executive, active in the American Legion.

5. Major General Amos Fries, of Washington, D.C.; retired U.S. army man, editor of *Friends of the Public Schools*, a periodic bulletin distributed to public schools and in which attacks have been made upon school practices.
6. Elizabeth Dilling, of Kenilworth, Ill.; wealthy author and publisher of *The Red Network*, lecturer on "un-Americanism" and the danger of Communistic tendencies in America.

These few persons make up the spearhead of the present attack on the schools. To this list must be added at least two professional writers who have prepared and published articles against progressivism in the schools in national mass-circulation magazines:

1. George E. Sokolsky, of New York City; wrote three articles in *Liberty* in 1940, reaching millions of readers and causing questioning about certain aspects of our work.
2. O. K. Armstrong, of Springfield, Mo.; active with Verne Marshall in the No Foreign War Committee, writer of the article "Treason in the Textbooks," which appeared in September 1940. This went into one million homes in several thousand American communities.

Inconspicuous though most of these persons are, they have created fear in many places. How was it possible for them to multiply their own personal influence so greatly? They have done it by using national publicity channels, especially the facilities of certain national organizations to distribute articles, letters, circular notices, what not. Among these are certain national patriotic organizations, certain business organizations, notably the New York State Economic Council (M. K. Hart's personal organization, reaching most New York State communities), and Hearst newspapers with their affiliated syndicated features, reaching several million readers each week.

In addition to these national agencies Hart, Rudd, et al.,

formed the American Parents Committee on Education in
the spring of 1940, with offices at Hart's headquarters, for
the purpose of co-ordinating articles and other materials
dealing with liberalism in the schools. This outlet is now
used for the distribution of their publications.

There are still other individuals and organizations involved, but these are the principal ones. The record before
me of their total work reveals a political and psychological
phenomenon of major significance. It can be sufficiently
illustrated by a brief statement. A single article distributed
by a national patriotic organization can alter, indeed has
drastically altered, the mood of the people in hundreds of
communities scattered widely over the country and has resulted in the censorship of schools.

★   ★   ★

A shocking example is at hand. In the first week of September 1940 O. K. Armstrong's article "Treason in the
Textbooks" went into a million homes. This is without
qualification the most unfair attack I have seen made on
schoolteachers in thirty years. "Treason" is a word one
doesn't lightly employ. Mr Armstrong, however, pretends
to find it "in textbooks." Can he escape the grave imputa-
tion of charging the teachers who use the books with being
traitors? He does not even attempt to escape it.

Two cartoons stretch across two facing pages. In one
a leering, bony teacher grins wickedly down at frightened boys and girls. From scrawny hands slime drips down
upon four books labeled *Constitution*, *Religion*, *U.S.
Heroes* and *U.S. History*. In the other the same teacher fits
black glasses on the eyes of a young boy and girl who are
reading books called *The American Way of Life*. A caption
reads: "The 'Frontier Thinkers' are trying to sell our youth
the idea that the American way of life has failed." In the

article itself a score of authors and books are blacklisted, although nine tenths of all illustrative references are taken from my writings.

What reception did this article find? In many cases it probably was not read at all; in others it was probably received with indifference. But a few subscribers who read it knew personally the editors and institutions it attacked, were filled with contempt for its defamations and protested vigorously to those who were responsible. Many non-subscribers, among whom were educational leaders all over the country, denounced it as vicious. Halfhearted retractions of the charges against *Scholastic* magazine and certain of the other blacklisted magazines began to be issued from the office of the periodical in which the Armstrong attack had appeared. There was no retraction at all, however, of the attack on my books. There was no apology for the cartoons, for smearing the teachers of our whole country.

It so happens that the organization in whose name the "treason" article was published has a special officer in each of hundreds of local communities throughout the country. These officers, disregarding protests and retractions, at once went into action—guided, as it appears, from headquarters. Many of them, bringing the matter up before local school boards and school superintendents, demanded that *the Rugg books,* Scholastic *magazine and other publications blacklisted by Armstrong be investigated. In some cases —we have clear proof of this—they demanded and secured the exclusion of the attacked materials from the schools.*

I have never witnessed such an astounding example of organized pressure on the schools in all my experience. Within two weeks from the time the article was published *Scholastic* magazine received four hundred letters cancelling orders for sixteen thousand subscriptions. In a score of communities around New York City, in Westchester

County, on Long Island and in New Jersey, school boards were compelled by the pressure to call special meetings to discuss "the Rugg books." In many places where this happened my books had been used for from six to ten years with wholehearted approval by students, teachers, administrators and parents.

I attended several of these meetings myself. In each case the local officer of whom I have spoken was the single protesting person and he admitted that his action was prompted by the "treason" article. In almost every case *he had not read the books, but*——

Thus the power of a million-circulation magazine together with the organization behind it is demonstrated. And, I repeat, any person who has access to such national means of communication and community action can disrupt community life in the entire country. Here is a clear example of dangerous concentration of power in the hands of a minority. And the only protection against it? Eternal vigilance!

★   ★   ★

From 1921 to 1926 and at times in the years since, other patriotic organizations have engaged in the same kind of hunt. Officers make repeated pronouncements in the press urging the removal of my books from the schools of local communities. Speeches are made before local, regional and national meetings. The most powerful weapon used, however, is the personal, face-to-face work of the local and district representatives. Letters have been sent from national headquarters, directing these people to find out if certain books were used in the local schools and, if they were, to exert influence to have them removed.

In April 1940 I personally met two of these district representatives, one in New Mexico, the other in Montana, at three-day regional meetings of the Progressive Education

Association. In each case the representative told me she had received a letter from "headquarters," urging the removal of the Rugg books from the schools of her region. In each case the representative had listened to my lectures with approval, found no basis for attacking my work, indeed decided to do all possible to keep me *in* the schools. But these were only two. How many "letters from headquarters" have had more successful results?

★ ★ ★

In the current attack on the schools the publicity officers of certain national business organizations—the "research directors," for example—work in exactly the same way as the "Americanism" officers of certain patriotic societies.

In some cases lecturers have been hired to go through the country from community to community, arousing clubs of citizens to "look into" their children's education. Investigation shows that their documentation of the presence of "subversive" and "un-American" activities in the schools consists largely of out-of-context paragraphs lifted from textbooks and other educational materials. In other instances professional writers have been employed to write articles for the million-circulation magazines. Chief among these is George E. Sokolsky, who published three articles in *Liberty*[2] attacking progressive education, with one devoted primarily to my books.

In the April 1940 issue of *Nation's Business* appeared Major A. G. Rudd's article "Our 'Reconstructed' Educational System,"[3] attacking the Rugg books. Its publication caused almost instant reverberations. In some cases school-

[2]George E. Sokolsky: *Liberty*, "Hard-Boiled Babes," March 16, 1940; "Our Children's Guardians," April 6, 1940; "Is Your Child Being Taught to Loaf?" May 4, 1940.

[3]This article is the chief source of many minor attacks made on the books.

board subscribers to the magazine, accepting the allegations made in this article as true, urged the elimination of the Rugg books and *Scholastic* magazine (these were specifically attacked in the article). In some cases superintendents who had read the article feared its effects and, wanting no repercussions in their schools, wrote to me and my publishers for "defense" material. It is known that agents for rival textbooks (not under attack) went out of their way to bring the article to the attention of board members, superintendents, principals and teachers. Citizens here and there began to discuss the contents of the article with the school people in their communities. In one way or another this single article caused many school systems to reconsider their retention of the attacked materials. In still other school systems an atmosphere of tension developed among teachers and administrators, and fear of the suppression of freedom of discussion spread.

Perhaps the best single example of self-appointed censors of the schools is Merwin K. Hart of Utica, N.Y., and New York City. His Who's Who in America record shows him to be a graduate of Harvard, a lawyer (specializing in taxation), a former captain of infantry in the United States army with service in France in 1918, an executive of insurance and other corporations and for a short time a member of the New York State Legislature. Since 1931 he has devoted himself increasingly to the task of keeping taxes in New York State at a low level. His chief organ in such activities has been the New York State Economic Council which he organized himself in 1931 and of which he is president. In one announcement the avowed purpose is "to curb public spending and to prevent legislation harmful to those who live by private enterprise." Through this organization he has so consistently opposed the progressive expansion of public education that many educational leaders now regard him as their chief opponent; he is indeed frequently referred to as "Public Education Enemy No. 1." In the past few years he has been perhaps the most vocal of the patrioteers who attack progressive educational developments, using my books as the chief target. In his biweekly "Economic Council Letter" he has repeatedly denounced the books; for example, in Council Letter 78, April 15, 1940, the following advice appears:

Are Rugg books in your schools? *We recommend* that our members and readers in all localities ascertain whether these Rugg social-science textbooks are in use in their schools. And if you let us know what you find we will try to make constructive suggestions.

He quotes from a newspaper item: "The loyalty of Dr Harold Rugg, the author of these textbooks, isn't above question . . ."

Council Letter 79 (May 1, 1940) carried a follow-up on the above:

The Economic Council . . . is setting up a special committee and is now prepared to assist any community in the United States with advice and suggestions and to furnish adequate booklets and other printed matter. *Inquiries are invited.*

On May 17, 1940, Hart announced the formation of an American Parents Council on Education with the object of "rooting out the subversive teachings which are taking place in many public schools." In the summer the committee sent out the announcement that George E. Sokolsky's four *Liberty* magazines were available in reprint form, together with reprints of addresses by Hart and Archibald E. Stevenson and a pamphlet containing radio speeches by A. G. Rudd, Stevenson and Hart—at a nickel a single copy and less for copies requested "in lots." Electrical transcriptions of the radio addresses (suitable for radio broadcasting) "will be sent to any interested person." Phonograph records of the addresses, "particularly effective for use with home groups," are also "available at the committee office."

That Hart, with his council and his committee, has been one of the chief "crusaders" against my books and my "Americanism" is a matter of record. One is justified, therefore, in raising questions about *his* "Americanism." Because it will illustrate the real attitude of these attackers of modern education, I refer to a single type of personal expression by him, namely, his assertion that America is not a democracy and never was so conceived by our great leaders until the crisis of the past few years came upon us. To illustrate I quote from his speech before the Nassau Club, Princeton, N.J., February 14, 1940.

" 'Democracy,' then, is the rallying cry under which the American system of government is being prepared for despotism. Its clear outline is already fashioned. . . .

"What started all this talk about 'democracy' in the United States? Beginning with the Communist International meeting in 1935 in Moscow, the representatives of that world organization began everywhere to speak of Soviet Russia as a 'democracy'—as one of 'the great democracies,' of which the others were Great Britain, France and the United States. Many organizations were formed forthwith in the United States, the name of each containing the word. These included the American League for Peace and Democracy, the North American Committee to Aid Spanish Democracy, the Church League for Industrial Democracy and many others. If you find any organization containing the word 'democracy' it is probably directly or indirectly affiliated with the Communist party."

Another chief source of fear and unrest in the schools is the Hearst newspapers, at the present moment the syndi-

cated column of B. C. Forbes. Day by day his recurring
blasts go into millions of homes. Following the publication
of each new outburst against me clippings of news items
and editorials based on his material have come to me
through the mails—from every section of the country,
north, east, south and west. Forbes's own magazine, carrying the same kind of attacks, also has influence, in spite of its
small circulation, because its clientele is made up largely of
the general group from which members of local boards of
education are appointed. Forbes's methods, I think, have
already been described sufficiently in Chapter II, so I shall
say little more about them here.

One important caution. The charges made against the
manufacturers of controversy are *not* meant to apply to the
memberships of the organizations whose facilities these persons have been able to use. Most of the Legionnaires, the
Daughters of the American Revolution, the Veterans of
Foreign Wars and the members of other patriotic and business organizations know nothing of the behind-the-scenes
activities against progressivism in the schools.

I have long been loath to deal with the attackers. Nevertheless, to do so now has, I feel, become an obligation to a
large sector of the American people. Several millions of
their children have read, perhaps are now reading, my
books. I feel now that I should tell them what the new education is trying to do for American youth. I feel, moreover,
that they should also know that the present dreadful wave
of hysteria is serving one good purpose—it is arousing adult
interest and building adult study in education infinitely
faster than any of our own organized efforts in that direction.

THE BUILD-UP OF UNREST

Understanding increases as we see the merchants of conflict at work. But first we need to know how the social soil is prepared for their sowing of the seeds of unrest in the school. People like Rudd, Hart, Forbes and company make headway only under certain social conditions. To see what those are we must examine the factors that contribute to the general build-up of unrest.[4]

1. The Kaleidoscope of Daily Events

No one factor taken alone accounts for the development of social tension. Only the cumulation and simultaneous occurrence of several can create the deep cycles of hysteria which periodically harass a people. The first is the moving flow of the daily current of events in the million neighborhoods of America. From morning to night, over the radio and through the press, the public mind is sprayed with a flood of episodes of personal stress and strain. To name a few:

A judge is convicted of a crime . . . a policeman commits suicide . . . a child is kidnaped . . . scandal breaks out in a school . . . a new sect splits off from a local church . . . a munitions plant blows up . . . a dam breaks . . . a business leader condemns the President . . . a corporation fails to pass its expected dividend . . . a mine is shut down . . . the racketeers in a labor union are arrested . . . a corporation defies the N.L.R.B.

Day by day the man on the street is pelted with these minutiae of personal strain. He may grouch a bit and grum-

[4]Chapter VII shows how cycles of witch-hunting rise and fall with corresponding cycles of social hysteria.

ble about this or that, but unless he or someone close to him is touched by the incidents, or unless he senses the curtailment of his liberties or the endangering of his security, he does little about it.

2. Periodic Events of Wider Influence

From time to time events occur which detonate more noisily through the culture. Examples are the conventions of such national organizations as those to which we have just referred. Keynote speeches, resolutions against this and for that, reports of "subversive" elements discovered and weeded out—all of these reflect the prestige and solidarity of the memberships and exert proportional social pressure.

The convening of a new Congress at the national capitol —the greatest single sounding board of American life—is another such event. New bills are proposed . . . lobbies harangue in the cloakroom . . . a senator excoriates the President. Blast after blast resounds and re-echoes in the twenty thousand American communities. The American listens, reads, discusses, tries to make up his mind.

Nothing perhaps contributes to the build-up of unrest more than the recurrent hearings and disclosures of state and national legislative investigation committees. Such agencies are powerful builders of tension. Note the procession of witnesses—renowned scientists, distinguished statesmen and judges, business experts, eminent workers in social welfare, employers and employees, renegade leaders welshing on former pals, patrioteers ranting against "the red network" or the Nazis, "front" members and their leaders.

The American is bombarded by documented facts, manufactured "facts," rumors and insinuations, displays of hate and spleen, talk of real and imagined sabotage against the

American way, charges and countercharges, denials and admissions, the smearing or "whitewashing" of personalities.

All of this is grist for the political mill and money in the pockets of reporters, news commentators, editors and publishers. And all of it makes for nationwide conflict and tension. Thus the daily pelting of news bullets on the American public becomes magnified periodically into a major shelling.

3. War, Panic and Other Great Crises

But the professional patrioteers need even more than this cumulation of unrest to thrive. Their success is limited until more powerful crisis situations come to spread a dangerous wave of public hysteria and to break down the whole temper of security among the people. In the past ten years we have lived through convincing demonstrations of two such crises—in the initial impact and persistence of economic depression and in the swift advance of the totalitarian menace.

Recall for a moment the effect of the panic of 1929 to 1933—the complete somersault in public mood with the collapse of stocks in October 1929, the shutdown of great manufacturing plants, the precipitous drop in production and sales, fear, bewilderment and anxiety of the throngs of idle people walking the streets, and so on. Three years of it—near panic. And then a great presidential election . . . one administration swept out of office and a new one installed. Who can forget the excited cry of business leaders, bankers, political bosses: "Let someone take the system and run it!" Who can forget the temporary but unprecedented concentration of power in the President and the swift passage of fourteen spectacular laws! Here was a major domestic crisis magnifying social fear and whipping the people into a state of near frenzy.

But, strangely enough, this crisis was insufficient in itself to start a sweeping and contagious spread of witch-hunting in the schools. Something still more terrifying was needed. And it has come—the fear of attack by a powerful alien foe.

During a single month, June 1940, came an almost instantaneous shift in the American public mood. Indifference toward "Europe's war" was supplanted by deep anxiety over the menace of totalitarianism to America. Millions of Americans stayed close to their radios; editions of the metropolitan newspapers were quickly snatched up. The frightening news poured out—another twenty-mile advance of the Germans into France, the capture of several more French divisions, the steady failure of the Maginot Line to hold, the rescue of the British from Dunkirk, the imminent fall of Paris, the escape of French divisions into Switzerland. Then came the real climax on June 18—the fall of France!

Almost overnight citizens on our southern border set up a cry for airplanes and tanks to guard against Nazi attacks via Central and South America. Government leaders began negotiating for a line of air and naval bases from Iceland to the West Indies and Argentina. One public leader after another proposed conscription. Billions were appropriated for defense. Thus within but a few days the hysteria which had swept over western Europe crossed the Atlantic and rolled through the United States.

Toward Total Crisis: The Coincidence of All Three Factors of Social Hysteria

Today in the early 1940s the American people are experiencing the simultaneous impact of all three of these factors of social unrest. They are living in the eleventh year of the Great Depression. Throughout it all they have been perplexed and troubled; some have been downright outraged by the "novel" ideas of "government in business" and "experiment in social control." The cumulating mood of bewilderment and drift has never been dispelled, and this, accompanied by the breakdown of many ancient and respected loyalties, has launched a questioning faith in the efficiency of democratic methods. The recent quadrennial struggle over another presidential election—perhaps the most important in three generations—has further fired the temper of the people.

But added to all this is the tumultuous effect of the collapse of democratic countries around the world and the alarming spread of the totalitarian revolution from one end of the globe to the other. Moreover, at the very moment when America is harnessing her national energies to the gigantic task of defending herself against the gravest foreign menace in her history, the security and confidence of her people are shaken daily by the incessant reports of fifth columnists, "Benedict Arnolds" and the insidious propaganda dispensers and *saboteurs* of foreign governments.

Out of the coincidence of these factors contributing to social unrest is rolling up the deepest cycle of social hysteria America has experienced for two generations.

The Build-Up of Fear in the Educational System

This combination of factors, I am convinced, accounts in very large measure for the success of censors of the schools today. To the seekers after publicity, to those who have "peeves" against the public schools, to the special-interest groups who fear the examination of their enterprises in the schools, to the rival authors and publishers desiring to make capital from the conflict—aided by the sincere defenders of authoritarian and aristocratic traditions in American life and education—the social soil could hardly be more favorably nourished.

The seeds sown by those who have attacked the schools have broken through the soil and sprouted in many places. I have explicit proof of this—from actual personal participation in several community controversies, from the written and spoken statements of teachers, administrators and citizens interested in the schools, from histories back of the elimination of the Rugg and other books and of *Scholastic* and other magazines and from school administrators' and teachers' confidential communications to me and my publishers explaining the nonrenewal of orders: "They must sit tight" until "things blow over" and "get less hysterical."

What Are the Charges?

Now we can come back to the charges made against the liberals in the schools. Our enemies have said "We accuse!" in a vast mass of words, ranging from "ringmaster of the fifth column of the United States" and "he is financed by Moscow" to the banal "un-American" and "subversive" against a large number of progressive educators. For a systematic outline of the charges we can go to statements written by Armstrong and Rudd.

First to Armstrong.

In his "Treason in the Textbooks" article he sums up the chief charges against the liberals by saying that they are working on four fronts:

1. To present a new interpretation of history in order to "debunk" our heroes and cast doubt upon their motives, their patriotism and their service to mankind.
2. To cast aspersions upon our Constitution and our form of

government and shape opinions favorable to replacing
them with socialistic control.

3. To condemn the American system of private ownership
and enterprise and form opinions favorable to collectivism.

4. To mold opinions against traditional religious faiths and
ideas of morality as being parts of an outgrown system.

Armstrong does not actually charge "conspiracy." The
chapter in *What Next, America?*,[5] on the other hand, comes
perilously close to it:

We charge that there is, throughout this country, a well-
organized and powerfully entrenched group of educators endeavoring to inculcate, in various ways, into a new generation
of boys and girls ideas and doctrines that are foreign and ab-
horrent to our American philosophy, as established by our fore-
fathers in the Constitution of the United States and the Declaration of Independence—and maintained over a period of one
hundred and fifty years.

These professors and teachers [Rugg and George S. Counts
are named specifically]—some of whom are known as the
"Frontier Thinkers"—are outspoken in their advocacy of a new
society or a new social order for the United States. This "new
society" which these theorists envision is, in reality, a very old
society, indeed. So closely does it resemble the threadbare
Marxian Mother Hubbard that it must inevitably have been cut
from the same pattern. We meet in their specifications our old
friend, "production for use and not for profit." They believe,
too, these "advanced" educators, in the elimination of competition, stifling of private enterprise, confiscation of wealth. All

[5]"The Inside Story of the 'Fifth Column' in America," Chapter III,
of *What Next, America?*, published by Maxwell Droke of Indianapolis.
No person is named as author of the book or of Chapter III. For the
particular section in the chapter named "The Communistic Trend in
Our Public Schools" there is the following footnote: "In the preparation
of this section we are deeply indebted to Mr Augustin G. Rudd, who
has made a special study of subversive activities in American public
schools. Many of the instances which we cite here are from Mr Rudd's
researches." Armstrong also gives credit to Major Rudd for the list of
names of textbooks and magazines to be blacklisted.

this of course leads inevitably to greatly enhanced powers for the federal government and the consequent regimentation of our people.

A little later it is stated that these "advanced" educators have five principal avenues through which they "can get and are getting action on their insidious ideas":

First, they *train the teachers* who are employed in our public-school systems. (Teachers College, Columbia University, is one of the strongholds of the group advocating "a new society." There are a number of others.)

Second, they *write the textbooks* which have been adopted by many states for use in our public-school systems.

Third, they write many of the books recommended as *supplementary reading* and exercise discretionary powers in selecting other supplementary readings which will guide youthful minds toward a regimented society.

Fourth, they *edit the magazines* which keep teachers and students conversant with the progress of the campaign for the new social order. These publications, used in library and classroom, include *Social Frontier* [no longer in existence, replaced by *Frontiers of Democracy*], *American Observer*, *Junior Review*, *Weekly News Review*, *Civic Leader* and *Scholastic*.

Fifth, they dominate or exert a powerful influence in national and state educational associations, as well as in various federal groups concerned with public education.

I hereby deny categorically that there is the slightest vestige of truth in these and other similar "charges."

It is to be regretted that a situation can be built up in our country in which it becomes necessary to deny charges of this kind. I do so only after years of silence and at the urgent request of publishers, colleagues and friends. Those who know me and those who *have* read and understood the books—and these include tens of thousands of students and teachers and parents who have used them for almost twenty years—know that the statements made above do not describe my philosophy or my work.

For example, take the ridiculous charge that I am a Communist and have a grandiose plan to overthrow the capitalist system by boring from within, through child and adult education!

I am not a Communist. I have never been a Communist. I have never been a member of or affiliated with the Communist party, directly or indirectly, in any way whatsoever. I am not a Socialist. I have never been a Socialist. I have never been a member of or affiliated with the Socialist party. Nor have I taken part in the work of that party.

I have never subscribed to such controversial tenets of the Marxist theory as the idea of the "class struggle." On the contrary, for years I have urged in articles[6] and lectures that students and teachers should not devote too much time to the study of Marxian ideas, since they were written in western Europe in the middle nineteenth century for European conditions. These ideas have never fitted American conditions, and certainly they do not fit them today in the middle twentieth century. I have urged instead that our students and teachers should concentrate most of their energies on preparing to lead young people toward an intelligent understanding of our own American civilization. This means direct and thorough study of American life— its history and its contemporaneous conditions and problems. They must of course study the history of other cultures and study also the theories of classic students of society from the Greeks to the present day, which necessarily includes Karl Marx. But their great task is mastery of all

[6]See, for example, *Social Frontier* for February and April 1936, "The American Mind and the Class Problem."

the significant writings of American philosophers of government and social life, from Jefferson, Hamilton, Madison, Marshall, Emerson, Whitman and their company down to and including the profound statesmen, scholars, poets and other thinking men of today.

I am accused of saying that the American way is wrong, that it is a failure. I have *never* said this. I do not believe it. On the contrary, the twenty-five thousand pages of my books have been written to build in youth and in adults an understanding of the fact that the American standard of living is the highest on the earth today and higher than that of any major country at any earlier stage of history. In book after book I have developed the fact that the United States is the greatest haven of liberty in the world. I have reiterated the view that the American people have the most favorable opportunity of any people in history to build a civilization of physical and spiritual abundance, of true democracy and of real integrity of expression. Persons who claim to have found otherwise from even a most careful search of my writings are guilty of outright falsehood.

I am accused of advocating the overthrow of the capitalist system. I have never done so.

Moreover, I have never believed in or preached social reconstruction by any means except through education. I do not believe and have never believed that the American people will ever resort to the use of violence or any other nondemocratic method to bring about social change. My entire professional career and my books—especially *The Child-Centered School, Culture and Education in America, The Great Technology* and *American Life and the School Curriculum*—have been devoted primarily to the building of a new and better education—for adults, for youths and for children. I think of this record as one of true Americanism and I am proud of it.

There is also the charge that the liberals in education "mold opinions against traditional and religious faith" and designate the ideals of morality as part of "an outgrown system." This is an absolute falsehood. Wherever the church and religion are discussed the presentation is always imbued with deep respect for and reverent attitudes toward the spiritual life of the people. As for ideas of morality being part of an outmoded system, I myself have been most persistent in pointing out the dangers to morality in the developing urban life of our times.

I could give many examples of the way in which outright falsehoods have crept into the charges against me, but my denial of these extends over all the others as well.[7]

Obviously a writer's meaning can be completely altered or destroyed by lifting statements out of context. Here is a single example:

From *A History of American Government and Culture*, page 141, I am quoted as saying: "The merchants, the

[7]Note also that ignorance of school practice determines some of the "charges."

Major Rudd, for example, claims that the Teachers' Guides to the Rugg social-science books are "not available to parents" and that the pupils' Workbooks are "not to be taken home." (Major General Fries's *Bulletin* and the Hearst newspapers quote the same thing.) Both of these statements are false. So far as my plan is concerned, the Guides can be made available to parents (or to children) and can be taken home at any time; the same holds true for the Workbooks. In this, as in so many other criticisms by laymen, there is complete ignorance of facts and conditions. Major Rudd seems to find something sinister even in the existence of teachers' guides in the Rugg program. Apparently he doesn't know that most textbooks are accompanied by such guides, given away by the publishers when the pupils' textbooks are purchased. Naturally there is only one copy to a class. This makes it physically impossible for the children to carry the teachers' guides home as a matter of routine. It isn't that the guides contain some secret and undercover advice only for the teacher; it is simply that there aren't enough of them to go around.

landowners, the manufacturers, the shippers and the bankers got what they wanted." This is offered as "proof" that I malign the Founding Fathers as a small moneyed power group conspiring to control the government solely in their own interest.

But note: this is only the first half of the sentence I had written. The other half is: " . . . namely, a government which would stabilize money and trade, keep order within the country and defend the nation against foreign enemies."

This and other half sentences and half paragraphs are quoted against me. Certainly it is clear that without the indispensable contexts such statements lose their meaning and validity.

★   ★   ★

In some cases the attackers have revealed a mastery of intemperate vocabulary and constantly resort to the tricks of the propagandist and the journalistic devices of creating prejudice by words. As proof I give the key phrases, picked out of hundreds of pages of their writings. I, they charge: [8]

am "subversive."

am "un-American."

"undermine patriotism."

"twit the Founding Fathers."

am "poisoning the minds of the young."

have an "alien ideology."

believe in "radical collectivism."

have an "outline for collectivist government."

sympathize with "the collectivation of agriculture."

am "Communistic."

have a "conspiracy" to "spread Communism."

emphasize the "classes" in American life.

am "socialistic."

advocate "state socialism."

am an "advocate of a new social order."

[8]See pages 230 to 235 for a discussion of the role of just such "stereotypes" as these in molding public opinion.

have a "plan to substitute a new social order for our American government."

would "regiment private enterprise."

"undermine the faith of pupils in private enterprise."

advocate "government bureaucratic control."

recommend a "complete planned economy."

have a "materialistic interpretation of history."

"belittle and malign America."

"tear up the Bill of Rights."

"insidiously teach false doctrines."

believe the "American way of life obsolete."

stress "errors and evils" in our civilization.

sow "discontent in the classroom."

have a "subtle and insidious scheme to undermine faith in America."

"delude" my readers.

use "underhanded efforts."

"cause pupils to rebel against all authority."

use "distortion."

★   ★   ★

One of the most common methods of attack is gross exaggeration of meanings. Here is a single instance. I am accused, correctly, of saying that democracy in the United States is an experiment.

As life on the continent changed the British emigrants into Americans, their government changed too. It became a new thing—partly British but essentially American. Decade by decade it changed, especially after the formation of the Constitution in 1787. Because it changed and is still changing, perhaps more rapidly than ever, we call it an experiment in government. . . .

This, it is said, indicates clearly my interest in Communism. The ridiculousness of this charge becomes obvious to those who go through the laborious task of searching for the facts as written.

★   ★   ★

Many examples can be given of twisting the author's meaning. A radio address[9] of A. E. Stevenson is a striking illustration. In it he said that the effort of the Frontier Thinkers "to indoctrinate the children of the nation with a new social creed would have failed to make its present progress" if I had not "implemented the program" with my social-science textbooks.

His purpose in writing these volumes, he says frankly, is to keep the "American problem" constantly before the school children. And that problem, he adds, is to substitute a "co-operate commonwealth" for the present government of the United States.

This is an outright twisting of meaning. Of course I have advocated the development of a co-operative commonwealth. But never in my statement of the American problem, never anywhere on the platform or in writing have I advocated that we *substitute* a co-operative commonwealth for the present government of the United States.

The Nub of the Attack: Our Social and Educational Philosophy

I am convinced that there is one deep-seated cleavage that lies behind the present attack and those which have recurred earlier. When the smoke screen of name calling is dissipated one central problem stands out: *What interpretation of "the American way of life" is to guide the study of civilization in the schools?* The real animus of the merchants of conflict is that we do not teach in our books *their* personal brand of the American system of private enterprise. Their personal brand, I say. To them—to judge from their statements—the American system means com-

[9]Archibald E. Stevenson, May 8, 1940, WIBX, Utica, N.Y.

petition without any regulation or control . . . old-fashioned laissez faire . . . "every man for himself and the
devil take the hindmost." They want this system taught,
and they would control the school and censor its books
to see that it is taught.

The Remainder of This Book Is Itself the Best Denial
of the Charges

The nub of the attacks upon me is, in short, my social
and educational philosophy. I cannot possibly state what
that is adequately in a few pages. For an understanding
of it I offer the rest of this book. I have no illusions that
its meager power will stop those who attack from grinding
their axes. Some of them are in the fight to make money;
some are in it for publicity leading to the power and the
glory. They are persistent men. I cannot hope to convert
them or even to defeat them.

But this book will, I hope, reach the people who want
to understand. That's why I've written it.

THE ORDEAL OF DEMOCRACY

THREE CURVES OF SOCIAL TREND

Out of the Dawn of the New Industrial Culture
Three Curves of Interdependent Social Trends
Traced Themselves on the Moving Record of History:
Economic Productivity ... Social Invention ... Popular Consent.

Throughout the First Day of Industrialism
It Was Taken for Granted That All Three Would Rise
Sufficiently Synchronized to Preserve Social Stability.
But under the Momentum of Expansion
Economic Productivity Was Sharply Accelerated,
While Social Invention and Popular Consent
Lagged Cumulatively Behind.

Meanwhile
Other Constituent Trends, Such as the Growth of Populations,
Which Had Given Life to the Advance of Man's Productivity,
Passed Points of Inflection
and Gave Fair Warning of Impending Social Change.

To the People Generally These Changes
from Positive to Negative Acceleration Meant Nothing,
but to the Men of Creative Design—
the Engineer, the Statesman, the Educator—
They Were Signposts of a Great Transition.

HYPOTHESIS

When, Therefore, in the Calculus of Human Events
the Curves of Interdependent Social Trends
Either Pass Points of Inflection
or Produce Equations of Different Orders,
Men of Intelligence Revise Their Systems of Thought
and Design New Courses of Democratic Action.

Chapter VI

THE LONG ARMISTICE

THE YEARS I have called the "Long Armistice" constitute the twenty-year period between the signing of the Treaty of Versailles in 1919 and the renewal of open warfare in Europe in 1939–40. I have so named them to convey the feeling of unbroken, near-war tension. Hardly a year has passed in which war was not being waged in some section of the Eurasian continent. The domestic life of many of its peoples has been constantly interrupted by the armed seizure of power by dictators, their undeclared war on civilization, their contempt for contracts and treaties, their stamping on liberties and their debasement of human personality. It so happens also that the construction of the Rugg books covers exactly the same period.

OUR TIMES, A GREAT TRANSITION IN INDUSTRIAL-DEMOCRATIC CULTURE

But even the Long Armistice cannot be understood except in the background of its antecedents—the events and circumstances which brought about its conditions and problems. These antecedents form the moving trends of history, some of short-term length and others covering many centuries.

In order to get at the roots of the Western conception of the "Individual"—the basis of present-day "democracy"— we should have to go as far back as the epoch-making days of the eastern Mediterranean cultures, twenty-five hundred to three thousand years ago. But a much shorter period provides enough background for understanding the unique problems of our times. The centuries when unmistakable signs of the development of modern industrial-democratic culture began to appear provide sufficient data. This means going back some eight hundred years to about 1100 A.D.

The sweep of Western history during those years can be divided, of course, in many ways, but I have found the following three periods to have excellent support in the facts of social change. Our times are a phase of the third stage.

I *Before the Machine Age,* 1100–1600 A.D.—centuries in which national states, languages and literatures slowly formed, the rudiments of science and inventions were achieved, the exploration of the physical earth was begun, and the individual man gradually discovered and asserted his personal powers.

II *The First Industrial-Democratic Revolution and the Great Expansion of Europe,* 1600 to about 1900—marked by the initial conquest and settlement of virgin continents and islands; the bold pre-emption of the "free land" of the earth and the exploitation of natural resources by "rugged individualists"; rapid advances in mathematics, science, invention and industrial technology; spectacular establishment of civil and political rights for the individual, and the development of literacy among industrial peoples through universal elementary education. It was in these three centuries that the framework of an efficient power-machine production system was built.

III *The Great Transition from the Machine Age into the Power Age, the 1890s to the present day—our own times.*

I have called this third period the "Great Transition" because it marks the passing of the first stage of industrial-democratic society and the emergence of a second.

Ten events of the past fifty years stand out conspicuously as witnesses. I do no more than enumerate them here:

1. Revolutionary inventions and their rapid integration in perfected machine technology.
2. Mass production of goods by corporations producing standardized products in increasingly manless straight-line production plants; a corresponding increase in the displacement of skilled craftsmen and unskilled workers.
3. The passing of the last frontier. The completion of the preemption and settlement of the "free land" of the earth formerly held by so-called backward peoples and taken from them by conquest.
4. A dramatic change in emigration from northern and western Europe to southern and eastern Europe—and with immigration into our own gates declining.
5. A change from a highly dynamic to a slowly growing population in industrial countries, with the statistical prediction in America that population will have stopped growing by the middle of the twentieth century.
6. The concentration of industrial peoples in cities with steady displacement of farm and craft labor and increasing anonymity and unresponsibility of personal and social life.
7. A marked decline in the size of the family and marked changes in its role as the chief cornerstone of national culture.
8. The complete establishment of formal reading-writing-arithmetic school systems in each of the major industrial countries, with ninety-odd per cent of the people becoming literate.
9. The suffrage provided for all, the end point of the seven-

hundred-year advance in the establishment of civil and political rights and the building of the machinery of democratic government.

10. First and Second World Wars, or, as some are saying, the modern "Thirty Years' War," brought about by such factors as world-wide interdependence of production and distribution, increase in rivalry for raw materials, markets and places of investment, competition in armament building, secret military alliances and corresponding propagation of hatred among national populations, devastating consequences in dislocation of economic world arrangements.

In very large part these ten examples of drastic change in the past fifty years—all revealed and documented by creative students of the social frontier—constitute the basis for my calling the period the "Great Transition."

OUR TIMES MARKED BY SWIFT INDUSTRIAL EXPANSION, 1860–

The true nature of our times stands out boldly if we look at the social problems pressing upon us today as the outcome of spectacular industrial expansion. My readers hardly need be reminded of the speed and the full-tilt drive under which the American system of private enterprise was built especially after 1860. It was a breath-taking movement in which every physical phase of industrial culture expanded quickly. Historical curves which portray the growth of all the vast industries rise with increasing acceleration.[1] Their equations are marked by high exponents—3, 4, 5, even 8 and 9 for some of extraordinary growth over short periods.[2] Such other phases of the cul-

[1] The generalized curve of production is of the form $p = kt^3$, where p = production, t = "time" and k = a constant. That of the productivity of the worker is $mh = kt^{-4}$ where mh = man-hours.

[2] See Bassett Jones: *Debt and Production*. The John Day Company, New York, 1933.

ture as the growth of population,[3] the concentration of people in cities, attendance in schools, literacy and the endowment of research advanced at similar rapid rates.

Three Trends Out of Step

The frontispiece of this chapter states one of the major theses underlying my work, namely, that our times constitute a critical period in American history because three basic social trends have gotten out of step with one another: (1) economic productivity, that is, the ability of men to produce economic goods and services, (2) social invention, especially that ability of society through its leaders to regulate and control the direction and extent of economic productivity, (3) popular consent, that is, the ability of our people to carry on government on the principle of consent of the governed. At bottom our current social problems hinge upon the lags between these three trends; put differently, upon three facts that emerge from these lags.

The first fact is that the Americans now possess an actual going economic system capable of producing enough goods and services to give every family in America the purchasing power needed to buy a decent standard of life.[4] The brains, ambition and energy of the American "free enterprisers" made this possible in the past century through their initial jobs of clearance and building. Their total contribution on the physical side cannot but arouse the

[3]The population equation is of the form $p = kt^2$, where p = population, t = time and k = a constant.

[4]Harold G. Moulton, et al. (1) *America's Capacity to Produce; America's Capacity to Consume.* Brookings Institution, Washington, D.C., 1934. (2) Harold Loeb, et al. *The Chart of Plenty,* Viking Press, New York, 1935, and the *Report of the National Survey of Potential Product Capacity.* (The New York City Housing Authority and the Works Division of the Emergency Relief Bureau, City of New York, 1935.)

excited admiration of the historian, and in my own books
I consciously try to cultivate that admiration in young
people.[5]

The second fact is that we simply have not yet devised
a way to give to the people generally sufficient purchasing
power to buy the maximum amount of goods and services
that the system can make available. In other words, distribution lags behind production. If one studies the authori-
tative government reports on consumer incomes[6] and with
them either the Brookings or the Loeb figure for potential
capacity—whichever personal assumptions and philosophy
lead one to prefer—the fact stands out that goods and services to the value of several thousand dollars per year per
family can be produced. But there is also the fact that in
the midst of this potential plenty many of the people actually get a niggardly purchasing power and live a near-
poverty existence.[7]

One explanation for this lag of distribution behind production is that the structure of our great producing industries was built so quickly after 1860 it was well-nigh impossible to invent at the same moment effective brakes with
which to regulate various parts of the gigantic system. So
it was that the goods actually produced and the services
made available failed from time to time to gee, on the one

[5]Again I deny the charge that I am a "past master" of the art of "be-
littling the American system, taking sly digs at capitalism, making a
studied effort to put American industry and business in the worst possible
light."

[6]For example, *Consumer Incomes in the United States*, National Resources Committee, Government Printing Office, Washington, D.C.,
1937.

[7]It is the insistence of the educational liberals that all such facts of
income and standards of living be taught in the schools. And it is this
that brings down upon them the attack of the merchants of conflict. The
latter do not want the deficiencies of American life taught, even though
the factors which caused them are made perfectly clear, documented
thoroughly and presented in an appreciative background of American
democracy.

hand with the needs and the purchasing power of the people, and on the other with the goods and services that could have been produced. And each time the disparity became especially marked there were "bad times" of unemployment, poverty and social tension. Witness the fourteen major recurrences of depression and the many minor ones in the past century.

There then emerges the third fact from the plotting of the three curves of social trend, namely, that popular consent has advanced less rapidly than either economic productivity or social invention. It is true that in creating the physical structure for universal education in the nineteenth and twentieth centuries our fathers made a spectacular achievement. In fact, in less than a century they built a literate world. Ninety-odd per cent of the eight hundred million people of industrial countries can now "read, write and reckon."

But literacy alone does not guarantee understanding, and understanding is necessary if the people are to "give consent" to the acts of their representatives in government. Actually the advancing curve of *literacy* from 1840 to 1940 does parallel the curve of economic productivity; it has a high exponent. But the curve of *understanding* for all the industrial peoples presents quite another picture. If we could write an equation for it its exponent would undoubtedly be very low. If we could plot it graphically we would not have a steeply mounting record of domestic and world problems grasped, of issues perceived, of data mastered; we would get, instead, an almost flat horizontal, representing relative ignorance, bewilderment and even indifference on the part of the people.

Many of the most pressing social problems of our times—among them the recurring disruption of the equanimity of the public mood—can be traced to the lags existing between these three social trends. But there are other characteristics of our times; there are other forces at play.

Sources of Social Tension

The frightening transition period through which we are passing can be understood only in the light of two important concepts[8] and their roles in the recent history of our industrial culture. One deals with our domestic life, the other with the world scene.

I   On the domestic scene—revolt and improvisation.

America is beginning to discover her creative capacity, rebelling against the grip of British-classical European tradition and improvising new forms to state every phase of her culture.

II On the world scene—the Long Armistice, an interregnum of dictatorship.

America is caught in the fragile interdependent world order, menaced by the advance of totalitarianism and gripped in the globe-encircling terror and fear of war.

I OUR TIMES, A PERIOD OF REVOLT AND IMPROVISATION

Many of the roots of the present confusion can be found in the infancy of our national culture, indeed in the very youth of industrial-democratic civilization around the world. America is a new country. Only ten generations have lived on its soil; only five on the land west of the Appalachians. Our history would not make a mark wider

---

[8]In a sense there is a third co-ordinate source of tension, namely, the awakening of our people to the impact on their lives of erosion and the violation of the sustained-yield principle. They are recognizing, first, that both their natural and human resources were extravagantly wasted and abused during the First Industrial Revolution and, second, that they must rebuild again on the principle of sustaining the yield. See Chapter XII.

than a razor scratch on the time line of man's culture building. In one sense, of course, all industrial civilizations are young, but certain ones—Britain and France, for example—are mature compared with the United States. They have a background of more than five hundred years of "national" life rising out of a preceding millennium of culture formation.

All these "new" civilizations are forms representing three stages of cultural growth: (1) the transplanting from the mother cultures, (2) appearance of partially indigenous improvisations and (3) emergence of native expression, creative and mature.

America's cultural development can be thought of as advancing roughly in that order—first, a "long" 250-year period of infancy, during which our ways of life were almost entirely imported from the European-British scene; second, a confused, transitional period of social invention, and, third, the dim beginnings of what now gives promise of being a mature organic expression of the people. At this moment America appears to be passing through the second and adolescent stage of revolt and improvisation.

The task of documenting this thesis[9] fully in the limited space of a few pages is impossible. I shall have to be content merely to point out briefly some of the confirming evidence, taking first the stormy economic scene of the decade following the World War.

The Boom Twenties

At no time in American history has there been a period of prosperity comparable to that of the 1920s. The World

[9] This is indeed one of the major purposes of a full-length book on the biography of the creative American mind which I have had in preparation for some years and which I trust will be the next publication forthcoming in my program.

War, which brought about a major shift in economic power among the industrial nations, served as a powerful impetus to the launching of a spectacular business boom in our own country. Our exports to Europe had mounted from $1,339,000,000 in 1914 to $4,062,000,000 in 1917. Total exports rose from $2,435,000,000 in 1914 to $8,439,-000,000 in 1920. Note the growth of our merchant marine —in 1914 the total tonnage of American-owned ships engaged in foreign trade was 1,000,000; in 1917, 3,000,000; in 1920, 9,500,000; in 1922, 11,000,000.

In 1914 the United States was a debtor nation, owing peoples abroad approximately $4,000,000,000; in 1919 we were the creditor nation of the world, to whom others owed about $22,000,000,000. Uncle Sam was becoming the banker of the earth.

Paper estimates showed our national wealth mounting at unbelievable rates: in 1912, $180,000,000,000; in 1920, $350,000,000,000; in 1929, $450,000,000,000!

Our industrial productive power, already growing rapidly in the early 1900s, was multiplied several fold to satisfy the demands of the Allied war machine, and production of the basic commodities continued to rise after the hostilities ceased. Witness, for example:

Value of Total Manufactures	Value of Production of Minerals
1914—$24,000,000,000	1913—$2,400,000,000
1919—$62,500,000,000	1919—$4,500,000,000

The steadily rising curves of business indices from 1922 to 1929 reveal an unparalleled advance in production. For seven years the newer industries whirled on in a major cycle of prosperity, although certain of the older basic ones sagged badly. For example: the farmer was severely hit by the pricking of the land-boom bubble after the war

. . . the coal mines were running only part time . . . cotton mills slowed down and population declined rapidly in New England textile cities. Throughout the decade of greatest prosperity there were never fewer than 1,400,000 to 2,000,000 workers idle. Nevertheless, the total national income in 1929 was very high, estimated by one agency to be $89,000,000,000 and by another $96,000,000,000, largely because conditions in the new industries were booming and wages were high. The popular demand for the automobile rapidly reduced it from a luxury status to a necessity; twenty-odd million families cruised over the country on wheels. In 1919 there had been only 6,771,000 passenger cars; in 1929 there were 23,121,000! Ten million radios had gone into American homes, an increase of 1400 per cent in seven years. A vast array of electrical household gadgets added to the comfort of the home. Some 50,000,000 Americans attended the movies each week. Great skyscrapers, apartment buildings and hotels shot up, proclaiming American genius.

The business world was in a whirl. Everyone seemed to be making "big" money, and everyone seemed to be spending freely what he made. Few were the people who understood or were troubled by the speculative character of the times. The future was being mortgaged to the extreme. It was not until the 1930s that the American people woke up to the fact that $6,000,000,000 worth of obligations had been contracted for through installment buying. Necessities and luxuries wore out and were scrapped long before the final payments had been made. It was not until 1929 that the dangers of uncontrolled stock-market speculation were seen—at one time in the late 1920s 2,000,000 people were playing the market. The boom twenties indeed!

The "New Freedom" in Social Customs

The rebellious and improvising tenor of these Armistice years can be illustrated also by the manner in which the mores of the people shifted. With the growth of great cities and the spreading use of the closed automobile (especially as an escape device for the bored and as a "get-away-quick" convenience for the criminal) the anonymity and lack of responsibility in urban life grew dangerously. Morals and manners changed drastically. A new "frankness" made its way into general conversation as well as into the theater, books, magazines, newspapers and the radio.

The war had precipitated a happy-go-lucky, "eat, drink and be merry" attitude. The saloon gave way to the speakeasy, with its gin and bootleg liquor. Crime and racketeering became flourishing businesses. It was an age of "jazz" and "wild youth." And as the younger people ran wild, so many of their middle-aged elders ran with them. The American woman especially became a new kind of person. Steadily she asserted her independence, entering business, the professions and the arts. She cut off her skirts and her hair and took off her corsets (corset sales dropped 11 per cent in the years 1924–27). She bought her bread and pastry at the corner store and spent a sizable part of her "budget" on the new beauticians. She smoked cigarettes and drank cocktails with her man.

The uproarious twenties they were—for old and young alike.

Rebellion and Improvisation in the Arts

Throughout the culture and revolt against the Victorian concepts of repression, authority and discipline was spreading. In the arts it was a protest against what George Santayana named the "genteel tradition." For two centuries, and especially in the nineteenth, architecture, letters, the graphic and plastic arts, music, dance and the theater were dominated by the styles and standards of Britain and Europe. Few artists in any media of expression freed themselves from the matrix into which they had been molded until the closing decades of the 1800s. Then there came the utterances of a few great forerunners: Sullivan "spoke" early in architecture; Isadora Duncan in the dance; Alfred Stieglitz in photography, painting and sculpture; from the 1890s on John Dewey in philosophy and education; Waldo Frank, Van Wyck Brooks, Randolph Bourne, et al., in letters and philosophy. These creative mutants built, wrote, painted or otherwise stated American life as they saw it being lived and with original thought and feeling.

Especially in the 1920s "Puritanism" in all its forms was vigorously attacked by the growing body of young intelligentsia congregating in the "Villages" of the large cities. They and their fellows over the country fought against censorship in literature, the theater and all other areas of expression and sought the abolition of established conventions of art. These, they said, repressed the artist's liberties. "Self-expression" became the new god. A great variety of improvised new forms and statements began to appear. They were sincere and indigenous but little more than casual improvisations.

The revolt against discipline and improvisations revealed itself in education as well—especially in the creation of the free-lance "progressive" or "child-centered" schools. During the period from 1910 to 1930 especially new articles of faith stressed child freedom at the expense of self-disciplined control. Emphasis upon teacher initiative came to be supplanted more and more by emphasis on child initiative. Child interests and the needs of society received greater and greater attention.

Revolutionary experiments and innovations were made with the materials of instruction. In the social sciences especially many new interpretations of the culture were introduced. The "new" history had shed new light, for example, on the Founding Fathers, and this sometimes got itself expressed in a negative "debunking" of heroes in the writings of certain free-lance biographers. And there were corresponding novel changes being effected in other aspects of education.

Lost Individuals . . . Disappearing Loyalties

Perhaps the most outstanding characteristic of our times is the deepening helplessness of a people who discover that their loyalties and ideas are inadequate to meet the new situations. The objects of allegiance in the Victorian era were sharp and clear—loyalty of children to their elders and of both to the home . . . loyalty to a clear conception of integrity in craftsmanship . . . loyalty to God and the church . . . loyalty to the Founding Fathers as a symbol of the American way. But this simple and easily understood agrarian world gave way to the complex and almost incomprehensible civilization of manufacturing and trading cities.

The industrial world became one of lost individuals. Emotional equilibrium was upset. The continuity of life was breaking down. People lost faith in their ability to master their own destinies; some resigned themselves to the fact that they were caught in a swiftly rushing social current which they could neither understand nor direct. They were cast adrift with no sure mooring masts. They could see their former allegiances to the idea of successful com-

petition, of obedience to elders and of a secure life in the
world to come, and even to the old idea of democracy,
crumbling before them. The young people were especially
confused—as F. Scott Fitzgerald put it in *This Side of Para-
dise*, "Here was a new generation . . . grown up to find
all gods dead, all wars fought, all faiths in men shaken."
And to take the place of the old loyalties the accepted
American philosophy had only the scientific method of
work to offer, and as an end, this experimental method of
inquiry was really no object of allegiance at all.

So much for the sources of social tension at work on
our domestic scene in this period of Great Transition.

Heaven knows that in such a rapidly changing civilization it would have been difficult enough for our people to
solve their problems and preserve at the same time their
treasured democratic processes. But their task has been and
is being made more difficult because of another factor—
the menace of the totalitarian revolution which is sweeping
around the world.

II An Interregnum of Dictatorship Sweeping around the World

The thousand-year-long march toward democracy of
the industrializing peoples of the earth has been interrupted
by a dangerous interregnum of one-man government. In
a score of countries ruthless rulers have seized power by
violence, by deceitful propaganda or by other dishonest
means. They have abolished parliaments and competing
political parties. They rule by fear and force. They persecute, banish and kill their opponents. They stamp on freedom of thought, research, speech, movement and productive work in general. They bait and persecute Jews and

Catholics, in some places all aliens. A century of efforts toward international co-operation has been nullified by their destructive wills. What an astounding setback this has brought to our complacent assurance that the world was made safe for democracy! Why this incredible interregnum? For "interregnum" I am convinced it is; I believe that after five, ten, perhaps even twenty-five, years of being throttled freedom-loving man will reinstate the free play of intelligence as the basis of government. But I also believe that he'll never be able to do so unless he first understands what has happened. He—and that means each and every one of us—must find the answer to the question: To what factors can the recurrence of one-man government round the world today be traced?

The Ordeal of Democracy and the Welfare State

No single answer can be given, for the nations of the world have varied in the degree to which liberty, equality, fraternity and other ideals of democracy have been implemented in their social orders. In three critical ways have they differed.

First, they have differed in actual experience with democratic processes. Only in America and a few other isolated spots on the earth has democracy been practiced *on the basis of popular consent with understanding* long enough to carry it through the terrifying, complex conditions of the Long Armistice. Those countries which have gone thoroughly totalitarian had worked at democracy very little before 1919.

Second, countries have differed in the success they have had in arranging their economic systems to give uninterrupted work and security to the people. At bottom the problem has been to provide people with purchasing power *commensurate with their resources,* though no government anywhere ever framed the problem in this specific form. Governments merely asked: "Can the economic system be kept going at all to give work to the people?" And the answers have varied. Facing cultural, economic and social confusion, faith in the effectiveness of democratic government to bring work and security to the people broke down in many parts of the world, causing peoples to shift their faith and confidence in divergent and opposite directions, but always away from democracy.

Third, national populations have differed in the presence within them of strong, active and determined enemies of democracy—men ready to capture the imagination of the people, to promise them a good life, to use every conceivable open and undercover means to enhance their prestige and gain power.

These three factors account in large measure for the halt in the world's march toward democracy—indeed for its actual collapse in many nations.

Varieties of Democracy

With the help of these three criteria arrange the principal industrialized nations of the earth on a scale. At one end put the nations in which "Democracy has worked!" At the very outside stands our own America, the world's staunchest haven of democracy—long experienced in carrying on the democratic way of life, enjoying a better internal economic situation than any other nation in the world and having fewer enemies of democracy in its midst. Even if the tide of totalitarianism should engulf Great Britain I am confident that America will live on as the glorious single home of democracy in the twentieth century. Next to America on the scale stand the British peoples—the United Kingdom and the Dominions—varying of course among themselves. These defenders of democracy have maintained the freedom of the individual man with great heroism in spite of the most trying conditions, in spite of the handicap of a dominant Tory group in government and in spite of a traditional class stratification of the people. The Scandinavians of the Long Armistice period—Sweden, Norway, Finland and Denmark—as well as the Dutch and the Belgians, would also stand fairly close to the "Democracy Works" end of the scale. Though living under constitutional monarchy they set the entire world admirable examples of "middle-way" experiments in economic and political co-operation. Heroic Czechoslovakia and little Switzerland also would be lined up on the scale's liberal democratic end.

Along the middle area would stand the democratic uncertainties. There would be huge China, the world's oldest continuous civilization, ravaged in recent years by the marauding industrial bandit from the eastern islands, but carrying within her social blood stream perhaps the greatest potential for working out the finest implementation of the man-man relationships (which is true democracy) that the world has ever known. France, too—the home of the Declaration of the Rights of Man, but beaten now to her knees by native renegades of Fascism as well as by foreign conquerors—would have to be put down merely as an "unknown quantity."

On the right side of the scale, approaching the "Democracy Fails" end, stand the Latin-American republics, struggling in a scene that may be as favorable to totalitarianism as to democracy. Except during short interludes of partially democratic rule in a few countries, these peoples have lived under "dictatorships" for the better part of four centuries.

Concentrated tightly at the "Democracy Fails" end of the scale the four big dictatorships loom large—Germany, Italy, Russia and Japan—flanked by a dozen lesser ones. In each of these the parliament has been dismissed and the dictator rules by edict. Elections are 98 per cent "pure," but the suffrage is a travesty. The Bill of Rights has been torn up. The dignity and worth of the individual have been destroyed.

This brings us back to the focus of the world scene during the Long Armistice, for it is the four big dictatorships—especially that of Germany—around which the current of world affairs has swung. It may even be upon them that the fate of American democracy in our generation hinges.

If the men of the twentieth century are to understand the rise of dictatorships and the fall of democracy they must center their study on this European focus. It was from there that the tensions of the Long Armistice emanated. It was there that the economic chaos was greatest. It was there that the enemies of democracy showed their power and influence most clearly. And within it all the real nub has been Germany—and Germany's relations with France and Britain and their empires. In comparison, Italy can be thought of as standing on the side lines with Russia, the latter until recently a huge, sprawling unknown quantity engaged in the business of industrializing her culture.

The periphery of the world struggle, perhaps later to become the focus, is eastern Asia. There we find Japan's War party moving step by step toward overlordship of the Pacific as well as the eastern part of the Asiatic continent. Distant, but occupying a strategic role in the periphery, are the United States and the twenty-one Latin-American republics, striving to remain aloof and partly isolated by geography but in the last analysis tied extricably to the world trends and bound up in the whole picture by psychology, tradition and economics.

So much for geographic orientations.

THE CONDITIONS THAT PRODUCED THE
TOTALITARIAN REVOLUTION

That men may understand . . .

That men may not let it happen here . . .

Let them learn a lesson from the ruthless destruction of democracy around the world. Let them go back, first, to the beginning of the Long Armistice, to the treaty making of Versailles. I was in Washington in June 1919 at the moment the treaty was signed and remember well how students of world problems in the capital shook their heads and prophesied that only more trouble would result. "It is a treaty of hate and vengeance," they said, "not a pact of lasting peace. These are only the terms of an *armistice*. War will start up again, certainly within twenty years."

It *was* a treaty of vengeance. The Germans were ordered to sign, to admit "war guilt," to agree to pay reparations. They were ordered to disarm in the midst of an armed world, to give up their merchant marine and to surrender valuable industrial resources and colonies.

The treaty makers created on paper a whole new European system. The lands of Europe, containing mixtures of differing and antagonistic "nationalities," were carved into a dozen new countries on the principle of "self-determination of peoples," and the world was told that control of the entire scheme by the League of Nations would forever keep Europe, indeed the whole earth, in order.

But the history of the Long Armistice proved that the League was really the imperial instrument of Great Britain and France. It solved several inconsequential minor disputes in the twenty years, but it was not permitted to succeed in a single major issue.

But back to Germany, the sharpest focus. Set up after the revolution of 1918 and the abdication of the Kaiser, the new German republic with its Weimar Constitution—called by historians one of the most democratic state papers in all world history—didn't have a chance; the odds against Ebert, Eisner and their colleagues were overwhelming. *All three of the defeating conditions, already set down, were in the picture:* (1) the lack of experience with democratic processes, (2) the near collapse of the national economic system and (3) the presence of enemies who hated democracy and at every opportunity sniped at the new government.

The story of the events by which the Weimar Republic became the total Nazi state are well known; the rehearsal of its chief chapters can be brief. With the old loyalties to emperor and state gone and with no strong, sure, new government with strong, sure, new policies, the people remained uncertain of democracy. The social and economic circumstances under which the new republic struggled for existence were against them too: incredible confusion . . . the terrible wreckage of the war . . . the breakdown of industry, transport and trade . . . the compulsion to pay the Allies a damage bill of $33,000,000,000 . . . the ruin of the currency . . . the millions of people out of work, poverty-stricken and bewildered . . . the millions of youth with no prospects ahead for careers, marriage and homes . . . all of this in a third-rate country, humiliated and disarmed.

Consider the powerful enemies at work within. There were the monarchists who wanted to see the Kaiser or one of his sons on the throne. There were the leading officers of the army. There were the bankers, manufacturers and great landowners, together with a fairly large number of people who worked for them and depended on them for a living. These were the men who took advantage of the chaos and misery of the common people and stirred them up against the new government. And these were the men who encouraged gangsters like Hitler and his Nazis in the 1920s to foment trouble.

The economic-social-political scene was just right for the rise of strong men, men of sudden drastic action, stubborn and persistent, brooking no interference, fanatically devoted to the supremacy and leadership of themselves and their party; men of ruthless hates, easy conscience, bad faith, no scruples; politically shrewd men, master strategists and propagandists with contempt for all agreements.

The strong men rose—Hitler and his Nazis, their National German Socialist Worker's party growing from a few scores in 1919 to 17,000,000 registered voters in 1932. Financed by the army, the monarchists and industrialists, Hitler played his brutal game—taking advantage of the hardened, cynical attitude growing among the people, promising much and giving little, playing one group against the other, moving step by step to power by dramatic oratory, skillful politics, trickery and sudden efficient action, using the terror and preaching hate for Jews, Communists and Socialists. By all these steps Hitler in his contempt for everything liberal brought about the destruction of democratic processes in Germany and became dictator, ruling by edict, in the summer of 1933.

That men may understand, I say, let them learn all these things.

And let them learn how by the same trickery, efficiency and dramatic action the Dictator Hitler proceeded to rearm Germany and remilitarize the Rhineland (1936), to take Austria and Czechoslovakia (1938–39), Memel (March 1939); how in 1939 he signed the Nazi-Communist pact with Stalin and conquered and divided Poland; and how with lightning speed he took Denmark, Norway, Holland, Belgium, Luxemburg and France in the spring and summer of 1940.

That men may understand let them also learn the play of forces behind the scenes in the foreign offices of the other Great Powers during all of this.

Let them learn the truth of the British and French domination of the League of Nations in its early attempts to settle major international disputes.

Let them learn from the experience of France and Britain the dangers of appeasement in the international scene of today.

Let them learn the dangers of a government's failure to implement its people's clear affirmation for peace by *making a fight for peace rather than by avoiding war at any cost.*

Let them learn the dangers of lack of preparedness.

All these things they must learn and understand. If they do not, it may happen here.

★   ★   ★

This, then, is the Long Armistice:

A period of drastic social change and continuous social tension.

A period in which three great social trends separated one from another by such vast gaps that they not only produced the critical social problems of today but also made it possible for us to see those problems clearly and with them the characteristics of each trend.

A period in which our people began to recognize, first, that they had violated the sustained-yield principle by permitting the widespread erosion of land and men and that now they must begin again.

A period of violent revolt against ancient and alien norms and hectic improvisation of new forms.

A period of ordeal for the democratic method, with an actual terrifying interregnum of dictatorship sweeping around the world.

This is the Long Armistice.

Chapter VII

THIS HAS HAPPENED BEFORE!

Hysteria and Witch-Hunting

ONE DAY in April 1927 the telephone rang in my office in Lincoln School of Teachers College.

"Rugg, this is Caldwell. Come down a moment. We have material here attacking your Social-Science Pamphlets. A director of research for one of the big corporations says your stuff is subversive."

I hurried downstairs. Many times since that day I have known that anxious sense of insecurity, that feeling of persons in high places watching and criticizing and questioning. This, however, was my first experience with actual "attack."

Caldwell handed me two "briefs," containing some two hundred short items lifted from the twelve volumes of my pamphlets.[1]

"They say the stuff is un-American. The brief was made by their Research director, who got hold of your pamphlets through the schools where they are being used experimentally in one of the larger Appalachian cities. He has characterized each of the excerpts; for example: here is one called 'unbalanced emphasis' . . . another, 'sensationalism'

[1]The story of the pamphlets is told in Chapter VIII.

. . . another, 'exaggeration' . . . others, 'misrepresenta-
tion,' 'generalization,' 'misstatements of fact' and the like."

I went upstairs to the office, called Hockett[2] off another
job and with him excitedly studied the briefs. For a solid
week all constructive writing and research in the office was
at a standstill while we gave ourselves to a painstaking
analysis of the attack. Every cited excerpt was located in
the pamphlets, the context in which each was used noted
and a critique of the criticism made.

This, as I have said, was my first experience with an attack upon my books, and I was startled at the methods employed. Since that day, thirteen years ago, I have examined
and studied many similar adverse criticisms of my work.
I am no longer astonished at the devices I find used. I was
then, however.

In only *three* of the two hundred-odd excerpts had we
made misstatements of fact (one was actually a misprint)
or, from the standpoint of the "new history" which we
accepted, had given misinterpretations! In ninety-eight per
cent of the items in the briefs the attacker himself was
guilty of misinterpretation of the author's meaning or gross
lifting-out-of-context or sheer ignorance of the purposes
and methods employed in the preparation and use of the
pamphlets in the school. For example, the briefs gave many
citations to show that we emphasized "the sordid side of
life"; but the voluminous materials portraying "the brighter
side of life" were completely ignored. In the ninth-grade
pamphlets, for example, we had deliberately used the paral-
lel-page method of presenting two "sides of a controversy"
or "points of view," but only one, the "sordid" side of each
pair, was taken.

[2]Dr John A. Hockett, my assistant in Lincoln School from 1924 to 1927,
and since 1927 a member of the Department of Education of the University of California at Berkeley.

A week later I went back to Caldwell. "Well, we've gone through the stuff and we're ready to deal with this matter."

"What's our next step?" he asked.

"I think we should have lunch with them—you, Doctor Flexner,[3] Dean Russell,[4] representatives of their organization, Hockett and myself. Let's talk it out face to face."

Caldwell smiled. "Good. We'll get Flexner to invite us to the Century Club."

It was done. A week later eight of us sat down together, ate lunch, got acquainted, sized each other up and frankly talked out the problem. One fact, more than any other, stands out clearly from that meeting. The real crux of the issue between us was the kind of interpretation of American life and especially of "American enterprise" that was to hold sway in the schools. From that day to this every episode within my knowledge of proposed censorship of the schools has revolved around the same issue—"Which brand of the American way are we to hold and teach?"

I shall never forget Dean James Russell's fine, clear statement that day and his forthright support of studying "problems" in the schools. A democracy can exist on no other basis, he said, than the fullest, frankest study of its problems by all of the people. Hence a full account of American life, unbiased as it is humanly possible to make it, should be presented. All sides should be studied. No problems and issues should be omitted. Nothing should be covered up, kept away from the young people. To this day that has been the policy of the administration of the Lincoln School and Teachers College. It is a fine example of the implementation in the schools of the great historic

[3]Dr Abraham Flexner, secretary, General Education Board, chief initiator, sponsor and "father-confessor" of the Lincoln School in its first ten years of life.

[4]Dean James Earl Russell of Teachers College.

principle of "government by consent of the governed," consent, as I shall discuss later, based upon a real understanding of problems and issues.

Dr Flexner and Dr Caldwell supported the dean. They didn't see how, in a democracy, the schools could do other than build understanding of American and modern civilization by bringing American life into the schools. They insisted that my social-science enterprise was one of the first attempts systematically to do that very thing.

My comments expanded that theme. There were really two things to be said. First, that the program of education must be built around problems. There is no other way to develop the knowledge and thinking of young people—describe American life fully, accurately, and present the problems. Thinking ability comes only from confronting problems and choosing between alternatives. *To keep issues out of the school is to keep intellectual life out of it.* Certainly more than one side should be told. Young people must be taught to take sides about American life only after they have taken thought.

The second point I had to make was even more important, namely, that we were reflecting a "new" point of view concerning the nature of the interpretation to be given to American life. This view, I explained, had been developed by careful historians in a half century of documentary research, and we were among the dozen text-writing groups who were bringing it into the schools. We believed with the "new" historians, not only that understanding of the "true" history was necessary to build integrity in the people, but that a far deeper loyalty to American institutions and heroes would be built at the same time.

The luncheon lasted three hours. By the time we were ready to leave, the "opposition" had slowly changed from one of carping criticism to one of co-operation: "He's not such a bad fellow after all!" Offers were made to supply us with photographs and other materials. This particular attacking group has never since voiced opposition or criticism of my work. Quite the opposite, they have helped from time to time, as have other industrial organizations, and for all of it I am grateful.

But one phase of the aftermath of this episode is important to put into the historical record. Although the leaders of this group stopped opposition to the Social-Science Pamphlets at once, the mood of tension and fear which they had stirred up in their own community kept the Rugg books out of their schools from that day to this. Two years later, when the commercial edition of the books supplanting the pamphlets went into five thousand places, this corporation's bailiwick would still have no "Rugg." Many times in the years since I have talked with educators and teachers of that community. They still "don't dare use Rugg." Why? I think it is because the very people of prestige who set the climate of opinion *against us* never actually set it *for us*. Rugg probably would have gone back into the schools there if the company's leaders had undone what they had done, if they had admitted they were mistaken, if they had made retractions of their attacks, if they had written to the schools emphatically supporting Rugg, urging the use of his books and advocating the discussion of problems and controversial issues in the classroom. But they never did that. So the emotional hang-over accompanying the stereotypes created by their first attack still remains.

★   ★   ★

I give this story merely to introduce the whole problem of "This Has Happened Before" in the schools. Certainly

the current attack upon liberalism in education is not the
first of its kind. It is true that this one is nationwide, more
virulent and promises to last longer and to set back the
work of the schools more than any previous one. But it
has happened before—five times since the World War!
In 1918 there was an isolated, short-lived attack on a single
small group . . . in 1921–26, a prolonged and fairly widespread one . . . in 1927 the "local" one upon my group
to which I have referred . . . and in 1934–35 a much bigger and more powerful one. Five times in two decades a
wave of censorship has rolled up on the schools.

And if these were plotted on a time line they would
coincide fairly closely with the ups and downs of the
curves of social hysteria and conflict.

WAVES OF SOCIAL HYSTERIA, 1919–41

Historians have long been aware of the tendency of domestic unrest to follow in the train of great wars or other
major crises. An hypothesis for a documentary study of
these periods might be something like this: Following or
in connection with each major war or domestic crisis there
ensues a dangerous period of restlessness, agitation, discontent and revolt. Labor troubles, strikes, riots, lynchings,
near-financial panics and witch-hunts of aliens, liberals and
racial and religious out-groups are all manifestations of
this unrest. If the rise and fall of these were shown on a
graph such a graph would, I feel sure, rise quickly to its
peak within two or three years then slowly taper off
through some years to a longer period of comparative quiet.

The Red Scare of 1919–21

This is what happened following the close of the World
War of 1914–18. Within a year a near panic had spread

across the country. A wave of labor strikes broke out in the stockyards, shipyards and subways, on the docks of the harbors, in the shoe factories and in the building-construction industry. At one moment in 1919 two million workers were out on strike. In Boston in September 1919 even the police went on strike, leaving the city defenseless. Violence was the order of the day, with hoodlums smashing windows and looting stores; state troopers and a voluntary police force were organized to keep order.

Labor leaders were not only asking better wages and working conditions, they were becoming socialistic as well. In the coal industry, for example, they were demanding government ownership of coal mines. Defenders of "free enterprise" marshaled their forces against labor, against "radicals," against "East Side Jews." The newspapers were blazoned with scare headlines. Parades of Socialists were broken up; riots occurred in which people were killed or injured. In New York, although Colonel Theodore Roosevelt, Jr, Mr Justice Charles E. Hughes and former Cabinet member Elihu Root spoke out against it, the state legislature passed the Lusk Bill. By means of this legislation five legally elected Socialists were refused seats, thereby disfranchising some sixty thousand electors.

In the winter of 1919–20 frightening rumors of impending attack on American institutions began to spread. These were accentuated by a series of bombings, in one of which the home of Attorney General A. Mitchell Palmer in Washington was damaged. Meanwhile the debates and acts of the Congress on the Volstead Act, the Suffrage Amendment and on what Lodge called "Wilson's Treaty" aggravated rather than calmed the public mood.

Raids were made by the attorney general on aliens. Using the wartime Sedition Act as authority, more than six thousand aliens were arrested and kept in jail.

Week by week the hysteria mounted. Owners of Liberty bonds, farms and savings accounts were warned that the "Reds" were coming over to destroy their property. The number of members in the Communist and related organizations was magnified to ridiculous totals, one "authority" estimating six hundred thousand Communists. Actually the aggregate of Communists and anarchists in the country was very small. In an issue of the *Atlantic Monthly* in 1919 Professor G. S. Watkins estimated the total Socialists at thirty-nine thousand, Communist Labor members at not more than thirty thousand and the Communist party members at from thirty thousand to sixty thousand.

Such liberal civic organizations as the Federal Council of Churches, the Foreign Policy Association, the National League of Women Voters, and even such art groups as the Moscow Art Theater, came under suspicion. So did such distinguished citizens as Rabbi Wise, Norman Thomas, Jane Addams, Paul Kellogg and Felix Frankfurter.

The Ku-Klux Klan reinforced the agitation. It had been organized in the South in 1915, but after the war it gained remarkable headway. In 1920 and the next few years it spread its terror across the South, into the Middle West, Northwest and Northeast, actually coming to wield political control over seven state governments.[5]

By the end of the summer of 1920 social conditions were getting better. Production was rising; the unemployed were going back to work. So also the Red scare began to lose momentum. Some witch-hunting of aliens and liberals continued through 1921, but by 1922—*except for the schools*—it had died out, not to appear again for over a decade.

---

[5]Estimates place the Klan's total membership by 1924 at over four million.

"Except for the Schools"

Attacks upon the schools started as the hysteria in other areas declined. Was this a phenomenal development? Yes and no. There is documentation for the hypothesis that trends for education tend to lag behind those affecting the people more directly. Take the well-known example of budgets. In a time of depression school-budget cuts lag behind curtailments and economies in other fields; school-budget increases also lag behind during recovery. So also with witch-hunting. It appears to follow, though lagging somewhat, the crest of the general wave of unrest and then far outlives it.

This is exactly what happened in the early 1920s. The school witch-hunters became active in 1921, and their hunt lasted until about 1926. It was manufactured in much the same way as the present one. It was kept going by persons with much the same kind of background, interests and philosophy. And the methods used in spreading and prolonging the attack were almost identical.

The Patrioteers Attack the "New Historians," 1921–26[6]

In order to understand this five-year attempt to censor the school program we must reach back into the 1800s, in fact, to the very beginning of history teaching in the American schools. The conflicts in those early years, however,

[6] I wish to acknowledge with deep appreciation the courtesy of my colleague in Teachers College, Professor J. Montgomery Gambrill, in giving me access to his large collection of source material from which this section has been written. It includes newspaper clippings, school reports and pamphlets by patriotic organizations, letters, magazine articles and book reviews by historians, reports by investigating committees of teachers, pamphlets by book publishers, reports and resolutions by state and regional committees of history teachers and other documents, covering the years 1920–27.

were largely "sectional." In the 1850s there was reaction in the South, stimulated especially by military and patriotic organizations, against textbooks made in the North and by Northerners. Pierce[7] gives examples. One Southerner writing in *De Bow's Review* of 1855 said: "Our textbooks are abolition works." Another suggested that an author would commit no offense if he should "step aside . . . to drag in" a *favorable* attitude toward slavery. In general the Southerners were eager to get rid of "the wandering incendiary Yankee schoolmaster" with "his incendiary schools books." Thirty years later the annual resolutions of such Southern patriotic organizations as the United Confederate Veterans were still demanding a "true and reliable history." From the 1880s on, similar organizations in the North became active. The Grand Army of the Republic was stressing the point that the schools should make sure that pupils comprehended "the causes that resulted in the war of the Rebellion."

After 1900 the issue over "what kind of history to teach" took a "racial," "nationalistic" turn. Although most of our people up to 1890 could trace their ancestry back to the British Isles, there were several million Catholics of southern Irish stock who held a long-standing animosity against everything British. Several million others were of German ancestry, and these, too, hated Britain. At certain times each of these minority groups, with the help of patriotic organizations, rose to "reform" the schools, to see that their people got due credit for their contribution to America and especially to see that their mother countries were presented in the proper light in the school histories. Sometimes the two were combined, as shown by this example:

In 1907 the German-American Alliance, in conjunction with the Ancient Order of Hibernians in America, resolved "to

[7]Bessie L. Pierce. *Control of History Teaching*, Chicago, 1925, pp. 4–8.

recommend a systematic investigation of the share all races had had in the development of our country . . . as the basis for the founding of an unbiased American history."[8]

During the World War years the German and Irish groups continued their attacks and opposition to British influence, while the pro-Ally forces did all they could to root out everything Prussian.

After the close of the war the social soil was perfectly prepared for the launching of a concerted successful attack upon the writers of school histories. The Red scare of 1919–21 had set the mood of many peoples; the defeat of Germany and the confirmation of British domination over the world stimulated the pro-Ally groups into increased activity. German-Americans and Irish-Americans in general were still alert to seize upon any chance to attack Britain; among these were politicians like Thompson in Chicago and New York City's Tammany Mayor Hylan, whose primary interests were votes.

Three additional factors helped to pave the way for the attack. First, the controversy had sharpened over the "new" interpretation of American history, evidence for which has been accumulating for several decades. Second, professional publicity persons were at hand, ready to dramatize attack and sell it to newspapers and magazines. Third, chiefs of "Americanization" units of national patriotic organizations were becoming increasingly active in propagandizing any actual or imagined "subversive" influence.

A brief word about each of these influences.

The "New History" Gets into the Schools

The attacks upon the school immediately after the World War cannot be understood unless one remembers that it

[8] Ibid. p. 9.

was in this period that the content of the history program was being made over. "History" had long been little more than a build-up of unthinking patriotism, a eulogy of patriots who had fought the Revolutionary War and founded the country. Bancroft's *History of the United States*, published in 1834, had set the tone of historical writing for more than a half century. Even in the colleges and universities the same uncritical attitude was prevalent.

With the establishment of the Johns Hopkins (1876) and Chicago (1893) universities and the modernizing of Columbia, a scientific spirit spread among the students of history. In 1883 the Johns Hopkins group began to issue the "Studies in Historical and Political Science." In the 1890s historians at the universities of Chicago, Columbia, Wisconsin and others began the publication of the findings of more impartial research. All of them helped to throw new light on the colonial period, the Revolution, the first administrations, the conflict over slavery, westward expansion and other aspects of American life. At Wisconsin Frederick J. Turner turned out his epoch-making studies on *The Significance of the Frontier in American History*. At Columbia James Harvey Robinson developed his studies of western European history and the making of the modern mind. A little later (1913) the younger Charles A. Beard published his now classic monograph on *An Economic Determination of the Constitution of the United States*. At Chicago J. H. Breasted was launching a lifetime of work on the origins of civilization in the eastern Mediterranean region; Franz Boas was developing his first anthropological studies on the mind of the primitive peoples. William I. Thomas was building the foundations for a new sociology; Thorstein Veblen was carrying on economic and social-psychological investigations which were soon to open up a more comprehensive view of the modern world. Taken all together, these students produced, between the 1880s and the World War, materials for a more complete interpretation of American and Western civilization. Indeed their work provided the basis for a whole new history of man.

Even by 1905 the point of view was so clear and the evidence so voluminous and well documented that a group of historians under the leadership of Professor Albert Bushnell Hart of Harvard issued the twenty-eight volume *The American Nation: A History*. For two decades this was the standard work read by college students and professors, and certainly it did much to give prestige to the new interpretation.

It was this "new history" that began to get into school textbooks by the 1910s. The colonial period, the Revolutionary War and the Founding Fathers were given a more objective treatment. Military exploits and political details were minimized. New viewpoints, and particularly new economic and social emphases, were brought out. New content was introduced. The frontier was played up, as were the westward movement, land and industrial history, even "the arts." It was this "new history" which became the target of attack.

Enter the Professional Publicist and the Patriotic Organization[9]

In the uncertainty brought about by the Red scare of 1921 Charles Grant Miller, a Hearst syndicate writer,

[9]This section has been documented from Bessie L. Pierce's *Control of History Teaching*, Association for Peace Education, Chicago, 1925; Chicago *Herald-Examiner*, July 3, 1921; October 15, 1922; January 14, 1923; Los Angeles *Examiner*, June 10, 1923; New York *American*, June 17, 1923; Harold U. Faulkner's "Perverted American History" in *Harper's Magazine*, February, 1926; Charles Grant Miller's *Propaganda in School Histories*, a pamphlet issued by the Executive Committee, Pennsylvania State Camp, Patriotic Order Sons of America, Philadelphia;

started an attack on the textbooks of no fewer than eight school historians: David S. Muzzey, W. M. West, A. B. Hart, A. C. McLaughlin, C. H. van Tyne, J. P. O'Hara, E. Barnes and W. B. Guitteau. Professor Muzzey, whose *American History* was being used in some five thousand places, bore the brunt of the controversy which arose.

Then, as now, the books were called "treason texts" . . . "unfit for public-school use because subversive of American spirit" . . . "un-American" . . . "grossly defamatory." It was said that they showed "alien allegiances," "debasement of American school history," "lack of patriotic spirit"; that they failed to "enthuse over American [colonial] victories," were "defamatory of our nation's founders" and "eminent Americans"; that they were filled with "distortions, perversions and outright falsifications of vital historical truths"; that they contained "offensive inaccuracy" and "sneering deprecations." These are the very same accusations made against the textbook writers under attack today. The only exception is that in the earlier controversy the books were also branded as being "pro-British propaganda textbooks" and "Anglicized histories."

Miller formed in 1922 the Patriot League for the Preservation of American History, a propaganda organization composed of the executive officials of such patriotic organizations as the National Society of the Sons of the American Revolution, the Veterans of Foreign Wars, the American Legion, the United Spanish War Veterans and the Early Settlers of America. For the express purpose of combating the "Briticized textbooks" and the writers who "undermine the foundations of our patriotic pride," the league published a pamphlet by Miller—*Treason to American Tra-*

descriptive literature issued by the National Historical Society, Chicago, publisher of Miller's book *The Poisoned Loving-Cup* (1928); descriptive literature issued by Miller concerning his organization, the Patriot League for the Preservation of American History.

*dition: The Spirit of Benedict Arnold Reincarnated in
United States History Revised in Text Books.* This was
widely distributed throughout the country, especially by
the Sons of the American Revolution in the state of California.

New York City Politicians Join the Attack

As early as October 1920, under the pressure of the patrioteers, New York City's superintendent of schools, William L. Ettinger, appointed a committee of teachers and
administrators to look into the "new history." From time to
time this committee held open hearings. At these Miller
and other publicists and several officials of patriotic organizations appeared and made charges, the same charges which
had already been printed in Miller's Hearst articles. In January 1922 the committee made a report, finding that: "there
is no evidence to support the charge that any of the textbook writers whose books were examined is unpatriotic"
and no evidence "of organized propaganda." The usefulness
of some of the books was questioned, however, first, "because the authors have written from the point of view of a
critical historian rather than from the point of view of a
teacher"; second, because pupils were taught "the mistakes,
weaknesses and blunders of the prominent characters of the
Republic," and, third, because the authors failed "to describe
adequately and vividly many of the inspiring events in our
history."

This report was accepted by the board of education, but
Tammany politicians were not satisfied; they wanted a report more clearly adverse to the new interpretation which
seemed to them to be pro-British. Mayor Hylan, recognizing that charges of pro-British and un-American attitudes
in schoolbooks could be used to his own political advantage,
ordered his commissioner of accounts, David Hirshfield, in

December 1921, to launch a new investigation. Again public hearings were held, and again Miller and the same group attacked Muzzey and the other historians.

One Joseph Devlin,[10] hired by Hirshfield to conduct an investigation of the books, cleared them of un-American taints. Hirshfield, however, shelved Devlin's report and engaged no less than the ubiquitous Mr Charles Grant Miller to make a new study. This time a denunciatory report[11] was forthcoming, and Hirshfield published it under his own name.[12]

This 1921–26 episode aroused a group in the Knights of Columbus to action. They decided to rewrite American history. They offered prizes of thousands of dollars for "sound," that is, anti-British, histories. In 1922 the Sons of the American Revolution, under the leadership of an Oregon federal judge, Wallace McCamant, passed a resolution of "protest against the use of any textbook which . . . censures the patriots, which maligns the memory of any of the great men of the Revolutionary period." In 1924 the officials of the American Legion, under the guidance of Garland W. Powell, the chief of the National Americanism Commission of the Legion, decided to write an American history. They secured the co-operation of some fifty patriotic organizations and hired Charles F. Horne, editorial director of the Legion and professor of English at the College of the City of New York, to prepare the manuscript.

[10]The New York *Tribune*, November 5-12, 1923.

[11]It is interesting to note that Major General Amos A. Fries is still using this episode and report to buttress his attack on the schools. See his bulletin, *Friends of the Public Schools*, March 1940.

[12]David Hirshfield, "Report on Investigation of Pro-British History Text-Books in Use in the Public Schools of the City of New York," May 25, 1923. See articles referred to in the New York *Tribune*, "Control of History Teaching," by Bessie L. Pierce and an article by Harold U. Faulkner, "Perverted American History," in *Harper's Magazine*, February 1926.

It was published in 1926 but in spite of wide publicity never obtained much use in the schools.

Thus we see that "this has happened before." And the attack on the schools since 1939 is almost an exact replica of the raid of 1921–26.

Then, as Now . . .

. . . it was initiated by professional publicity men and patroteers.

. . . the charges were "un-Americanism," "subversiveness."

. . . Hearst newspapers, national popular magazines and the "Americanization" chiefs of national patriotic organizations broadcast the attack.

. . . it was kept alive artificially.

. . . special propaganda organizations were formed.

. . . new "patriot leagues" inspired and sponsored bills censoring the schools in the legislatures of various states.

. . . publishers of competing texts sent their agents into schools armed with detailed materials to keep the strife stirred up.

. . . local political factions used the fight to aid them in ousting local school officials.

. . . associations of teachers and other liberal groups appointed committees and passed resolutions counterattacking the accusers and supporting the historians.

. . . The Teachers Union of New York City and local committees of teachers in other places rose to the defense of freedom of teaching.

For About a Decade No Attacks on the Schools

Following the attack upon Muzzey, et al., there was a decade-long lull in witch-hunting. As for my own work, I recall no more than four or five instances in the seven years from 1922 to 1929 in which the Social-Science Pamphlets were seriously questioned. This is surprising, too, for they were going into the schools at the rate of a hundred thousand a year. Even the 1927 episode described at the opening of this chapter caused no regional or nationwide repercussions. So far as I know, no other community was ever influenced by what was done in this one town.

Authors of other textbooks have reported to me approximately the same findings with respect to their own enterprises. Attacks upon teachers and professors and upon academic freedom in general were practically unheard of. The Scopes "monkey" trial was perhaps the only conspicuous exception.

The chief explanation for the lull in the late twenties, I feel confident, is the nature of the period. It was an era of optimism, of speculation, of ebullience. The times were "prosperous"; there was little tension among the people. The mood was feverish, but this was more from overindulgence than from fear of insecurity. Actually the people were much more inclined to rebel against troublemakers than to spend their lives clamping down on the accused, including the "subversive" ghosts in the schools. Witchhunting was out; bigotry was at a new low. The public was tolerant.

In education, as in the business world, these were the "good years."

Then came the shocking events of 1929–33: the collapse of the stock market, the suicide of ruined men, the closing of factories and banks, the mounting unemployment from two million in 1929 to thirteen million in 1933 and the disintegration of the morale of the people. By 1933 the country was in the depths of the worst depression in its history.

And yet there were almost no attacks on the schools. Why? I think that those who manufacture them and keep them alive were otherwise engaged—saving the wrecks of their own enterprises, their fortunes, their minds, their souls. The publicity men were silent; the patrioteers were quiet; annual conventions of patriotic organizations made no denunciations of "subversive" un-Americanism in the schools.

It was in this period that the Rugg social-science enterprise came on the commercial market. The first volume of Man and His Changing Society (made out of the first two of the seventh-grade Social-Science Pamphlets) was issued by Ginn and Company in September 1929. At six-month intervals thereafter the five other large junior-high-school volumes appeared and were adopted for use. To the amazement of all concerned these large and expensive books— much more expensive than the conventional histories, geographies and civic books which they replaced—were bought in large numbers, the total sales annually during those years being more than one hundred and fifty thousand copies. It is not known exactly how many young people used the books; certainly three and a half years after the first publication of the junior-high-school series they numbered not less than a half million and probably nearly that many homes knew about them. Yet throughout this time not one word of opposition to their content reached either me or my publishers. And so far as I have been able to discover, opposition to other schoolbooks was also practically nil.

This situation leads me to pose another hypothesis for the psychologists of the public mind to document and refute or confirm. It is this: *Witch-hunting in the schools flourishes neither in times of great prosperity nor in times of great depression.* In the one period excitement brought about by the promise of personal gain is so intense that people cannot be bothered with "trivialities in the schools." Their attitude is: "Our youngsters are well cared for. Our schools are fine." On the other hand, in the period of unrest, of panic, of economic anxiety, of breakdown of the entrepreneur, of widespread stalling of industry and business, of unemployment, the interest of the people in such campaigns just cannot be captured. They are too worried over other matters. The very economic-social scene itself is so "subverted" that the interests of the hunters themselves are diverted in other directions.

Whether the hypothesis be proved or disproved, the fact remains that neither during the "good years" of 1924 to 1929, nor during the "bad years" from 1930 to 1933, were there any major questionings of progressive developments in the nation's schools.

But the thing was to happen again.

THE GREAT TECHNOLOGY

The first epoch on the time line of history in which
man can bring forth
a civilization of abundance, of tolerance
and of beauty.

A potentially great culture, because, having invented
efficient prime movers, man need no longer be a
cringing slave of nature.

Great—not because the twelve-hour day can become the
four-hour day, but because work of any prolongation
can become a happy and creative experience.

Great—because of the possibility of the successful union
of technology and democracy.

Great—because the scientific method can at last be
applied to the man-man relationships as well as
to the man-thing relationships.

In a word—great—because man can live creatively
both as artist and as technologist.

We stand at the crossroads to a new epoch; in one direction
lies the road to the Great Technology; in others lie
various pathways to social chaos and the
possible destruction of interdependent ways of living.

Chapter VIII

THE NEW STATECRAFT: EDUCATION FOR CONSENT

THE AMERICAN SCENE on March 4, 1933, was tense almost to the point of panic. A third of the nation's banks were closed, and every economic group was demanding relief from the new government—farmers, industrial and professional workers, businessmen and political leaders, indeed the whole consuming public. Conservatives as well as liberals, all deeply troubled by the gravity of the situation, recognized that something more than an ordinary depression had come upon the nation. A hitherto unknown combination of factors had thrust up a baffling and staggering problem. The tragedy of millions of people in distress stirred the liberal forces of America—students of the social scene, economists, industrialists, political leaders and educationists—to do something about it, vigorously and with dispatch. The people as a whole were ready to resort to almost any action which promised relief, even if this meant "experimenting" with new kinds of governmental machinery. There was general agreement, even among conservative politicians and economic leaders until 1934–35, that government should try something new. Try anything at least once was the mood.

144

The new government did. It acted with dispatch in meeting problems of morale and relief. It worked quickly at the task of remedying certain obvious evils in the operation of the social system. Small bank deposits, savings and investments were safeguarded. A program of social security was built up, including compulsory unemployment insurance, insurance for widows, mothers and the aged and accident and health insurance. Some advance was made toward regulating speculative enterprises and protecting buyers of securities. Other immediate needs received some legislative and executive attention—through the protection of small-home, farm and shop owners, the inauguration of a national system of employment exchanges, the modernization of the machinery of government. And meager beginnings were made in the study of deeper-lying problems of social reconstruction.

THE ENGINEERS AND THE NEW STATECRAFT

Of all the novel phenomena of the Long Armistice, and there have been many, none is of more importance than the entrance of a new statecraft upon the social scene. It had been building up slowly throughout our generation, made up of scientific men from many professions—physicists, chemists, engineers, social and political scientists, social psychologists and statesmanlike administrators in government. Conspicuous in this new statecraft were such world-renowned figures as Frederick Soddy, Nobel prize-winning chemist; such masters of the new physics as P. W. Bridgman, A. S. Eddington and A. N. Whitehead; such analysts of power-machine production as Charles P. Steinmetz, Bassett Jones, Frederick L. Ackerman, Richard Tolman, Fred Henderson, Walter N. Polakov, Major C. H. Douglas; such creative students of the economic and social

system as Thorstein Veblen, John Dewey and R. H. Tawney and leading social psychologists, political scientists and
other students of changing cultures.

This new statecraft was the product of many forces, but
two especially—science or technology and welfare. And the
fusion of the technological way of working with human-
itarian outlooks led to social engineering in government.
In limited ways it had been *in* government for two generations—making research contributions to the improvement
of agriculture, health, coast and geodetic surveys, the development of a vast range of standards, divisions of engineering, and the like. But if the decade since 1929 is to
stand out on the time line of our history, and I believe it is
inevitable, it will be because at last the *social-engineering
mind* was given a conspicuous role in government. Certainly more creative imagination was applied to social life
in this period than in any earlier one of similar length.

It seemed to be in the cards that I should play a part in
the discussion of the social-engineering approach to the
pressing economic and political problems of the day. I had
come back from the Far East in the late summer of 1932
with definite plans to write a memorandum on social reconstruction in China. But I found that I couldn't go forward. Steadily and with increasing insistence the growing
chaos in America pulled me away from my intriguing Chinese material. I couldn't escape the reproaches of my own
mind that I was doing nothing to help get us out of the
dreadful slough into which the country had fallen.

From the literature of "planning" that had piled up in
my absence I could see that many people were thinking out
and proposing plans for economic rehabilitation. Important
suggestions for a new economic state had come and were
coming from the minds and pens of scientific students of

the economic system. Indeed, from a wide range of individuals and groups were coming adverse appraisals of the old order and outlines of designs for a new one. College presidents were writing papers on "a planless world." Prominent bishops of churches, industrial leaders, notably Mr Daniel Willard, president of the Baltimore and Ohio Railroad Company, were publicly questioning the soundness of certain phases of capitalism. Journalists were exposing the false advice of business forecasters. I read and studied this whole library of criticism and protest as it came from the press.

There were also constructive proposals and plans for a new system—Governor Roosevelt's agricultural reconstruction proposals . . . the plan of Gerard Swope (president of the General Electric Company) for the stabilization of industry . . . Stuart Chase's and Charles A. Beard's comprehensive plans for the general reorganization of the economic system . . . John T. Flynn's "Security Wage" plan . . . Wisconsin's Governor Philip LaFollette's state unemployment-insurance plan . . . the pronouncements of the American Federation of Labor and the United States Chamber of Commerce. Altogether I reviewed more than thirty publications which were presented for criticism and discussion.[1]

One thing struck me as significant in all these proposals. The writers had no desire actually to abolish private capitalism; they saw, instead, the urgent need for imposing some kind of control—either by industry itself, by national government or by both. All insisted upon the principle that the purchasing power of the worker as well as of the owner and manager must be protected by building reserves in "times of prosperity."

[1]See Chapter IX of my book, *The Great Technology*, the John Day Company, Inc., New York.

A Program for Adult Education

Through all of this I was growing more and more rest-less. In the autumn of 1932 I came to the conviction that there was one thing seriously needed that I could help do. A generation of psychological research had shown that not only could the general "social instincts" of the American people be trusted, but, more specifically, that there were certainly not less than twenty-five to thirty million Americans who by hard study could be counted on to come to a fairly good understanding of what was happening to industrial civilization. On the sound judgment of these persons government by consent of the governed really hung in the balance. This was my cue. Turn mental capacity into dynamic understanding and will to constructive action. Adult education! Emergency adult education! Long-time continuing adult education! So I went to work to do what I could to help men understand.

Under the auspices of a committee on adult education of the Progressive Education Association, of which I became chairman (soon after merged with an "independent economic committee" chaired by John W. Herring), a systematic proposal[2] for nationwide adult study of the economic situation and the preparation of study materials for citizens was drawn up. It was a plan by which the tens of thousands of local branches of national organizations already in existence could be brought together under a central national clearinghouse in New York City, with regional and state offices stimulating and co-ordinating the work throughout the country.

[2] As presented to the financing foundations, *A Proposal to Establish a National Clearing House for Social-Economic Education,* by Harold Rugg and John W. Herring, under the auspices of the Progressive Education Association, 1933.

From the start the executives of forty national organizations[3] showed interest and actively co-operated for many months in the formulation of our plan. How many of the estimated fifty thousand of their local branches (in 1933) and their total membership of over fifteen million persons could be galvanized into prolonged study of economic-social problems we could not tell, but some were already carrying on this kind of work, and certainly many others could be led to do it if effective central and regional agencies could be established. The outlook, therefore, seemed bright. As for financing the enterprise, we hoped that grants could be secured from the foundations or sponsorship obtained from the federal government at Washington.

The plan itself comprised five major proposals:

First: that a central planning agency be established for social-economic education . . . to be governed by the representatives of forty or more co-operating national organizations and by competent persons in the fields of economics and the related social sciences.

Second: a central publications and information service to serve the current demand of millions of lay readers for clear, timely, concise and inexpensive materials on the vital social-economic issues before the nation.

Third: the establishment of regional, short-term institutions for the training of teachers and leaders . . . opportunity for measuring results and shaping the program of the central agency to meet the local need.

[3]Leading examples of the most active were: General Federation of Women's Clubs, National Congress of Parents and Teachers, Young Men's Christian Association, Young Women's Christian Association, American Association of University Women, National Federation of Business and Professional Women's Clubs, International Federation of Home and School, Workers Education Bureau of America, Council of Church Boards of Education in the United States, Association for Childhood Education, Child Study Association of America, National Association of Jewish Center Executives, National Council for Jewish Education and National Association for College Women.

Fourth: the development of radio and press educational services . . . the co-ordination of a radio service with the building of audiences and the dissemination of literature seen as a task for which the national organizations were splendidly equipped.

Fifth: the measurement of results and the appraisal of methods.

It was this plan that I presented as the report of my Adult Education Committee at the Cleveland meeting of the National Education Association in February 1934.[4] Largely because of the gross exaggeration in the interpretations of what we were trying to do, it created a sensation in the national press. The financing foundations which had shown interest were scared off.

I think of this whole effort as a capital illustration of one of the chief points I am trying to establish in this book. Here was a dynamic attempt by persons in education to do a constructive piece of work in the field of adult education. It was a sincere effort to build a better understanding among a compact minority of the people. But coming when it did, at a moment when all "liberalism" was beginning to be suspect, when many of our people were becoming frightened by the Roosevelt administration's experiments in government, the ever-alert haters of new ideas found receptive ears and succeeded in crushing what at another time no doubt would have been regarded as a sound educational venture.

"The Great Technology"

In the meantime as a contribution to adult study groups I wrote a small book and two "Study Guides." As a result of my reading of the cumulating literature I could see the

[4]In more recent years M. K. Hart, et al., have pictured the whole plan as a subversive, nationwide effort to overthrow the government!

need for a synthesis, presented fairly simply, of the tangled economic and psychological factors which had caused the recurring "jams" in our modern society. So I decided, with Richard Walsh's friendly enthusiasm as publisher, that I would prepare such a synthesis in a "long pamphlet" for adult study groups. In it I indicated that crucial problems had burst upon our people and that nothing short of heroic measures could meet them successfully. Its purpose was to describe the scene which had been ushered in by the new industrial revolution, to show clearly its unique character and to suggest the possibility of a potentially great culture looming just over the horizon. I called it *The Great Technology*.[5] The central theme of the book is given in the prologue statement on the inscription page, which is quoted in the frontispiece of this chapter.

Today isolated statements lifted from *The Great Technology* constitute the basis of much of the attack upon me and my schoolbooks. The attackers do not make clear that the book was written for adults, that its primary aim was to stimulate adult study and discussion. Moreover, they do not judge it in the light of the distressing conditions existing in late 1932 and early 1933, the very moment when it was being written. They conveniently forget the terrifying paralysis which gripped the nation during those months. They forget that they themselves accepted, even welcomed, the acts of the welfare government as it rescued them from the brink of collapse on which they tottered on March 4, 1933—the very acts which they now so violently condemn.

But as I wrote, urging the quick building of adult education, these things were constantly on my mind—the thirteen million to seventeen million people who were out of work,

[5] *The Great Technology: Social Chaos and the Public Mind*, the John Day Company, Inc., New York, 1933.

the hungry people pleading for food, the bread lines, the distinguished but poverty-stricken engineers and professional men who were begging for help and advice. I was deeply moved, intellectually and emotionally, by the spectacle of a powerful producing system standing stalled in the presence of mass misery, and I wrote vigorously in that mood. I feel sure that the statement stands as valid today as when I wrote it.

It is satisfying to see how much of the thesis has stood the test of the swift-moving social-economic trends. For example, the estimate of future unemployment—that six million would remain unemployed even when the index of production returned to the norm of pre-depression years—has since been proved to be conservatively sound; actually the number for the years 1937 to 1940 was ten million. That we have long been moving through a great transition into a new stage of industrial civilization is today becoming a truism to students of modern society. That America has potential physical and human resources to give every family an "adequate-diet" standard of living was later confirmed by the four famous volumes of the Brookings Institution and by reports of the National Survey of Potential Product Capacity. I believe that it can be said that the general soundness of *The Great Technology's* analysis of the social-economic problem has not been seriously questioned.[6]

★   ★   ★

In the autumn and winter of 1932 technocracy captured the headlines and was discussed by millions of people as a

[6]Following the publication of *The Great Technology* in March 1933, I prepared and published, with the collaboration of Marvin Krueger, two guides for directed study for adult discussion groups: (1) *Study Guide to National Recovery: An Introduction to Economic Problems*, (2) a longer and more fundamental booklet, *Social Reconstruction: Study Guide for Group and Class Discussion*, both published by the John Day Company, Inc., New York, 1933.

possible "plan." Governor Roosevelt listened to its advocates with interest, although his political instinct told him
that our people would not be interested in the "rule-by-
engineers" implication which seemed to be in it and which
Howard Scott, its chief propagandist, probably had in
mind. Langdon Post, later a member of the Roosevelt government, and others formed the Continental Committee on
Technocracy to further Scott's researches. The enterprise
was housed at Columbia University under the sponsorship
of my colleague Walter Rautenstrauch, professor of mechanical engineering. At the same time the ideas behind the
sensational movement caught the interest of Mr Frank A.
Vanderlip and other financiers, as well as economists and
publicists.

I studied technocracy carefully and agreed with three of
its concepts: (1) that the American people had within their
grasp a civilization of abundance in natural and human resources and in technology (and I insisted on adding—in
democratic tradition and in creative capacity); (2) that
neither on the side of production nor on the side of distribution was the social system designed or actually working
to fit the needs of the people, and (3) that the major task
before our people was one of becoming aware and studying
the problems of design. I sensed in Scott's version, however, an "authoritarian" tendency—a dictatorship by technicians—and I rejected that phase of the scheme. I note that
Jay Franklin (John Franklin Carter), who was a part of it,
did too.[7] It was for this reason that I never accepted the
movement *in toto*. I made the differences between conceptions of technocracy and my own clear in *The Great
Technology*.

Nevertheless, it was sad to see technocracy die a sudden
death in the winter of 1933. Here were practical business-

[7] Jay Franklin, *1940*, the Viking Press, New York, p. 22.

men, political leaders, engineers and other students of the
social system coming together eagerly (they were eager
that tragic winter!) to study and implement one of the
most profound ideas of modern times, an idea jointly produced over many years by the new statecraft to which I
have referred. Scott had kept it alive and was now giving
it national publicity. But all too soon he alienated businessmen, engineers and educators by his personal idiosyn-
crasies.

I remember well sitting with Harry Elmer Barnes and
Waldo Frank at that final technocracy meeting in the Hotel
Pierre in midwinter 1933. Mr Vanderlip was presiding and
Walter Rautenstrauch and other engineers and economists
had spoken. The crucial moment arrived—Howard Scott,
wandering in casually and late as usual, was to be the last
speaker on the program. His words were to go over a national radio network estimated to reach thirty million
people. But Scott failed completely. He repeated a few
platitudes on abundance and tried to speak extemporane-
ously on a problem which could have been compassed only
by an effort of supreme creative talent. In company with
others I left that meeting with the feeling that one of the
greatest opportunities of our generation to bind the people
together quickly in support of the scientific method in
government had been missed; probably never in our times,
I thought, would that moment be recaptured.

Harold Loeb, Walter N. Polakov, Felix J. Frazer and
other engineers went forward with the technical research,
and under the sponsorship of the government three years
later produced the very important volumes of data and conclusions to which I have had occasion to refer elsewhere.[8]

[8]The Chart of Plenty, Viking Press, New York, 1935. Also The Report
of the National Survey of Potential Product Capacity, New York City
Housing Authority and Works Division of the Emergency Relief
Bureau of the City of New York, 1935.

The Teachers College Group

Among the professors in education, I think I can say that few made a more serious attempt to build understanding among adults and children than a score of my colleagues at Teachers College, Columbia University. I had the good fortune to witness their gathering, one by one, in the college, in a small way actually took part in the assembling of some of them. Except for Dr William Heard Kilpatrick, who antedated my arrival by a decade, I was the first to come.

Moving away from mathematics and through the history of education into the philosophy of education, Kilpatrick had by the 1920s made of himself the natural "elder statesman" of our group. By 1930 he was recognized as one of the nation's greatest leaders in the open forum. Indeed, through the whole Long Armistice he has always been a champion and stanch defender of frontier movements. Long before Counts, Childs, Raup, Watson, Johnson, Clark and the others joined us I found in him an honest and wise elder brother and counselor.

Except for my association with Kilpatrick and occasional contacts with Gambrill, I worked almost alone in Teachers College. Then, one by one, and from various fields and backgrounds, the others arrived. Slowly our thinking brought us together and we built around Dr Kilpatrick a discussion group which, I believe, has been one of the best stimuli to our own intellectual development. Regularly from 1927 to 1934, intermittently from 1934 to 1938 and again regularly since September 1939 we have held our bi-monthly dinner-discussion meetings, canvassing informally, without programs planned in advance, the roots of every phase of our culture. In hundreds of hours of friendly argument we dug to the social foundations of education. Even by 1932 we had become a fairly cohesive group, taking our stand together for the general conception of a welfare state, agreeing fairly closely on the constituents of the democratic principle, avoiding membership or participation in political organizations but studying and critically appraising all platforms, creeds, strategies and tactics. This was practicing what we preached—vigorous adult education.

The Kilpatrick Discussion Group was also the nucleus which in 1935 established the John Dewey Society for the Study of Education and Culture, whose primary function has been the preparation of yearbooks. To date (through 1940) four have been published,[9] and all are fresh and direct studies of education in the actual framework of our changing American life. No important problems were dodged; no conditions which could be documented were ignored. With the Progressive Education Association the publications and meetings of this organization now lead the educational profession in bringing into the schools for study and discussion American life as it is actually lived.

Scholastic 1920–41: Creative Journalism for Young America

Almost from the beginning of the Social-Science Pamphlets my associates and I planned to build a journal of understanding for young Americans to accompany the books. In 1921–22 my brother and I discussed it and made preliminary inquiries, cost analyses, investigations of dis-

[9]First yearbook: *The Teacher and Society* (1937); second yearbook: *Educational Freedom and Democracy* (1938); third yearbook: *Democracy and the Curriculum* (1939); fourth yearbook: *Teachers for Democracy* (1940). All published by D. Appleton-Century Company, New York.

tributions methods, and the like. The task of preparing and handling the first two editions of the pamphlets was too great, however, actually to extend the enterprise in this way. Again in 1924–26 I talked with Hockett, Galloway, Washburne and others about it, but we were still unable to move because of the insistent demands on our energies by the research and writing. Still later, when the first commercial edition of Man and His Changing Society appeared, my publishers and I discussed the founding of such a magazine but finally decided against it.

Almost at the very moment when we were first considering these things Maurice R. Robinson was pioneering in this very field. His Volume I, Number 1, of *The Western Pennsylvanian Scholastic* appeared in the fall of 1920—a little five-column, eight-page weekly devoted chiefly to sports news of the high schools around Pittsburgh. For two years its subscription list consisted merely of a few thousand students in some fifty high schools. From these meager beginnings and out of a precarious infancy *Scholastic* became what is today a nationwide weekly educational magazine bought by over two hundred thousand high-school students. From a one-man organization in 1920 the staff enlarged and today numbers fifty-five.

In 1931 Scholastic Corporation began the publication of *Scholastic Coach*, a monthly magazine for directors of physical education and high-school coaches. *Junior Scholastic* was announced in the summer of 1937 and has become an established weekly magazine for the seventh, eighth and ninth grades. In addition *Scholastic* issues from time to time books and pamphlets of special classroom usefulness.

With the years many new features were added to the

magazine. In 1933 *Scholastic* began to issue separate editions for its two main subscriber groups—one for English classes and the other for the social studies. Since then, and in addition, a combined edition is also distributed for use in correlated or combined high-school courses or for those wishing to use one magazine in both English and social-studies departments.

Moreover, *Scholastic* has become a truly national sponsor of creative effort in youth. It not only has opened its pages to short stories, plays, essays and special articles by hundreds of great names in modern literature;[10] it has encouraged its own youthful readers to write, paint, compose music and otherwise express themselves. For years *Scholastic* awards have been a talent searchlight. Each year the best high-school writing is judged from thousands of manuscripts; since 1926 a representative sampling of the best work submitted has been gathered together in an annual anthology called *Saplings*. Later a division devoted to the arts and crafts was added to the awards project. Beginning in 1929, with the aid and guidance of a committee of prominent artists and art educators, annual national high-school art exhibits have been held in the fine-arts galleries of the famous Carnegie Institute in Pittsburgh. Beginning in 1937, the awards were expanded still further, adding a division and offering prizes for musical compositions by high-school students. In the spring of each year the *Scholastic* awards in this field are broadcast over a nationwide network.

★   ★   ★

[10]To name a few: Sherwood Anderson, Dorothy Canfield Fisher, Zona Gale, Hamlin Garland, Anne Parrish, William Saroyan, Elsie Singmaster, Henry Seidel Canby, Hughes Mearns, William Lyon Phelps, Channing Pollock, Agnes Repplier, Louis Adamic, James Truslow Adams, Harry Elmer Barnes, Charles Beard, Omar and Ryllis Goslin, Ernest Gruening, Hubert Herring, Quincy Howe, Howard W. Odum, William F. Ogburn, Hendrick van Loon and many others.

Maurice Robinson came to me in the spring of 1931 with the proposal to expand the social studies section of the magazine, inviting me to serve as a contributing editor in that field. It happened that within the same month Mr Walter Meyer of the *American Observer* asked me to join Charles Beard and David Muzzey on his editorial board. I looked into the two propositions and decided for *Scholastic*. I have never regretted the decision. For ten years, since September 1931, although I have made almost no editorial contribution to the magazine, I have written regularly for it—altogether a hundred-odd articles ramifying over the domestic and world scene. It has been a joy to work with Ken Gould, the brilliant and indefatigable managing editor of the magazine since 1926.[11]

Robbie and Ken and their weekly *Scholastic* brought into my life another one of those insistent deadlines; every year Ken's schedule kept me alive to the significance of the current of events as nothing else could have done. The articles have covered the entire range of world problems and their historical backgrounds; for example: industrial civilization at the crossroads . . . the undeclared wars on civilization and the struggle for eastern Asia, the Mediterranean and the British Empire . . . the current conflicts on the European continent . . . the world-wide struggle of dictatorship and democracy . . . American economic-social problems . . . appraisals of the New Deal and its opponents . . . studies of the work of creative Americans.

It is my considered judgment that *Scholastic* has made a profound contribution to the social education of young America. It has kept our youth in touch with their times

[11]Kenneth M. Gould, frequent contributor to national magazines and author of *Windows on the World* (Stackpole Sons, 1938; rev. ed. 1940), the latter, one of the best available introductions to the trends and forces playing on the world scene in our times.

and their culture—describing, analyzing and interpreting the events, problems, personalities and writings which are molding their world. Its accounts of events and problems in contemporary history are comprehensive and clear. It offers a rich supply of counsel about living through reading material which fosters an appreciation for the best on today's creative frontiers.

ANOTHER WAVE OF ATTACKS

As I appraise the work of the new statecraft and the dramatic action of the liberals in education during the early 1930s I can see more clearly than ever before how inevitable it was that witch-hunting would begin again. Indeed, even then we predicted that it would happen.

By the autumn of 1934 the public mood was properly prepared. Suspicion was in the air. Growing numbers were beginning to cry out against the "experiments" being tried in Washington. Groups like M. K. Hart's were out to cut taxes, even if that meant hampering the schools. Businessmen had begun to talk about being "hamstrung." In education sincere defenders of the disciplinary tradition sought to put "progressivism" out. These and other factors paved the way for the fire of the opponents of change in educational practice.

The targets had become conspicuous enough to hit. And hit they were—by the Hearst newspapers, Elizabeth Dilling, the Americanism units of the American Legion, the Sons of American Revolution, the Daughters of American Revolution, the Veterans of Foreign Wars and other patriotic organizations. A brief word about several of the attacks.

The Red Network

In 1934 Elizabeth Dilling, a Middle West concert harpist and housewife, published a little handbook called *The Red Network*. It was a kind of Who's Who of Radicalism for "patriots." It listed four hundred and sixty suspected organizations and thirteen hundred persons, including, in the words of one reviewer, practically everyone in America who "has ever worked for social progress, freedom and humanitarianism." I am listed in it because of my reference to the Russian youth movement in my 1933 *Herald Tribune* speech which was quoted in *The Daily Worker*. I must confess that I should now be quite chagrined had I been left out of it; after all—thirteen hundred liberals!

A ridiculous book? Yes—and no! As Leon Whipple wrote in the *Survey Graphic*, it is

. . . not without portent. Already there are signs that it is used as a guide for attack on certain groups; in a crisis that might become the index of proscribed activities and people. And the substratum of fear and ignorance it reveals points to one of the danger spots in our social geology.[12]

Here is a bit of the story behind Mrs Dilling and her book. After seeing conditions in Russia in 1931 and being told there that the Communist world revolution would start in China and end with the United States, she returned home to study the subject. She began to give lectures on Communism before patriotic meetings. She wrote articles for a local paper, among them one called "Red Revolution, Do We Want It Here?" These she had printed and distributed, ten thousand copies at cost. The Daughters of the

[12] *Survey Graphic*, January 1935, p. 39.

American Revolution sent them to every one of their chapters throughout the country.

In 1939 at a Senate hearing Mrs Dilling vigorously opposed President Roosevelt's nomination of Professor Felix Frankfurter for the Supreme Court. *Life* said of her performance:

> After dismissing Professor Frankfurter as a tool of "Red revolutionaries," fast-talking Mrs Dilling informed the committee that both President and Mrs Roosevelt are "dangerous radicals," offered to prove it in fifteen minutes. [Asked what] did she think about the Republican party's Number 1 brain-truster, Dr Glenn Frank, "He is a very dangerous man," snapped Mrs Dilling.[13]

The Red Network ridiculous? Yes, but probably no single publication of the superpatriots during the past decade has exerted more damaging influence upon liberal forces in America.

Hearst's 1934 Attack upon the Schools and Colleges

In December 1934 faculty members of Teachers College, New York University and Union Theological Seminary sent to the McCormack-Dickstein Committee on Un-American Activities evidence of the efforts of William Randolph Hearst to incite a Red scare through attacks in his newspapers upon university professors. Here is some of the basis for their action.

Hearst reporters obtained appointments with Dr John N. Washburne[14] at the University of Syracuse and Dr Kilpatrick and Dr Counts of Teachers College, describing

---

[13]*Life*, January 23, 1939, p. 16.

[14]A member of my research group in Lincoln School from 1923 to 1926 and professor of psychology at the University of Syracuse since 1926.

themselves as American Communists and students who wished information about going to Russia to study. Among other things they asked such questions as: Are there students at the university who admit being Communists or Socialists? Do some of them preach pink or red doctrines? Are there Communists on the faculty of the university? Are the courses for the students more or less radical?

Washburne was visited first. To his utter amazement the (Hearst) Syracuse *Journal* for the next day, November 22, 1934, called him a "Red" and stated that during the reporter's interview Washburne had admitted that his and other professors' courses in American colleges were "radical" and "communistic." Washburne immediately sent other papers categorical denials of ever making such statements. He also sent out warnings to his friends in other institutions to be on the lookout for the Hearst trick.

It was fortunate that he did, for sure enough, in a few days a Hearst reporter came to the offices of Kilpatrick and Counts and gave much the same story as was given to Washburne. But they were prepared for his visit and had a stenographer record every word that was said. A few sample lines of the conversation[15] are revealing.

The reporter started out by telling Dr Kilpatrick:

"I am in the peculiar position, in talking with you, of Red baiter. Personally I am not in sympathy with that sort of thing —in fact, quite the opposite—but Mr Hearst wants to get material along this line. Let me ask you first how you feel about things—do you believe in studying the Soviet Russian experiment, for example?"

When Dr Kilpatrick asked him later if he didn't "feel ashamed to come and talk . . . this way" the reporter answered: "I'm not ashamed for myself but for the situation

[15]These quotations are taken from the private stenographic transcripts made by Dr Kilpatrick and Dr Counts.

that makes it necessary to do this in order to keep alive." In the interview with Dr Counts the reporter openly admitted that "Hearst is engaged at present in conducting a Red scare."

As a result of these methods the liberals led in a nation-wide discussion of the Hearst attack upon the schools. Transcribed reports of the interviews were given to the press and were reproduced in several non-Hearst newspapers. Such persons as Charles A. Beard and John Dewey made statements condemning the methods used and warning

"that a campaign of terrorism against teachers in American colleges, universities, schools and even private schools is getting under way. Such repressive efforts are not only directly contrary to American democratic tradition but, if successful, would make it impossible for schools to do their proper work."[16]

Hearst fought back on February 24, 1935, publishing in his New York *American* the names of a score of nationally distinguished educators who he said were

authorized disseminators of Communistic propaganda in the United States, who deliberately and designedly mislead our fine young people and bring them up to be disloyal to our American ideals and institutions and stupidly to favor the brutal and bloody tyranny of Soviet Russia.

During the next two months the fight of the professors to eliminate Hearst from the Red-baiting scene went on. In February they organized an independent meeting at the midwinter superintendents' convention at Atlantic City on Red baiting in the schools and colleges. Not one who attended will ever forget the magnificent speech made by Charles A. Beard.

[16]Appeal to the McCormack-Dickstein Committee.

The Patriotic Organization Again

A year later the patriotic organizations began to get active again, this time in Washington, D.C., and in several small communities from Montana and Iowa to Massachusetts. In Washington, D.C., a so-called Federation of Citizens Associations of the District of Columbia asked the board of education to eliminate three books from the public schools. Two of these were mine—*Introduction to American Civilization* and *Changing Civilizations in the Modern World*—and one was *Modern History*, by Carl L. Becker of Cornell University. A similar attack was made upon *Scholastic* magazine about the same time but not because of my connection with it. As soon as this was known in New York and other parts of the country a committee of the federation itself reported that "the board of education is now receiving a deluge of telegrams and letters regarding Professor Harold Rugg, similar to those previously received on behalf of Carl L. Becker."

A committee appointed by the Washington Board of Education investigated the books and reported later that the accusers had repeatedly changed the author's interpretations by lifting out of context. The committee concluded with regard to my work:

We find no mention of Communism in this textbook, not even a suggestion of it. The description and discussion of the manner in which the American people have lived and now live are not herein associated, even remotely, with the subject of Communism, and we consider criticism of the book on this ground unfair and unjust.[17]

No more was heard from this quarter.

[17]Minutes of the tenth meeting of the Board of Education, December 18, 1935, p. 44.

1935–The Hand of the "Americanism" Headquarters Again?

In the spring of 1935 I began to get letters, telegrams and telephone calls from various parts of the United States, telling me that attempts were being made to eliminate my books from the schools. On a single day four such letters appeared—one each from Montana, Illinois, Indiana and Massachusetts. Many of the features of the earlier "un-Americanism" baiting were repeated. The Boston *Post* gave a double-page spread in two Sunday issues to the controversy in Boston and vicinity; one against me, and one for me.

To this day I have been unable to get to the exact source of these attacks, but word-of-mouth confirmation and the very simultaneity and similarity of the attacks seem to indicate clearly that the national headquarters of one or more of the patriotic societies must have been involved. I do know that members of certain of these organizations had made demands that the Rugg books be eliminated. In only two communities to my knowledge were they successful.

Certainly President Hopkins of Dartmouth described the situation well when he was giving me an honorary doctorate degree in June 1935:

". . . in the forthrightness of your utterances you have aroused the disapprobation of intolerant minds and you have incurred the hostility of advocates of special privilege. . . ." The two days in Hanover, coming as they did in the midst of attacks on several fronts, were indeed a welcome interlude of friendship and encouragement.

★   ★   ★

There were a few other sporadic and local attacks, but I think these are enough to show how a new wave rose and fell in 1934 and 1935.

THAT I MAY UNDERSTAND

Chapter IX

ACADEMIC MIND, 1918

How did it all start—this writing of books to bring American life into the school? An episode, recalled over the years, helps to fix a good beginning point. I was walking with John Coss in Rock Creek Park, Washington, the day after the "real" Armistice in November 1918, and we had been reminiscing about the work of our army personnel organization. Suddenly he asked: "What are you going to do when you get back to Chicago?"

"I'm not sure," I said; "probably more of what I've been doing, at least for a while. I think I'll write a primer to precede my statistics book[1] and make some intelligence tests; and I'll probably publish this army rating stuff to show how the rating of human character is askew. After that—I don't know. Pope[2] has me all stirred up about Van Wyck

[1]My *Statistical Methods Applied to Education* had been published in 1917 as we went into the war; the *Primer of Graphics and Statistics* was not actually published until 1925. *On the Rating of Human Character* ran in serial form in 1920–21 in the *Journal of Educational Psychology*, of which I was editor for eleven years.

[2]Arthur Upham Pope, formerly a member of the philosophy faculty of the University of California, brilliant and stimulating colleague on the Committee on Personnel of the United States army, later distinguished authority in Iranian art and now for some years director of

Brooks's new stuff—stirred up and mixed up. But what are you going to do?"

John was quiet for a time, but finally he said, "Well, I'll tell you. I am going to put through just one job—if it's the last one I do. I am going to help make a big orientation course for the undergraduate students in Columbia College."

We talked about it. Here was a new idea, at least on the college level, although it had antecedents in a generation or reorganizing work in the sciences and mathematics for the secondary schools. It was to bring the social sciences into one overview "introduction to contemporary civilization course" required of all freshmen. It was still nebulous as to detail, but the key idea—the "integration of the college curriculum"—was of enormous importance. I think it is not too much to say, from the perspective of 1940, that on the side of the developing organization of the educational program of school and college since 1919, this conception has been of real significance.[3]

For a year after I left Washington in late November 1918, I did go on teaching and researching with Judd at the University of Chicago, carrying on from about where I

the Institute of Iranian Studies. It was long trips and exciting talks with Pope around the cantonments of the army in 1918 that first introduced me to Van Wyck Brooks's *America's Coming of Age* and *Letters and Leadership,* as well as the *Seven Arts* and *New Republic* groups of young social critics.

[3]John Coss carried out his plan. He returned to Columbia College and for fifteen years was chairman of a faculty group which developed the famous "CC" course, Introduction to Contemporary Civilization. After Washington his and my paths parted, later to come together again when I became educational psychologist of the Lincoln School of Teachers College in 1920. Now he is gone from us—in the middle of life—but his influence and his contribution to collegiate education will long be recognized.

had left off. I think we all did for a while. I remember that a score of war psychologists rushed a score of new intelligence tests into press. With their new tests and scales in hand most of the measurers hurried to publishers, and a mountainous literature of measurement and statistics piled up. Scott[4] and company sold "personnel" to industry as never before.

But only for a while, for in some of us a new leaven was working. The war had jolted many of the middle-of-the-road academicians out of the ruts in which they had been plodding; the changes that they brought in scholastic programs stand as witnesses. And the war raised questions in the minds of the more sensitive technicians—questions of *values* that hitherto had not been raised. Although we were not aware of it at the time the impact of the new contacts and experiences brought by the war really launched many of us on a new quest for understanding of self and society.

A Backward Look: Before 1918

As I inventory the academic mind of 1918[5] and its antecedents in home, school and occupation, one distinct lack of mental equipment stands out above all others—a profound naïveté about the social scene and lack of independence in thought and action. As word came through in the spring of 1919 of the kind of treaty President Wilson was letting Clemenceau dictate at Versailles, few of us in the academic world had any really critical insight about it;

[4]Walter Dill Scott, chief of our Committee on Personnel and later president of Northwestern University.

[5]I recognize the danger of rationalization in any retrospection which supplies the data of autobiography. To help minimize that I am writing Chapters IX to XI from a manuscript hitherto unpublished, of a "mental" autobiography entitled "Stephen Cross." I wrote this in 1925 on my return from the Far East and the survey of the educational system of the Philippine Islands. The manuscript has been supplemented by notes and records made each year from 1920 to 1925.

and it must be confessed that several years more passed
before I myself had much competence. Among my university colleagues there was little evidence that they understood the transitional nature of the epoch through which
industrial nations were passing, the behind-the-scene forces
playing on foreign offices, international trade and finance,
the making and breaking of secret alliances or the long-time
trends that had already brought the international world to
an economic and political stalemate. And yet by that time
the "new history" had long since passed out of its adoles-
cence and America had been in the throes of a transitional
period of cultural revolt and improvisation for two decades. The lag of the academic mind behind the creative
mind of America in 1919 was wide, and, I think, thoroughly exponential of university pedagogy and school
practice. I cannot recall a single professor of education or
teacher in school history or the social sciences who was
aware of the forces, trends, attitudes or ideas set down in
Chapters VI and IX–XI of this book or who took steps to
bring them into the life and program of the schools. In
1919, I say.

Our naïveté and conformity were perhaps not astonishing, considering the cultural deficiencies of the middle-class
homes and the communities in which most of us had grown
up. The college-bred Americans of 1918 largely lacked a
thorough understanding. Certainly my own youth and
young manhood had given little promise of such fruition,
and I am confident that much the same could be said of my
neighbors. Home, school and community had not only
failed to build understanding and a sense of values but had
actually worked against their development.

In my own case, at least, they conspired to fix attitudes

of conformity and inferiority, for in the lower middle-class homes in the New England mill city in which I lived most personal courses of action were dictated by two deep-seated fears—the fear of not having enough and the fear of "What will the neighbors think?"

For nine generations the homesteads of my people had grayed under the chill of New England hills. For nine generations my pioneer forebears had planted their orchards, skimmed the boulderish soil, repaired their stone walls each spring, walled their neighbors out and their spirits in. The narrow physical inheritance had produced its counterpart in the circumscribed mental horizon of the people. Life was thin and arid like the soil; norm domineered over the spirit. All social forces—home, community and education—made for acquiescence, molding my contemporaries and myself to the standards of adult life. Independence of thought was minimized; loyalty was canonized. Indeed life was regarded as an existing fact, not a vivid experiment; it was accepted, questioningly and even despairingly by some, but nevertheless, accepted by all who clung to the ancestral place. Certainly for most of us in the Neo-Victorian era conformity, not adventure, was the governing criterion of conduct.

A widespread climate of inferiority also pervaded the hierarchy of neighborhoods that made up that mill city of hills and valleys; certainly it was the mood created by my years of child-youth experience and one which held long over into adult life. As I feel my way back now over those years at the turn of the century I see that life in those parental homes was dominated primarily by the quest for food, the benumbing effect of fatigue and an acute class consciousness. The latter, I think, was caused partly by the daily routine of life in an artisan home and partly by such spontaneous economic symptoms of inferiority as vocal outbursts of tired elders. It was fatigue, I think, caused by the attempt to make ends meet, that lay at the basis of much of the inferiority. The environment assailed the individual from every angle; home, neighborhood and the town co-operated in the unceasing endeavor to put each in his place. Young minds were molded, stamped and labeled—each with an economic and social status. Thus the sense of inferiority accumulated, and attitudes of conformity solidified.

Even in childhood—and in spite of a temperamental re-belliousness which I am sure was not altogether environ-mental—I learned that liberalism of thought and speech brought its aftermath in insecurity of income and the in-evitable risk of physical danger. Refusal to join the car-penters' union and criticism of employer or of his politics produced the same result—loss of job. I remember well examples of the ruthless action of both during the long years of struggle between an independent-minded father and a rigid economic order.

The constant reiteration of economic danger in the plastic years of youth taught the wisdom of acquiescence. Repression filled the place of creative joy in living. The march of life was regimented. It became a lock step. The herd was produced.

The New England grammar of life produced, I think, the grammar school—or was it the Western man's grammar of life? Certainly the episodes of the twelve-grade mass school were replicas of the mass mind. The high school merely continued the regimented curriculum which the rapid rise of the graded school had precipitated. I can see now that the teachers were not only dull—which I knew then—but they were uninformed concerning both the problems of modern life and the trends and factors that produced them. I marvel today that it was possible for my fellows and myself to live in the midst of the changing industrialism of northeastern America at the turn of the twentieth century and remain entirely untouched by it. Never once, except from my unlettered father—I like to remember him as the last of the New England artist-craftsmen—did I hear of the industrial revolution, the frontier of American life, the "new" immigration of eastern and southern Europe, which was utterly transforming our very state, or the maelstrom of economic imperialism which was bringing on the World War. Never once was I urged to read a contemporary American writer. Never once did I hear of American architects, painters, sculptors or other artists, although the creative spirit was even then beginning to break through the encompassing matrix of Victorian British-classical culture into which we were being poured. Although in the 1890s and early 1900s America still continued to take its arts as it had its common law, its language, its customs and its religion from Great Britain and Europe, creative native genius had already emerged, but we never heard of it. Henry Richardson had long since put up his famous stone churches and railroad stations in Massachusetts, and Louis Sullivan was then creating a new architecture in Middle Western cities. Isadora Duncan had danced her way, unheralded, across America and was being acclaimed in Europe. Stephen Crane's *Red Badge of Courage* was becoming a vogue—and New England letters, even in its twilight, had much to give New England youth! Edward Bellamy had written *Looking Backward* and *Equality* only forty miles from my home in Fitchburg, and Henry George's name and theory were on millions of lips. But not a word did I hear of anything native and contemporary; nor, for that matter, did I get any critique of the very lack of native artists, a critique of the kind which had been made for sixty years by Emerson, for thirty by Walt Whitman.

Not only did the school fail to develop understanding and sensitiveness; it thwarted expressive capacity as well. I don't recall a single experience in school or college which stimulated really creative production on my part; there was not one instructor who suggested that I "say what I saw *my* unique way."

All of this was characteristic of the education I got in a well-financed Massachusetts school in the last decade of the nineteenth century. I cannot resist adding that my home was only thirty miles from the famous village of Quincy, where Francis W. Parker—under Charles Francis Adams's tolerant and stimulating lay sponsorship—had only recently become a storm center of educational reform. I think my story at that point could be duplicated by most of the post-war academicians.

In 1902, at the impressionable age of sixteen, I left high school and for two years earned a meager "living" at the textile trade. I learned more than hand skill. I was plunged from an "other-worldly" scholastic atmosphere into the stark mercenariness of industrial mass production. From before dawn until after dark I stood in the din of clacking looms, shoulder to shoulder with a dozen races and nationalities from eastern and southern Europe. There I not only sensed the struggle of the "new" immigration for a safe place on the ladder of economic life; through first-hand contact with piecework I saw the ruthlessness with which an uncontrolled industry could exact precision of skill in a world in which dividends apportioned bread. I moved later from the weave room into the office, and the new contact with accounting orders and sales revealed to me the discrepancy between the wages of the herd, the salary of the white-collared executive and the dividends of the owner. And firsthand I was learning that immigrant

families of ten did find it difficult to live on nine dollars a
week.

★   ★   ★

For two years another person of greater vision and courage and initiative prodded me to get out of my rut and make
something of myself. "Go to college. Go to Tech—where
you've always wanted to go"—and where examinations
had already been passed. At last I shook myself out of the
conformity and inertia to plan somewhat more definitely
the course of my life. Education—as always with the
American—was to provide the leverage to pull me up the
ladder of opportunity. The college was viewed as the road
to economic salvation, the bachelor's degree as a commercial asset; they were the prestige symbols of the upper
middle classes from which I had been brought up to feel
that I was set apart—excluded.

Then followed five years of college and technology at
Dartmouth where both liberal arts and civil engineering
were offered. The football was superb, as was the total
"life" of the institution; the curriculum was as good as
any of that day, I think. So my professors—a few are still
living—will forgive me if I say that only a modicum of
approval can be given today for what took the place of
"the effort of reason" and "the adventure of beauty" for
those six hundred young Americans.

I hardly need remind my readers that the curriculum
of the liberal arts college at the beginning of the twentieth
century was focused primarily on technique, and academic
technique at that. It satisfied practical measures as little as
did that of the secondary school. Indeed, it must be recorded that the outcome of my own nine years of secondary school, college and technological study was but a
superficial smattering of knowledge about a variety of

academic things, a fair amount of competence in certain limited engineering skills, almost total innocence of the fundamental forces playing upon the domestic and international scene, lack of acquaintance with the essential principles of behavior and a distinct want of mental ballast.

For the "educated" man who was to live in the violent cultural mind shifts of a dynamic and changing civilization this lack of intellectual ballast was perhaps the most important deficiency. Like tens of thousands of other American youth, I was turned out of college with no sure sense of personal values, no clear basis for making economic-political decisions. As a consequence, for some years·after leaving college I lurched violently from one political and economic faith to another. I think most of my contemporaries did too; we were indeed fit subjects for the organized propaganda of editorial opinion. Higher education in those days surely produced no generation of informed, thinking men and women, guided by clear disinterestedness of purpose with respect to national and world affairs. It succeeded in doing little more than develop partisan loyalties and a vague discomfort on hearing the first strains of the national anthem. My citizenship enthusiasms during the next decade spent themselves on superficial differences between the major political parties and the reform of obvious social evils; I was a "progressive" in politics. And as for the attitudes of conformity, inferiority and desire for social approval generated in childhood and youth, college and technological training served chiefly to rivet them more tightly.

Passage from the arts college into the graduate school of civil engineering made one significant contribution to my education; it made me a technician, fairly competent in measurement and statistics. The "reduction of error" became my chief pursuit. I remember "Bobbie" Fletcher, our revered ex-army-officer professor of engineering, appearing the very first class meeting with these words (he repeated them again at our graduation): "Young gentlemen, for you, all your lives, there will be no such thing as 'truth'! There will be only practical approximations. Your endeavor shall constantly be to cut down 'error'—to reduce error in measurement by repeated measurements, error in interpretation by the statistical averaging of measurements and by the application of theoretical corrections." We believed him, and the mastery of technical competence became our obsession. In 1909 the intellectual prewar equipment of the academic mind certainly bulked large on the side of the consumption of technique.

Five years before the war I left my books to spike rails and tamp ties on one of the great Middle Western railroad systems. I surveyed track, ran hundred-mile lines of levels, fitted railroad spirals on sharp curves to the nice adjustments of speed, rolling stock and curvature. And there I made at last the shocking discovery that the handbook formulas of Searles and Trautwine which I had learned in college actually worked! The equations of algebra and analytics and the integrations of calculus had never appeared to fulfill the pragmatic sanction, but the formulas really worked! With them one could make concrete briquettes, counteract rabies or diphtheria and communicate around the world. With them—the young engineer believed what he had been taught—you could save America; maybe, indeed, the world. Fifteen years later I was to be shown how inevitable it was that Charles Sanders Peirce, engineer, statistician and professor of logic, should have fashioned the mold for America's first philosophic statement—pragmatism.

In that year of work on the railroad precise measurements were supreme. Bobbie was right; my job was to reduce error and I practiced it with a vengeance. Happily not much thinking was required—just precise measurement. But there was one conspicuous constructive outcome of the experience—attitudes of precision were engendered by hours of standing behind a transit, reading elevations on the cross hair of an instrument, making, checking and rechecking numerical computations, using the slide rule, the computation machine and the handbook, my constant companion for many years.

Salvation via Fact Finding

The practice of engineering construction held me for only a short time. Once more I made an original decision, left my work and turned to the field of engineering education. Then followed two years in a small new college in Illinois where I was half the Civil Engineering Department[6] and four years at the University of Illinois, combining the teaching of engineering and the graduate study of education, psychology and sociology with Bagley,[7] Coffman, Whipple, Hayes and their associates. Gradually, aided by a Ph.D. in education and sociology in 1915, I made the

---

[6] In the James Millikin University, Decatur, Ill. It was there and at the moment of my going there that James Hessler was writing the first general-science book for high schools. It was there that Thomas Walton Galloway was laying the foundations for his important work in sex hygiene, which he later developed in New York under the American Social Hygiene Association.

[7] William C. Bagley, later professor of education and my colleague and friend for many years at Teachers College.

Lotus D. Coffman, later president of the University of Minnesota.

Guy M. Whipple, for twenty years secretary of the National Society for the Study of Education.

Edward Cary Hayes, professor of sociology at the University of Illinois.

transition to the general field of education. It must be recorded that, looking back today, I see it as merely changing the job, the data with which I worked—not my fundamental outlook or interest. Society had made me a technician, and the change from engineering to education left me still a technician—and to a very considerable extent ignorant of the new world order that was being fashioned all around me.

Many of my readers will no doubt remember that at the moment of my shift the new field of general education was in the throes of a great fact-finding movement. The new "child accounting" was being born: Thorndike had just published his original studies of the school population. Strayer, Elliott and Cubberley had question-blanked school finance in cities and states. Courtis was making his original series of arithmetic tests. The new science of educational psychology was emerging from the pioneer laboratory studies in learning; experimental methods of laboratory psychology were being taken over into education; the concept of the active school was ousting that of the listening school. Thorndike, Judd and company were producing monographs and articles dealing with the transfer of training, the practice curve, eye movements in meaning and reading; Freeman was initiating his studies on rhythmic movement and posture in handwriting.

This stage of tabular analysis was probably a necessary first period in the development of the "science of education"; in spite of the jeers of the established academicians—the physical and natural scientists and the classicists—the infant of the human technologies, "education," was being born. But chiefly because of the infancy of the work, the processes of survey, inventory and rearrangement took precedence over controlled experiment, scientific law, re-oriented philosophy and thoroughgoing reconstruction.

We lived in one long orgy of tabulation. Mountains of facts were piled up, condensed, summarized and interpreted by the new quantitative technique. The air was full of normal curves, standard deviations, coefficients of correlation, regression equations.

I was only one of a very large band of intellectuals, outside the universities as well as inside, who with Lippmann and company were proclaiming salvation through fact finding. The decade just passed had witnessed the establishment of one great foundation after another and the setting aside of hundreds of millions of dollars, the income from which was to be devoted to finding the facts of life. The Russell Sage Foundation was launching its surveys of the community. The General Education Board, the Rockefeller Institute for Medical Research, the Rockefeller Foundation, the Rosenwald Fund and others were stamping the heel of knowledge upon disease the world over. A hundred corporations were setting up research divisions. Half as many universities had long since set trained minds at finding the facts of agriculture, industry, health, education, what not, and five times that number of school systems had already introduced departments of research. The first third of the twentieth century was indeed a great fact-finding era in American intellectual life.

I spent four years of graduate study at this kind of thing at the University of Illinois and five years more teaching and researching with Judd at Chicago. Then in 1918 came the jolting interlude of the war, my revolutionary meetings with Arthur Pope and at last, and by imperceptible stages, an introduction to a whole new world of creative American life. The war had broken upon a nation, which, while traditionally organized for peace, had been accustomed by three centuries of pioneering to swift readjustments. Overnight the nation harnessed itself for war, and overnight the intellectual world of America responded to the call to arms by organizing a fourfold brigade of technicians. Even before Wilson's actual declaration of war Leonard Ayres, reporting to us in Judd's living room that memorable evening of April 5, 1917, had launched his statistical division to inventory the needs of the army. Shortly after, under the leadership of Walter Dill Scott, Edward L. Thorndike and Walter V. Bingham, a hand-picked lot of psychologists, educationalists, statisticians and industrial and business personnel executives were organized into the army's Committee on Classification of Personnel, of which I became a member. Yerkes, Terman and other psychologists had set up the psychological division of the army. Walter Lippmann and other free-lance publicists had enlisted in the various intelligence divisions of government agencies. And all of us practiced the "philosophy of the existing fact" more exhaustively than we ever·had done in civil life. There is perhaps no comparable precedent in history for the volume of quantitative analysis of human and material needs which was made by these four groups in a year's time.

The total effect of all of this on most of the academicians was certainly not to release them from their consumption of technique. They believed more firmly than before that social and personal problems could be solved if one could "find the facts." The dearth of vision and value seemed as profound as ever.

As I try to look back at myself and the other academicians of 1918 there is danger, of course, of magnifying our inadequacies. And yet I am amazed at how seldom most of us fact finders really found the "right" facts. I give here a single example—others will emerge later. For a full half century before the Long Armistice a whole new organic outlook and understanding had been building among students of American life. No fewer than ten groups of creative workers[8] had already brought about the essential transition in point of view from that of animistic theology and an absorption in mechanistic science to a more organic and modern outlook. Of this important achievement my colleagues and I in education were fairly innocent. I, for example, while spending four years (1911–15) at Illinois with Bagley, Whipple and Coffman on a study of mental discipline in school studies and reporting my findings in a dissertation, was literally surrounded by a library of the very physiological and psychological monographs which would have obviated the need for even making the study. Some of these materials I had actually read, but their real significance for my research problem I didn't understand until ten years after the doctoral dissertation was completed. And I doubt if my various professors did either, for they certainly did not point the way. How well this illustrates the difficulty "educated" human beings have in lifting themselves out of habitual mental-emotional ruts in which their minds insist on moving.

Moreover, in 1918 there was a goodly company of intellectuals, a small liberal Left—some inside, but more outside the colleges—who knew a good deal of what the social-economic-political to-do was all about. They could have told us if we had cultivated them. This group comprised those who wrote for and a few who read *The New Republic, The Nation, The Dial* and, for a short time after the war, *The Freeman*. They were the rebel pragmatists who had been educated by James, Dewey, the "Hopkins" group and other liberal teachers of the 1890s. They were evolutionists and students of the scientific method. Al-

[8] I discuss these more fully in Chapter IX.

though they accepted democratic industrialism, for a quarter century they had been trying to reform it, knocking the props out from under monopoly, cleaning up housing and city government. They were social and economic pathologists—stirring little groups, led by such people as Woodrow Wilson, Tom Johnson, Frederic C. Howe, Willard Straight and Oswald Villard.

Still farther to the Left were incisive critics, liberal and pragmatic novelists and poetic reflectors of the current of American life. There was Frank Norris, writing *The Pit* and *The Octopus;* Upton Sinclair with his *Jungle, Money Writes* and *The Brass Check;* Theodore Dreiser producing clumsy, verbose word portraits of American types—*The Financier* and *The Genius;* Sinclair Lewis describing Main Street, making up composite pictures of the middle-class businessman Babbitt, the technical research specialist Arrowsmith and the organizing middle-of-the-road pulpiteer Elmer Gantry. A valiant company they were, calling to account the opportunistic administrators of our industrial and political regime.

At that same time there was still another company of creative minds, about whom most of my colleagues and I knew practically nothing—an obscure nucleus of creative America, working chiefly in our largest cities but occasionally in isolated small communities. Some in the groups were making a new cultural criticism; others were searching for means of self-expression in the imaginative realism of story telling, poetry, the drama, painting, sculpture, music and the dance. Before and during the war many of them were separated from one another, pioneering more or less alone. Others had been brought together by several great focusing centers: Alfred Stieglitz and his "291" and other "American Places"; Harriet Monroe and *Poetry* (1912); Frank, Brooks, Bourne, et al. and *The Seven Arts* (1916);

Eastman and *The Masses* (1911); Reedy and his *Mirror* (1911). Thus even before the war the creative mind of America had organs through which to herald the new day and give substantial support and encouragement to isolated artists.

But of all these things I knew almost nothing on Armistice Day, 1918—or even a year later. I had been left untouched by the intangible orienting fundamentals of life—philosophy, psychology, music, literature, painting, indeed the whole realm of the creative and appreciative processes. I was innocent of the study of human behavior and the orienting study of contemporary civilization. I admit frankly that the reverberations of the creative revolution even then rolling up in America registered not at all on my mind.

★   ★   ★

Then came a sharp turning point in my life, marking the beginning of a new period—many years of unlearning and an exciting search for understanding. On January 1, 1920, I went to the Lincoln School and to Teachers College, Columbia University.

Chapter X

THE BIOGRAPHY OF IDEAS:
SCHOLARS OF THE SOCIAL SCENE

I'LL COME for freedom."

That was the idea struggling for utterance from the back of my mind, even though in the autumn of 1919 the larynx was unequal to the demands on it. Caldwell and I had walked the long trail from his house through Van Cortlandt Park, talking out the possibilities of my coming to the new "modern school" that the Rockefellers, Mrs Dorothy Straight and others had launched under Dr Flexner's inspiration. Finally I found myself stipulating freedom in a nebulous and naïve way as a necessary condition:

"I think if I were sure I'd be left really free to work as I wish, I'd come. I'm happy with Judd and his men, although I'm not sure that I'm really free. Judd is pretty dominating, whether he means to be or not. What I need most now is a little leisure to study the total problem of America and education and make up my mind what should be done about it. I need to be let alone to choose my job and work at it as I see best."

This seemed to bother Caldwell at first; then it began to intrigue him, but he wasn't sure what this freedom meant.

"Well," I went on, "when I say 'free to choose my own job,' I mean I should like to select that part of the school's task that I feel I should work on and then be left free to go ahead. I don't want anybody telling me: 'You can't say that,' or 'You can't do that.' "

What I was searching for was rather vague even in my own mind, but I knew that I wished to be free of unspoken pressures as well as word-of-mouth admonitions and interferences. I didn't want to live and work in a climate of opinion which would be forever trying to warp me and label me in its image.

Soon afterward I left Judd's ordered team of "scientists" and joined Caldwell's company of creative individualists. I've never once regretted it. I became free as probably no other person working on the controversial frontier in America has been free. In the autumn and winter of 1919–20 I measured and charted the abilities of every child in the school, coming to grips for the first time with the intimate problems of child growth. I built up the Lincoln School's first system of records and worked with the teachers at bringing up the achievement of a "child-centered" school not sufficiently concerned with "social needs." Then I retired for a half year to the seclusion of my new laboratory to begin the greatest adventure in ideas of my life. There in the summer of 1920 I began the "life sentence" with a blank sheet of paper.

For nine years I stayed at Lincoln and at Teachers College,[1] designing and building the new social-science pro-

[1]Throughout the nine years I held the positions of educational psychologist at Lincoln and professor at Teachers College. Since 1928 my connection has been that of professor at Teachers College.

gram, experimenting with new ideas in educational practice, writing and speaking both at home and abroad.

And through it all I was left free to work—at enterprises
of my own design.

Sixteen years later Dean Will Russell and I were ex-
amining a batch of articles I had written for *Scholastic* (I
wrote a hundred in ten years) when he suddenly said to
me, referring to my freedom to work: "Harold, you've got
the best educational job in the country."

"I know it, and don't think I'm not grateful for it. These
many years in Lincoln School and Teachers College have
been years of comparative security. In spite of all the
harassing pressures from many directions I know no other
place in the country where I could have worked as freely
as I have here."

This is still true. I have never ceased to give thanks for
these two institutions in which those who are determined
to do so can exercise the freest play of the experimental
method of inquiry and the creative spirit. (Naturally to
get such freedom anywhere there must be determination
to have it.) In spite of the social foundations to which our
studies carried our minds and our utterance, in spite of
the barrage the two Deans Russell have received across the
country about the "subversive" group at Teachers College,
they have always risen to an unswerving defense of the
right to speak. Dean Will Russell deserves a place in the
annals of American civil liberties for having maintained in
Teachers College a conspicuous haven of free utterance
during the Great Depression—a time when hysteria and
bigotry have been rife. This is especially significant because more often than not he differed with the views of

those he protected. That's more than theorizing about democracy—that's maintaining it in action.

★   ★   ★

Actually the experimental spirit was emphasized in the Lincoln School from its very beginning. It had been established two years before I joined the group, largely to implement the theories expressed in two memorable essays which appeared in 1914: one Dr Flexner's "The Modern School," the other President Charles W. Eliot's "Needed Changes in Secondary Education." These publications led the General Education Board three years later to set aside a large sum of money to finance an experimental school.[2]

Opening in 1917 with a staff of twenty-five and a pupil body of a hundred and sixteen in the first five grades, the school grew rapidly to a staff of over seventy and a pupil body of nearly five hundred, the students divided about equally between boys and girls and between the elementary and high-school grades. Matthew Willing[3] (in 1926) described the teachers thus:

"Some are enthusiasts. Others are skeptics; some *live* with children; others *investigate* children; still others drill them—when they can. . . . With all their individual differences the members of the staff are highly sensitive to this much of a common

[2]". . . for the purpose of endeavoring by experimental methods to assist in the reorganization of subjects and methods of study which was already under way in the fields of elementary and secondary education" —as Otis W. Caldwell, the director, rather hesitatingly stated the purposes of the school in the first descriptive booklet issued in 1918, following the establishment of the school. As I watched the developments in Lincoln for nine years I came to feel that the phrase, "reorganization of subjects and methods of study which was already under way," was a much too limited interpretation of the far-reaching experiments which were tried there.

[3]M. H. Willing, "The Value of an Experimental School," *School and Society*, May 15, 1926. Willing was brought to Lincoln in 1922 after many years as professor of English in the University of Wisconsin. Later he went to George Peabody College of Teachers in Nashville.

purpose, namely, to find out something about education that will be sound and usable."

The atmosphere of the school was certainly one of freedom of imagination and willingness to experiment. No matter how unworkable a suggestion appeared to be upon first impression it got a hearing. Although a proposal generally received initial opposition at the office, the final answer always was: "All right, go ahead. Try it! See how it will work." Everything educational under the sun was tried.[4]

I doubt if there was a single member of the faculty in those early years who wasn't a rank individualist—the director, the educational psychologist and all the researchers and teachers. It was laissez faire in education, every man for himself—from the standpoint of productive imagination a good setting; from that of co-operative teamwork of doubtful value. Eventually the school—like America—came to exemplify both "I" and "We," but not in the earliest years!

After the first few years both the "child centered" and the "society centered" in philosophy were represented in the staff, and that was unusual in the early 1920s, for most of the "progressive" schools ignored the concepts of social use and the scientific method. I fell into the habit of calling the two groups the "scientific methodists" and the "project methodists." The former were those interested in measurement and controlled experiments, still working for salvation via the tabulation of social needs. They wanted teachers to

[4]At one point in my own experimentation with historical materials I tried to put into practice a notion that history should be taught "backward." I doubted that it would work, but it had been advanced by one of our academic psychologists and I decided to try it. I prepared some materials that way and tried them with a group in the junior high school. I shall never forget the maze of bewilderment in which those young people struggled to bring a sense of order and continuity out of anarchic discontinuity. Anyway, we tried it—and discarded it.

become students of the social order. The others, most of them readers of Dewey and students of Kilpatrick, were advocates of a "child-centered"[5] school.

The nine years were ones of revolutionary, stimulating interchange of minds and moods and of friendly but vigorous controversies. Noon after noon Billy Mearns ("Hughes" Mearns of the now-famous *Creative Youth,* 1925, which literally launched a whole new approach to the creative act), "Ros" Clark, Raleigh Schorling, Charley Finley and I would go out around the corner to a luncheon of beer and sandwiches and two hours of provocative talk. In not less than two hundred major faculty meetings and hundreds of other conferences, group discussions, luncheon-table meetings, and the like, the opposing methodists on the staff fought and argued, presented statistical charts and dramatic word pictures of child growth, deficiencies of learning, estimates of content and method, proposals and plans, counterproposals and counterplans—each side struggling to get inside the other's minds. Slowly each group came to see a little more truth in the other's position, and its own became new and more profound. As I think back over those years I believe that this merging of the two strands of educational reconstruction in Lincoln School's dynamic faculty was one of the first examples of what proved to be the trend which integrated the ideas and the techniques of the "scientist" with those of the "activist" into a sound, balanced, *new* education. The same thing was, of course, happening but to a lesser extent, I think, in other laboratories and schools.

[5]Ann Shumaker and I coined this phrase in 1928 when we published *The Child-Centered School* together. (World Book Company, Yonkers.) Miss Shumaker was a member of my staff in Lincoln for several years; later she became editor of *Progressive Education Magazine.* What promised to be a brilliant career was cut short by her death in 1935, a great personal loss for her friends, I think a loss to creative America.

It was in this climate then that the making of the new social-science books began and flourished.

Then the Vista Widened

By the spring of 1920 I was permitted really to be free to put my heels on the table and read and think. I had already made up my mind about what I was going to work at—the social studies. My decision was due in part, no doubt, to the hang-over of the talks with Pope and Coss and my reading of the new social criticism of Van Wyck Brooks and company. One thing was certain: I was through with statistics and tests and the reorganization of school mathematics.[6]

Others had predicted that I would turn back to my first intellectual love—"history and the social sciences." History and the social sciences had long had a prior claim on me, even in college days. As a junior in college I had published my somewhat absurd *Complete Outline of European History*. (I still flinch at the title, but it and my lectures did coach Dartmouth sophomores successfully through Eric's dreaded History I and History II!) Four years of work on my sociology minor in the graduate school at Illinois (1911–15) with Edward Cary Hayes and Arthur Todd had given me at least a crude outline of nineteenth-century social speculation from Comte and Spencer through Sumner and Ward to the social psychology of Thorstein Veblen and the "new" historians.

Caldwell and Flexner had asked me in our first interview: "Social studies? What is that?"

[6]My friend Ros (John R.) Clark and I had collaborated in writing a monograph and textbook: *Scientific Method in the Reconstruction of Ninth Grade Mathematics*, University of Chicago Press, 1917, and *Funda-*

I didn't know exactly myself. "In general," I said, "all the materials that have to do with how people live together."

"You mean the facts of history and geography and civics?"

"Yes, and economics and sociology and anthropology—everything that has to do with social life."

I reminded them of a report of the National Education Association on the reorganization of secondary education (1916) which had a section called "Social Studies." "But even that," I said, "is merely a general caption to group together under one name the existing materials of history, geography and civics. It represents essentially no change in content."

"What changes would you make?" one of them asked.

"I don't know—yet. But I'll try to find out in the half year of leisure you're going to give me. I think now that there will probably be two kinds of changes: first, the new content will deal with conditions and problems of modern civilization that have never been in schools at all and second, there will be a new organization of the materials—probably a kind of 'general' or 'unified' social studies."

Caldwell smiled. "Oh, you mean something similar to what has been done in the general-mathematics or general-science movements?"

"Perhaps, but yet not quite the same, for they have merely scrambled the content of several 'subjects.' I think now that I wouldn't take the existing materials of history, geography, civics, economics, sociology, and the like, and put them into one course. Some of that content is obsolete;

mentals of High School Mathematics, World Book Company, Yonkers, N.Y., 1918. Ros joined me at Lincoln in 1921, has taught there and in Teachers College ever since, being at various times principal of the high school and director of the entire school. He is a friend as well as schoolmaster of the clearest integrity and intellect.

in fact, much of it never was worth teaching in the school!"
(Flexner liked that!)

"We need a new principle," I continued. "Something
like this: that all the facts, ideas and generalizations needed
by a child's mind or an adult's mind, for that matter, should
be brought into close relationship with one another. This
would necessitate going straight across the boundaries of
the academic subjects whenever the indispensable facts for
understanding are needed."

"Does that mean that you may still have separate units
of geography?"

"Yes, I think so. And very likely long stretches of history too. But I can't imagine history being taught so that
young people really understand the development of the
people in question unless it is taught in the scene in which
they live, in the geography of their habitat. It's what Robinson has been writing about in his *New History*. The
'new' historians are trying to describe life as it was and
actually is lived in America and the modern world. That's
what I'd like to explore."

That much I had known in 1919, and the idea grew
on me during the measuring period. So when the moment
came to leave the tests and the graphs I started on the
thrilling quest for understanding of modern industrial civilization.

It was fortunate for me that I began during the years of
the Long Armistice; a decade earlier I would have been
definitely thwarted by lack of materials. Occasional essays like Turner's "Significance of the Frontier in American History" (1893) had appeared. Beard's *Economic Interpretation of the Constitution of the United States* had

come out the year before the war began in Europe (1913). Veblen's *Theory of the Leisure Class* (1899) and Cooley's *Human Nature and the Social Order* (1902) could have given some basis for a truer picture of the times than the one we held in 1918.

The war served many of the "middle-of-the-road" students much as it did me. It shocked them into a new outlook on industrial civilization and its impact on other cultures. It led them to collect new data and create new categories. It jolted them into seeing new hypotheses. But all these materials taken together were a meager shelf of sources compared with the library which came from the presses during the years following the war. The peace had scarcely been signed when Europe's foreign offices rushed out their special pleading documents—the White Books, Red Books and others. Monographs and reports by scholars and publicists' pamphlets with new interpretations of all phases of Western culture began to appear.

The "new" historians and other scholars of the social scene on both sides of the Atlantic were able to say, "We told you so," for the war had proved that they had been essentially correct in their predictions. And they did say so, even by Versailles. John Maynard Keynes left the British Treasury and told the world flatly what he thought of it all in a vigorous book *The Economic Consequences of the Peace* (1920). (Ralph) Norman Angell (Lane), who had warned us of what was coming in 1913 in *The Great Illusion*,[7] now said: "You see!" in *The Fruits of Victory* (1921). In the first year of the war (1914) H. N. Brailsford had clearly stated some of the economic factors leading to the outbreak. Bertrand Russell, who had been interned in Britain during the war, reviewed the various "Proposed

---

[7]And Dr Butler's Carnegie Endowment for Peace had distributed it free to college professors all over the United States.

Roads to Freedom" in 1919. And there were others who, with E. D. Morel, had seen long before 1914 that swift industrialization and the mad race for natural resources, markets and a place to invest surplus capital would destroy a tipsy balance of power between the European countries and bring on war—a series of wars.

As I delved into my reading I found that a quarter century before the war, young British enthusiasts—Frank Podmore, Bernard Shaw, Beatrice and Sidney Webb, Graham Wallas and others—had built a common reconstructive faith through their Fabian Society. With financial endowment supplied to them they had founded the London School of Economics and Political Science at the turn of the century.

Even before that time (1906) John A. Hobson had produced his brilliant interpretation, *The Evolution of Modern Capitalism*. Now in 1920 came his *Taxation in the New State*. Both were a revelation to me, as was Harold Laski's *Foundations of Sovereignty* (1921) and his *Studies in the Problem of Sovereignty* (1917), written while he was here in America. Perhaps the most profound interpreter, certainly the most dogged scholar of the London school group, was R. H. Tawney. I read his little book *Acquisitive Society* the moment it came in 1920, and six years later his magnificent summary of twenty years of research into the background of Western industrial culture, *Religion and the Rise of Capitalism* (1926). This still seems to be one of the two or three profound revelations of the history of individualism and of modern culture.

Graham Wallas, grown middle aged since the days of the Fabian Society, had brought out *The Great Society* in 1914. Now in 1920 I got his *Social Heritage*. A half-dozen years later I spent a week with him in a group at Hanover where Dartmouth had brought him for a part of the summer. I had a grand time, hearing at firsthand the experiences of the little group of British liberals.

The American scholars were also giving their minds and energies to the social scene. I had known vaguely of Turner, Robinson and Beard, had read Veblen and Cooley equally vaguely and had known the Chicago group personally as a younger faculty member of the Quadrangle Club.

But now I was to get my first real introduction to the "new" historians of the United States. As I dug into what had come out of a quarter century of researches I began to find them, to know them. The schools of thought and work were already forming—determined, I was to observe later, partly by geography. At Wisconsin Turner's "Frontier" essay was republished in my red-letter year of 1920 but now in company with the more mature interpretations of his middle age. More than all else this material helped to set for the next twenty years the frame of my interpretation of American land history, the economic mood and factors behind it and the traits of the American mind. I wrote *Westward Movement* (1922) and *Explorers and Settlers Westward Bound* (1924) largely in terms of the perspective it helped to build.

I found the two-volume *History of Labour in the United States* which John R. Commons and his associates had just produced (1918) at Wisconsin. And their President van Hise's *Conservation of Natural Resources*, in its successive editions from 1910 to 1934, has remained a standard source and resource ever since. Edward A. Ross had turned out his new volume *Social Control* (1901). The Wisconsin group was important for me.

Six years before I began my work (1914) Walton Hamilton had published his readings book *Current Economic*

Problems. In 1918 Leon Marshall, as he started his war-labor work for the government, published his *Readings in Industrial Society* (1918). Harold Moulton was issuing his huge tome *Financial Organization of Society*. The last mentioned was used by my Lincoln group as a mine of valuable material for years. All three were to move East later—Hamilton went to Amherst; Marshall to make a new interpretation of the relation between law and economics at Johns Hopkins and to help the National Council of Social Studies for years; Moulton in 1922 to organize his Brookings Institution staff at Washington, which in the last decade and a half has done more to document the economic foundations of modern industrial society than any other single research group.

Meanwhile Charles E. Merriam, for years alderman in the City Council of Chicago and professor of political science at the University of Chicago, was completing his *American Political Ideas*, the first of the classic interpretations of government with which my research group and I kept in touch. As for the ancient roots of our culture, Breasted and his Oriental Institute at Chicago were launching epoch-marking expeditions and studies into the eastern Mediterranean civilizations, pushing back the threshold of recorded history and throwing light on man and his changing society.

At the same time I didn't miss the work being done by the British, especially Elliott Smith, who published his *Human History* about the time we began to know him personally at Locarno and in New York.

As for the Columbia University faculty in 1920, we had lost James Harvey Robinson and Charles A. Beard, who had resigned in 1917 at the dismissal of J. McKeen Cattell and Henry Wadsworth Longfellow Dana. They had joined with Alvin Johnson and a score of other liberals to form the

New School for Social Research. Robinson's splendid *Mind in the Making* came to us in 1921, but even from the beginning of our work we had used the outline of his famous Columbia course—*The History of Western Civilization.* Beard produced *Cross Currents in Europe.* Carleton Hayes's *Political and Social History of Modern Europe* appeared just in time for me to come to depend on it, along with Gooch's *History of Modern Europe,* which gave new "social" emphasis and interpretation.

Veblen was in New York writing for a year or so for *The Dial* and meeting with the Technical Alliance (Steinmetz, Jones, et al.). His articles, reprinted as *The Engineers and the Price System* in 1921, were the cue to the ideas of the technocrats in 1933.

There were many others—Fay at Harvard and . . . but I must not enumerate more of the sources. These were the "frontier thinkers"—those who were building a new understanding of the Western world.

★   ★   ★

What came out of all this surge of new ideas?

Several things: First, with the new literature at hand I started to piece together, bit by bit, a mosaiclike picture of increasing industrialism around the world. Chiefly I began to see the intricate ramifications of the factors and trends that produced our machine civilization of the twentieth century: the partial releasing of man from his bondage as a draft animal, the herding together of human beings in cities, the disappearance of handicrafts, the terrifying search for food by isolated island manufacturing countries (land, raw materials and trade were essentially "bread" to nations like England and Japan), the seizure of huge territories by Great Britain, France and Germany and of smaller ones by lesser industrial nations, the subjugation of "backward" peoples. For the first time I peered a bit beneath the surface of the modern world at the effects of the impact of agricultural and industrial nations upon each other. From the analysts on the frontier of economic and political thought I began to see that industrial civilization was something novel in world history. Its basic themes were beginning to appear.

Paralleling the study of world industrialization, I began to explore the chief characteristics of the American scene. Concentrating at first on industry and government, the most overt outposts of American life, I noted that the America of 1919 reflected some of the same problems which existed in its British and European counterparts. In this area, also, I found books dealing with the impasse between employer and employee, with trends in industry, the interrelations of business and national politics. It was the year, for example, of the Interchurch World Report and the books of Elbert Gary, president of the United States Steel Corporation, and the extremist William Z. Foster. I put one view against the other.

So it was that I waded into a mass of articles, books and monographs by engineers, social workers and economics professors, as well as the publications of mining, railroad and trade commissions, all of which contained data covering the entire field of American industrialism.

A new vista of possibilities as well as problems of man and his civilization opened before me. The very discovery of the deeper-lying trends and movements of the modern industrial world served as urge and impetus to master the chief concepts and generalizations of economic, political and social life and to phrase the fundamental problems and issues of our time.

But this study was more than a joy ride through the new literature. I must confess that a good deal of mental and emotional discomfort accompanied it all, for attitudes of long standing had to be uprooted. I think I was by nature somewhat of a "constructive antagonist" (as Thorndike had exclaimed to me one day at a luncheon conference). I had always been to some extent a protagonist of change, but while I was rebellious at injustice and temperamentally for the underdog, nevertheless, if one had dug to the roots of my attitudes during this reading time he would have found there great uneasiness caused by the things I read. My first glimpse into the library of social criticism disturbed as much as excited me. Lacking historical and world perspective, I felt these questionings of monopoly and the inequalities in the distribution of the social income as attacks on my personal sense of security. I had always believed that the machinery of industrial civilization was essentially admirable and that capitalism was to be accepted on its proved merits and not really to be challenged. The Webbs's *Decay of Capitalist Civilization*, to name a single example, was certainly not pleasant reading for one of my background. I had never been much concerned with the underlying forces at work in the industrial world. My mind had never endeavored to discover the basic economic and psychological determiners of the contemporary situation. And here was a questioning of the whole current industrial order, with proposals for its radical reconstruction!

These mental and emotional disturbances revealed well the danger of a little knowledge and the unsureness of mind that is born of inadequate education. The discomfort created by opening the mind to the new criticism led first to instant denial of the attacks upon industrialism. Then a smattering of knowledge brought me to wholesale acceptance of the new view. With a gradual accumulation of more knowledge came broad swings with the radical and conservative pendulum. As my researches developed, as I

saw forecasts borne out by historical events, as I encountered instances of agreement in generalizations arrived at
by impartial critics among divers nations and groups, stability of judgment began to grow. I think I do not exagger-
ate in saying that during the next few years the swings from
left to right became fewer and shorter. Steadily a better
grounded knowledge of the history of evolving civilizations
and an understanding of long-time trends brought a clearer
and surer outlook and a more definitely marked-out position.

Day after day during this intense period of reading and
study I kept saying to myself and to Mearns and Clark at
our luncheon talks: "Something must be done about this!
Our youngsters must know these ideas! The high school
should build an understanding of the rise and spread of
industrialism around the world!"

Clark especially was interested. "What ideas?"

"Such ideas as these: the great human migrations of the
world, the multiplication and concentration of populations
in the nineteenth century, man's increasing control over
nature, the crucial importance of trade, the increasing
dominance of 'distribution' over 'production' in economic
life, the tendency in economic life toward concentration
in the ownership and control of wealth, income and credit,
the changing psychological effects of increasing industrialism, the transportation of self-sufficient peoples into
a fragile society of interdependent peoples, the spread of
economic imperialism, the world-wide rise in economic
standards of living." They were skeptics, as I had been, but
the argument was good, I think, for all of us.

Clearer and clearer it became that to introduce twenty-
three million young people (1920) to an understanding of

America and its development would require the making of a dramatic and thought-provoking curriculum of understanding and tolerance—no mean order for the American public-school system. Take the magnificent account of the building of America—the startling story of the mechanical conquest of the continent and the other remarkable achievements about which youth can justifiably thrill; the story of a century and a half of courageous clearance of soil and forest, of the mining of coal, iron and other raw materials; the story of the complicated mechanism of industry and business, of the invention and development of artificial power, of transportation and communication, of finance and credit; the story of the production of food, shelter and clothing in quantities not known by earlier civilizations and only suspected by the other half of the human race; the story of man's transforming of luxuries into necessities in but a century. Here were the materials for a fine new curriculum with which young people could be helped to solve America's critical problems.

The need seemed obvious. But how could it all be done? How could even part of the story, the part describing merely the physical characteristics of the developing drama of American life, be brought into the school? The American school curriculum was crystallized in its rut—it was a slave to political history, to locational and encyclopedic geography, to suppression of living under the widespread disciplinary regime of memorization and recitation. How, under the geographic and psychological limitations of the people and their school, could the directors of America's educational system hope to succeed at this staggering curriculum task?

THE SOCIAL-SCIENCE PAMPHLETS

In that Lincoln atmosphere of 1920, to be aroused mentally and emotionally was merely a stimulus to action. I could not wait until we began to do something about it all. The first step would be to try something in Lincoln, then extend its use into public schools. We never forgot that we were set aside "to experiment for public schools." So during the spring of 1920 I persuaded the historian in the high school, a geography teacher, a history teacher and a "room" teacher in the elementary school to join forces. The plan was to teach the history and geography, together with contemporary community life, in one long class period in the fifth and sixth grades. In September we began. My plan wasn't too clear, even to me, and to the teachers it was utterly nebulous. We were certainly not equipped to do the difficult task of assembling new reading and study and work materials in a vast field where there was almost nothing. It meant mimeographing and graphing, making bibliographies, planning excursions for the children to various parts of the city, keying in the work of the "arts" teachers, the "science" and "industrial arts" teachers and others to see our new program, holding round-table discussions, providing for sufficient practice on the "skills," and what not. I had never taught in the elementary school —and yet had to teach, to illustrate to the other teachers what I was talking about, improvising a good deal of it as I went along. The elementary teachers had never worked at research problems; neither had they acquired a clear conception of the "new history" or of my theories of integration of the "social studies." And the high-school history man was downright opposed to the whole idea. He is to this day, I think.

Under such conditions it was to be expected, perhaps, that the prima donnas would find we couldn't work together. We pulled and hauled each other through a crude year of trial and error. Then three of them agreed with me to disagree, each to go his own way in the school. One remained with me for several years as teacher of the new materials that developed.[8]

But we learned much from the year's experiment. In 1921–22, with my brother's[9] help, I recast the plan, assembled more new materials and started out again in the fifth, sixth and ninth grades. Nearly a thousand pages of mimeographed copy—quoted excerpts and original writing—were put together for children of these ages. It dealt with problems of immigration and population, industry and business, municipal and state and national governments, all in the new historical setting. Through the daily trials with the new content, through discussions with college classes and my colleagues, new principles in the selection and organization of the social-studies curriculum took more definite form.

SCHOOLTEACHERS AND ADMINISTRATORS UNDERWROTE THE SOCIAL-SCIENCE PAMPHLETS, 1922–29

By the middle of the school year of 1921–22 it was clear that wider experimentation with our plan in public schools would be futile so long as we continued to use mimeographed materials. They were hard to read and generally uninteresting. With them clear pictures, photographs,

[8] Emma Schweppe, Lincoln School, East Orange, N.J.; Hunter College.

[9] Earle U. Rugg, assistant in the Department of Education in Teachers College and a part-time teacher in the Horace Mann School, member of Lincoln School staff (1922–24); doctor of philosophy at Teachers College, 1924; professor and head of Department of Education at the Colorado College of Education since 1924, also librarian there since 1936.

graphs and other illustrations were out of the question. Public-school experimental work required large editions, also impossible with mimeographing. I proposed to the director, therefore, that we print experimental editions and have them tried out in a considerable number of public schools. A budget was prepared, and funds were sought from one of the foundations, but the requests were not granted. Being convinced that the entire experiment would fail unless we could print experimental editions, I suggested to Dr Caldwell that I be permitted to try a plan of public-school co-operation.

"How will you do it?" he asked.

"I think I can get school men whom I know to 'underwrite' small editions of these pamphlets."

"Underwrite them? What do you mean?"

"I mean, ask a number of superintendents and teachers to subscribe for enough copies to supply one experimental class for each school."

Clark and I had done that with a course in mathematics while I was at the University of Chicago and he was a teacher in the Parker High School. Even in that instance sixty school men and women had worked with us.[10]

Caldwell finally agreed, and during the spring of 1922 I sent to some three hundred superintendents, principals and teachers in public and private schools—most of them had been my students in graduate classes at Chicago or at Teachers College—a short mimeographed announcement of a *proposed* printed edition of a new general social-science course for the junior-high-school grades (VII, VIII and IX). Since no samples could be printed to illustrate, the superintendents were asked to co-operate "sight unseen." I

[10]Out of that experiment came the Rugg and Clark *Scientific Method in the Reconstruction of Ninth Grade Mathematics* (University of Chicago Press, 1917) and the *Fundamentals of High School Mathematics*, World Book Company, 1918.

explained that I would write and publish "social-science" materials (history and geography, economics, and the like) in the form of small printed booklets to be called the Social-Science Pamphlets. I asked each one if he would subscribe for enough pamphlets to equip one or more experimental classes in either one, two or three of the junior-high-school grades.

The response was not only encouraging; it was astonishing. Day by day the replies came: "We'll take twenty" . . . "Count on me for enough for three classes—one hundred copies of each pamphlet" . . . "I'd like to have enough for my whole junior high school" . . . "Send me five hundred copies!" We could hardly believe our eyes. School people *were* interested in educational experiments! Or was it their very great need of new materials which the conventional texts did not satisfy? I feel sure now as I look back on it all that both answers were correct.

★   ★   ★

But there might be difficulties! Several added the proviso: "*if* you are sure the whole series will be shipped, pamphlet by pamphlet, on time; the classes must not be held up."

We had not counted on making materials for all three grades; pamphlets for one grade were all we could manage each year. But by June we had to our amazement actual orders for four thousand copies of each of twelve pamphlets—four to each of the seventh, eighth and ninth grades. We *had* to come through. So with Earle Rugg as assistant and several stenographers, I assembled a library, isolated myself completely and started to write—what was to be the first of three editions of the Social-Science Pamphlets. It was the first of 750,000 experimental pamphlets distributed to co-operating schools in nine years; the first of 25,000 pages of a portrait of man and his changing society published for young people.

The First Edition of the Pamphlets

We girded ourselves for the task; Earle[11] did the research and documented the material; I wrote, and Marie[11] revised and read proof. By the end of the summer (on time) we sent the co-operating schools *America and Her Immigrants*, the first seventh-grade pamphlet; *The Westward Movement and the Growth of Transportation*, the first eighth-grade pamphlet; and *The Americanization of Our Foreign-Born*, the first ninth-grade pamphlet. The schools began to use them early in September 1922. Thereafter, every two months they received another; while they tried out one we wrote another. The original plan had been to make eight small (seventy-five- to one hundred-page) pamphlets per year. The schools reported that they could not handle so many separate items. As a compromise we produced four larger pamphlets per year for each class.

★   ★   ★

In April of 1923 the eleventh pamphlet was shipped. Drawing several deep breaths, we took account of stock.

I put away the writing table, and Earle and I relaxed and planned for a slower reconstruction of the materials in the years ahead. Marie went to her ancestral Norway for a holiday and on her return the following year taught the social sciences in a near-by school system. The first siege was over.

[11]Earle Rugg worked as research associate and collaborator in preparing the first edition of the Social-Science Pamphlets.

Marie Gulbransen, a former student and assistant at Chicago became editorial assistant to revise manuscript and see the copy through the press; during the ten months until April 1923, she worked heroically at that task.

Chapter XI

THUS WIDENS THE VISTA

IDEAS RULE the world or throw it into chaos!"

Thus Auguste Comte stated his now-famous dictum of social change. I heard it first thirty years ago from Edward Cary Hayes as he lectured enthusiastically to our tiny seminar in his Urbana living room. The conception never left me even during my technician years. A decade later I was to make it the chief plank in my platform for the reorganization of the life and program of the schools. I think that I can honestly say that my own whole search for understanding has been a tracing of the life history of those great ideas to which Comte referred, those that really rule the world or throw it into chaos.

As my Social Science Research Group settled down to plan in May 1923, I was sure that we had chosen the most insistent problem for our research. America's greatest educational need was an honest and intelligible description of our social order. Adults needed it; young people needed it. The school people were ready and eager for it; that had been shown by their instant response "sight unseen" to our announced "new social-science" program and the enthusiastic acclamation of approval after its actual trial in the school. And I knew it from the reverberations of my own thrill over the discovery of its basic concepts.

But what a task! It would be a staggering job. It would mean nothing less than writing and printing a total word portrait of contemporary society. A *total* portrait, I say; one that would deal with all phases of culture, inner as well as external. In the pamphlets the portrayal of the obvious *material* civilization had been uppermost in our minds, and the bulk of the content depicted modern industrial peoples in action—man making and doing, producing food, shelter and clothing, transporting and communicating, buying and selling, moving about and governing. We scarcely touched the esthetic and "cultural." I had a vague notion, however, that the social frontier alone was too limited a territory. A total portrait would have to include man meditating, man contemplating, man appreciating, man creating with esthetic materials, with light and shade, with tone and stone, copper and steel. To paint such a picture of total culture and expression—of man living—would take us into many new areas; social institutions, for example, would have to be set forth, man's language, his ways of measuring and recording facts, his use of science and art. The psychology of the people would have to be presented —all the subtle processes of thinking and feeling, what people have in their heads, their foundational attitudes and ideas, what they want most and what they fear most, the climates of opinion in which they live. Clearer and clearer it became that we had concentrated far too much on the material economic world. A total portrait was needed if men were to understand.

Moreover, we would have to guard against a narrow

chauvinism. All world cultures would have to be presented
—the agrarian and more primitive ones as well as the industrial ones. And all would have to be seen in historical
perspective. To understand civilization changing our
young people must see it changing. The conditions and
problems of today are but the product of the moving
trends and factors of yesterday. Every area of the social
order would have to be put both in its long-time and short-
time historical setting. Moreover—and I said this hundreds
of times—every bit of history given would have to have
some clearly established functional justification—if not an
esthetic one, then at least one which was crassly utilitarian.

Of course our minds didn't open to all of this at once.
Even the twelve volumes of the second edition of the
pamphlets were still heavily weighted on the side of economics and politics and geographic background. In academic jargon—they were largely economics, government,
community life, geography and, of course, history. This
was perhaps to be expected, for the world impasse over industrialism was in the center of our consciousness. Indeed
the "new" historians themselves had concentrated practically all of their energy in that direction, and I was guided
by them more than by any others during those early years.
It was not until later that I made my first hesitating contacts with the artists and social critics who later became my
friends.

So we confronted the bewildering maze of episodes, historical narratives, generalizations and facts—geographic,
economic, political, statistical, what not—which had been
put together in the first eleven pamphlets with a somewhat
new approach. These would have to be organized so that

their significance would be made clear, first to ourselves and then so stated that they would become clear for young people. The bewildering industrial society would have to be reduced to meaningful order. How could it be done? During the next several years we tried and discarded one lead after another.

But the cue came from Comte's great generalization. *The whole social order would fall into a clear picture if we would organize it around the great ideas that "rule the world or throw it into chaos."* The ideas! Of course. We should have seen it at once, for that was really the stock in trade of the university—the discovery and expression of ideas. We hadn't, but the light had come at last, and since that period in our work there has never been any doubt that the intellectual outline of the story of man and his changing society must be the great concepts. The "good concepts" I came to call them, in the sense of the "good life." They were the ones which are absolutely indispensable to understanding the modern world and to living in it as informed, tolerant and co-operative participants.

I started on the documentary trail of the "good concepts" in the summer of 1923 and have been following it ever since, using every method I could discover from the archives of the scholars. I knew that the ideas I sought were so foundational in nature that I must not trust a limited validation. Certainly my own subjective judgment and that of my educational colleagues were inadequate. Upon what, whom, then, was I to rely?

Five Frontiers of Study

I turned first (in 1923) to the workers on the social frontier—those I have called the scholars of the social scene. Then within the next few years, as my story shows, their company enlarged to include all workers on several frontiers of thought and feeling—the "poets," the psychologists and the philosophers as well as the "sociologists." In fact, I found that without having distinguished them very clearly I had already been working on several creative frontiers at one and the same moment. It was at this time indeed that the term "frontier" began to come into our jargon to denote the unexplored nature of the intellectual regions in which we were blazing new trails. Certainly we were working in unblazed educational territory.

Thus though our major field continued to be the educational frontier, we moved on to several others, for we found that the educational frontier could be explored successfully only with the concepts and outlooks of the creative workers on other fronts.

In all there were five frontiers:

The educational frontier—studying and building the story of man and his changing society.
The social frontier—the study of man and his culture.
The personal frontier—the study of the organic life of the living creature.
The psychological frontier—the psychology of man and his changing society and the study of his methods of inquiry and work, especially the creative act.
The esthetic frontier—the study of man's statement of his view of life.

There were no less than five frontiers then, and our educational one could be explored only with the intellectual and emotional tools acquired in the other four. Again I remind the reader that I had no clear understanding of and was not working on all of these in 1923 or in 1926 or on all of them even when Man and His Changing Society was in preparation in 1928 and 1929. I was at home on the social and psychological frontiers by the middle 1920s. The trails

of the esthetic and personal frontiers were becoming fairly
familiar by the early 1930s. But the synthesis—the interrelationships—of all five clarified most of all in the decade
just passed.

Our chief reliance then became these frontiersmen of
thought and feeling. We fell into the habit in those early
days of calling them the "frontier thinkers."[1]

Taking the social frontier first, they were the all-inclusive
social-science group of "new" historians, to whose works
I have so frequently referred and upon whose vision and
technical researches we depended for the skeleton of our
description of modern society. In a statement written at the
completion of the second edition[2] I described four of their
special and conspicuous qualifications. I repeat them here:

First, their persistent attempt to see life whole, to maintain an overview, searching constantly for interrelationship
between academic fields. Second, their honest tracing of
factors, causes and relationships to their inevitable ends;
this they did without regard for conflicts with prevalent
concepts and norms. Third, their experience in documentation, in the handling of carefully recorded and classified
data in several related fields; they were critics of validity,
well grounded in the commonly known facts and generalizations of several areas. Fourth, their ability to stand aloof
from the surface pathology of current problems and movements, searching for underlying trends and deep-founded
traits and causes.

We turned to these scholars incessantly to help us see as
much of life *whole* as the slowly widening horizon let in by
our opening mental blinders would permit . . . to guide

[1]The Forbes-Hart-Rudd group apply this name to all the liberal educators whom they attack.

[2]Published in *Culture and Education in America*, p. 274. Harcourt,
Brace & Company, New York, 1931.

us in following honestly the ramifications of interrelated factors . . . to help us document our conclusions in a scholarly way to achieve as near valid generalizations as possible. Thus my whole enterprise rests upon twenty years of research and is in large measure the result of culling out the essence of the research products of a half century of work by the pioneer trail blazers and scholars on the five frontiers.

★   ★   ★

Our constant effort was to design, to plan carefully. "Remember, design comes first, in social engineering as well as in any other phase of technology," we warned ourselves repeatedly. We knew that to build a program of *guided living*—the essence of a good education—we would have to design carefully, despite the cries of the "free-the-child" evangelists. As an engineer habituated to meet situations as problems and to design before building, I tended naturally to regard curriculum construction as a technological process, not an act of sentiment or evangelical faith.

Certain data were "given," and with them we had to solve the problem. The "given" were (1) children and youth of known heritage, home environment, capacities and abilities, (2) community and national life, changing swiftly with seventy-odd other competing national cultures —all with histories already known or that would become known, (3) a body of experience and documented data on growth, behavior, intelligence, interests and the learning process.

The task was clear: Taking the young people and the society as they were, we had to paint the comprehensive portrait of man and his changing civilization by designing and building as vital, as exciting, as mind stretching and as valid a program of materials and activities as was possible. But I repeat—we were facing a problem which had to be solved, not a tradition to be perpetuated. It was to be a job of *design*, an imaginative and creative job.

A designed school program, then, was our goal, one created from the very life of American children, the very life of all the American people, from their historical and contemporary doings and from the deep-seated current problems and issues and the social trends that have precipitated them. The activities and materials were to be designed carefully and scientifically in terms of the levels of the school in which they were to be used, but all were to be built straight out of *the culture*.[3]

Coming back again to May 1923: My brother Earle and I saw that even if we rebuilt the three-year scheme of materials more slowly, a year's stuff at a time, the schedule would still be a very tight one. Each pamphlet had to be longer, and a vast amount of research had to be done on a score of phases of the local culture which we had not touched before. The materials had to be much better organized and written better, or perhaps I should merely say in good form. That they were *not* in the first edition is a certainty.

There were really three jobs to be done. The first was

[3]I should add that even in the midst of the hectic writing program it was necessary to give some time to publicizing and financing the enterprise. It was evident even in 1922 that if the printing of the pamphlets, editions of at least seven or eight thousand of each, was to be financially possible we would have to raise funds and to publicize our work. Between 1922 and 1926 we did so in several ways. I wrote articles on the new social studies for *The Historical Outlook* and other magazines, lectured in many parts of the country on the new program and gave a regular course in Teachers College on the modern school. I also took the responsibility for organizing and editing two yearbooks of the National Society for the Study of Education: Part II of the twenty-second (1923)—"The Social Studies"—and Parts I and II of the twenty-sixth (1926)—"Foundations of Curriculum Making." The nationwide reading and discussion of these yearbooks stimulated interest in the social sciences and brought many school men to co-operate financially and otherwise in the pamphlet enterprise.

the building of insight concerning the "good concepts"—
the ideas that rule the world. That we all contributed to,
but perhaps I took more responsibility than the others. The
second was the technical job of locating and documenting
thousands of generalizations. The third was the writer's
task of finding the most favored "words" to convey the indispensable meanings needed to build understanding. To
help me in this latter job Elizabeth Galloway, daughter of
my Decatur friend Thomas Galloway, joined us in June
1923. She stayed three years, helping me write most of the
twelve large volumes of the second edition, three hundred
thousand copies of which were in use in schools by 1926.

For the research task we needed a number of competent
and technically prepared workers. It seemed that the demand for more and better pamphlets would be large
enough to finance them, so I borrowed several thousand
dollars and expanded the staff. I brought sixteen research
assistants[4] into my group during the four years 1923–27.
Most of them stayed several years, working at the same
time toward doctors' degrees in Teachers College, and then

[4] They were:

Research Associates

Earle Rugg, 1921–23	Louise Krueger, 1926–
Elizabeth Galloway, 1923–26	Laurence F. Shaffer, 1926–29
John N. Washburne, 1923–26	Bertha M. Rugg, 1926–28
Hyman Meltzer, 1924–25	
John A. Hockett, 1924–27	*Editorial and Research Assistants*
Neal Billings, 1924–27, 1928	Frances M. Foster, 1923–27, 1928–30
Chester O. Mathews, 1925–27	Ethelwyn M. Mendenhall, 1926–28
Benjamin R. Showalter, 1924–25	Frances Youtz, 1927–29
Helen M. Lynd, 1926–27	Elizabeth Morey, 1927–28
James E. Mendenhall, 1926–30	Joan Walker Coyne, 1929–30

Gertrude White was the efficient manager of the office throughout
the writing and publishing enterprise, 1922–29, preceded in the prepub-
lishing days by Anne Brown. The salaries and research expenses of these
staff members were paid from the research fund which I set aside from
the income received from the sale of the Social-Science Pamphlets. The
total spent for research for the years 1922 to 1929 was approximately
$90,000.

moved on to college and university posts of distinction.[5]

Eight of us took over the major research tasks. Earle, Hockett and I worked on "the problems of American life as the basis of the social-science program," and Hockett and I produced the *Objective Studies in Map Location.* Hyman Meltzer and Neal Billings studied basic concepts and generalizations. John Washburne, Chester Mathews and Laurence Shaffer investigated problems of learning, organization and age-grade placement of materials.[6]

Did we make a "scientific" validation of the concepts and generalizations? Yes, as far as possible. As I said in a report of 1926, we sought to maintain a critical attitude

[5]For example, Earle U. Rugg, at the Colorado College of Education; Helen M. Lynd (coauthor of the *Middletown* books and teacher at Sarah Lawrence College; John A. Hockett, University of California; John N. Washburne, universities of Syracuse and Chicago; Laurence Shaffer, Carnegie Institute of Technology; Chester O. Mathews, Ohio Wesleyan University; Hyman Meltzer, St. Louis.

[6]Altogether the technical monographs and articles in which results were published are as follows:

Harold Rugg and John A. Hockett: *Objective Studies in Map Location* (Bureau of Publications, Teachers College, Columbia University). Neal Billings, *A Determination of Generalizations Basic to the Social Studies Curriculum* (Warwick and York, Baltimore, Md., 1929). John A. Hockett, *The Determination of Major Social Problems of American Life* (Bureau of Publications, Teachers College, Columbia University). Harold Rugg, *Twenty-second Yearbook*, National Society for the Study of Education, Part II, "The Social Studies in the Elementary and Secondary School," Chapter XV: "Problems of Contemporary Life as the Basis for Curriculum Making in the Social Studies." Earle Rugg, *Curriculum Studies in the Social Sciences and Citizenship* (Colorado State Teachers College, Greeley, Colo., 1928). H. Meltzer, *Children's Social Concepts* (Bureau of Publications, Teachers College, Columbia University). C. O. Mathews, *Grade-Placement of Curriculum Materials in the Social Studies.* J. N. Washburne, "An Experimental Study of Various, Graphic, Tabular and Textual Methods of Presenting Quantitative Material," *Journal of Educational Psychology*, September–October 1927. J. N. Washburne, "The Use of Questions in Social Science Material," *Journal of Educational Psychology*, May 1929. L. F. Shaffer, "A Learning Experiment in the Social Studies," *Journal of Educational Psychology*, December 1927. L. F. Shaffer, *Children's Interpretations of Cartoons* (Bureau of Publications, Teachers College, Columbia University, 1930).

toward the reliability of our sources, using only factually documented materials. We resorted to the most valid judgments we could find, multiplying cases and searching for unanimity in generalization. Thus we tried to portray with fidelity current and earlier modes of living by utilizing the statistics of social life and the judgments of frontier thinkers. Wherever numbers of similar identities could be found these were tabulated and classified in frequency distributions and rank orders.

As for statistical methods, wherever the form and structure of our data warranted it, we applied the statistics of averages, dispersion and reliability. It is significant, however, that on the whole we found comparatively little use for the intricate technical methods of determining "probable errors," "correlation" and "reliability."

In short, we strove to maintain the attitude of experimental inquiry: confronting problems, collecting objective data, classifying and grouping them to discover similarities and dissimilarities, seeking recurrence and yet remaining skeptical of it, attempting to reduce errors of observation and judgment, generalizing and yet testing reliability.

★   ★   ★

The job ahead was clear. Elizabeth Galloway and I sat down, with the help of my large staff of research associates, to write the second edition of the pamphlets. We had formulated the best theory we could about content and organization. We had conducted the necessary researches. We had studied and profited from the schools' criticisms of the first edition of the pamphlets.

We scrapped the nearly nineteen hundred old pamphlet plates which I owned out at the *Gazette Press* in Yonkers and replaced them with some thirty-three hundred plates of the new description of society. In 1929 and 1930 all of these were also scrapped as Ginn and Company published the first six big volumes of Man and His Changing Society. Counting the mimeographed "first edition" and the reconstruction of the first commercial edition after 1936, I estimate that not less than ten thousand pages have been discarded to take advantage of new-found understanding, data and historical developments. I state this statistical and "research" fact for the benefit of those who jeer at the attempt to paint a comprehensive portrait of American culture and its roots in the world setting.

But back to the making of the second edition of the pamphlets. Regularly and on schedule, four times a year for three years, a new and enlarged pamphlet was sent to the co-operating schools; in all about one hundred thousand copies a year—the seventh-grade ones in 1923–24, the eighth-grade ones in 1925–26, the ninth-grade ones in 1925–26.

Twenty years of hard study, research and scientific experimentation have gone into the social-science enterprise. Experimentation, yes. Time after time we threw away the old material and began again. It was part of our creed to refuse to accept any concept or organization as fixed and final. We were tolerant of new ideas. I personally searched the wide world and the reaches of the past for the needed ideas and illustrative material to portray all contemporary civilizations. All these things we did.

The jeerers, however, do not base their objections on this kind of scientific study. They are not historians; they are not educators; they are not scholars of the social scene. Most of them have not even read the books. They merely repeat or pick out some bit of content which rubs their own personal philosophy the wrong way. Certainly the question should be raised: "Are they qualified to judge, and do their judgments merit unquestioned support?"

★ ★ ★

The pamphlets were finished and delivered. June 1926 came. For four years the treadmill had been run; the schedule had been met. Regularly and on time children and teachers in nearly four hundred school classes could say: "The pamphlets have come!" I confess my New England conscience gloated, as well as my pride, in having created a new instrument to help American youth make democracy work.

The respite which followed was welcome. I was now to have a real interlude for mental inventory, months in which I could take account of stock. I was to be free to canvass and clarify my theories and write them. Except for the two National Society yearbooks, for eight years I had produced nothing in book form for grownups on theory or technique, except the delayed *Primer of Graphics and Statistics*. I had piled up some twelve hundred pages of lecture notes and magazine article material and from time to time had announced my "American life and the school" (variously titled). But the pamphlet dead line, the blank-sheet-of-paper grind, always thwarted me. Now perhaps I could do it.

But first something drastic had to be done about my finances. The lavish use of pamphlet income on educational research had produced the inevitable deficit,[7] one so large, in fact, that it was clear that the pamphlets would have to be turned over to a publisher and an edition of commercially sold books made. I felt sure that this could be done

[7] I report below the financial facts involved in carrying through the experimental editions of the pamphlets. Because one of the chief Red baiters in the present attack intimated to me that he was astonished that

because the nationwide use and discussion of the materials had led already to the expression of interest in a dozen publishing houses. Several of the larger ones had actually asked for the opportunity to discuss contracts.

I think there was never any real doubt in my mind about whom I'd turn to first; Henry H. Hilton, Dartmouth, '90, and a Ginn and Company partner, had long been my friend and a kind of elder-brother adviser to me. I submitted a comprehensive plan for the publication of a big series of social-science books, and Mr Hilton and Charles H. Thurber, another partner, approved it. The other partners joined, and in the autumn of 1926 an agreement was drawn.

The first volume, *Introduction to American Civilization*, was published and distributed to the schools in August

anyone should use his own personally earned funds for such a purpose and risk his own security, perhaps some of the others also will come to understand that there are actually people in the world—and, I think, a good many—who are doing that very thing.

SUMMARY OF RECEIPTS AND EXPENDITURES IN CONNECTION WITH THE SALE OF SOCIAL-SCIENCE PAMPHLETS

1922–32

(Taken from Harold Rugg's annual reports to the United States Collector of Internal Revenue)

YEAR	RECEIPTS	EXPENDITURES
Prior to		
1922	———	$ 5,000.00 (est.)
1922	$ 7,855.42	10,276.34
1923	30,401.09	27,840.15
1924	39,292.85	38,306.81
1925	44,479.46	44,214.67
1926	63,803.51	60,349.57
1927	55,197.10	59,617.58
1928	49,811.22	53,289.73
1929	36,141.46	33,491.38
1930	16,801.76	18,916.96
1931	1,970.35	14,631.26
1932	1,088.14	12,763.07
	$346,942.36	$378,697.52

Deficit (January 1, 1933) $31,755.16

1929; thereafter every six months the next one in the series came from the presses. The last one, *Changing Governments and Changing Cultures*, was published on January 1, 1932. *A Workbook of Directed Study and a Teacher's Guide* accompanied each of these six junior-high-school volumes.[8]

The interlude beginning in the spring of 1926 was a real one. I was able to turn my mind to the theory of the enterprise at last, to work at philosophical and psychological foundations. Indeed, I had to do this before the experimental materials could be made over into a really effective instrument for general use in public schools.

So another period of reading and reflecting began.

Exploring the Problem of Consent

It was at this time that the concept of the great social trends and their relations was beginning to intrigue my mind. I had encountered the idea of the "lag" of one part of the culture behind others in my first reading of our colleague William Ogburn's *Social Change* in 1922. My engineering and statistical habits of mind and work had even led me to express the concept graphically—to plot the lag of one "trend" or movement behind another. In my laboratory we had explored this for years, plotting "growth" curves for various parts of the social system as best we could—population, production, literacy, growth of cities, corporations, what not, and the results of this had actually gotten in a crude way into the second edition of the pamphlets. Elaborate documentation of the work came with the publication in 1929 of the Hoover committee's *Recent Economic Changes* and, four years later, of the valuable *Recent Social Trends*.

[8]The titles of the entire series appear on pp. 46–47.

But by that time I had met Bassett Jones and was using his mathematical papers to define the basic trends more precisely. They led me to the concept of "The Three Curves of Social Trend" which I have restated on page 98.

The chief point for the educator in all this study was the clarification of the doctrine of consent. One baffling question was provoked in our minds: Under what conditions does a people really "give consent"? We wrestled with the problem for years.

Even in the social-science books we had gone about as far as the professed "political scientists" had in presenting the story of consent. For example, in the first edition of *Changing Governments and Changing Cultures* and in *History of American Government and Culture*[9] we traced the emergence of civil and political liberties, the advance of the Bill of Rights and the development of the mechanism of the suffrage. But this, my associates and I found, was about where everyone stopped.

Now we began to see that our problem was a far more fundamental one, and we were convinced it was the chief political problem of the American people also. It all revolved around the idea of "the psychology of consent." Evidently Locke had the cue way back at the turn of the eighteenth century when he wrote his "classic" *On the Conduct of the Understanding* and his *Two Treatises on Government*—that the basis of democratic government is *the consent of the governed*. I had read *The Conduct* in Lewis Anderson's course at Illinois in 1912 but regarded it only as an "educational classic." Not until the middle twenties did I see that here was the cue to the real meaning of "consent." And here, I decided, was the great principle upon which we would base our work in making the school program.

[9]Later in *Citizenship and Civic Affairs* (1939).

THOSE who are engaged in the making of these materials of instruction believe that the future of representative democracy in America depends upon the intelligence of the common man. They believe that the known facts of intelligence are worthy of the hypothesis that there is in the group mind sufficient capacity to express its will effectively through industrial, social, and political machinery. This means that potential capacity must be transformed into dynamic ability. They are equally confident that, although America has practised universal education on a scale never before attempted by a large nation, our instruction has fallen far short of preparing the rank and file for the intelligent operation of democratic government.

After more than a century of democracy, there are signs of serious import that we are facing a near impasse in citizenship. The impasse, if such it is, is undoubtedly the natural outgrowth of our spectacular conquest of vast material wealth; of our reception into the country of thirty-three millions of people of diverse races, nationalities, practices, and beliefs, and of the massing of human beings in cities at a rate of which we had hitherto not dreamed. The present crisis has been brought about in large part by the mushroom growth of a fragile and highly specialized mechanism of industry, transportation, communication, and credit. With these stupendous material advances, resulting in the artificial inflation of our economic and social standards of living, there has not been a parallel aesthetic, spiritual, and cultural growth.

To relieve this impasse, we must substitute critical judgment for impulsive response as the basis for deciding our social and political issues. The thoroughgoing reconstruction of the school curriculum is a necessary first step in the process, for the reason that the public school is our most potent agency for social regeneration. Especially through the curriculum in the social sciences must we subject our youth to a daily regimen of deliberation and critical thought. Only those who have been trained through years of practise in the analysis of facts, in the making of decisions, the drawing of inferences and conclusions, will resort to intelligence instead of to predisposition as their guide for conduct.

H. R.

Facsimile of the Frontispiece of the First SOCIAL SCIENCE PAMPHLET, *Distributed August 1922.*

This fundamental detonating concept seemed obvious enough once it got stated; *a people give consent only when they understand*. If democracy is to work the Bill of Rights must be established and must be kept alive, and the people must be provided with the mechanism of registering their collective "Aye" or "Nay" at the polls—all of that, yes. But even though those two criteria *are* satisfied—and my books teach that they are for most Americans—nevertheless, a people cannot give consent unless they really understand their conditions and problems, the issues which must be met and the alternative pathways to tomorrow.

Understanding, the basis of consent—this was one of the great ideas that "ruled the world or threw it into chaos!" I had known it intuitively from the making of the "first edition," as the inscription page of the first pamphlet, *America and Her Immigrants* (August 1922), showed. I reproduce it on page 226. But now, more than ever, it was to be the chief intellectual nub of my work.

The problem of "government by the consent of the governed" sent me on a long and mostly futile search for material on the "psychology" of consent. To my amazement I could find few studies and not much theory—even by searching the material from Locke to Laski, Merriam and Beard. So for ten years this realm of the basis of understanding became an uncharted frontier on which my own group attempted to blaze new trails.

We charted the obstacles to building understanding among the people:

The sudden rise of a complex, interdependent social life.
The scattering of the people over a vast territory.
The rapid concentration of population in cosmopolitan cities.
The decline of personal, face-to-face contact and the dependence upon long-range, impersonal agencies of communication.
The increasing resort to the printed word.

The enormous diversity of language, social background and
economic interest in the population.
The lack among educationalists themselves of understanding
of the psychology of meaning.

We knew the enormity of the obstacles. But we knew
also that unless at least a large minority of our people came
to understand our civilization and its problems they could
never boast a government based on their own consent.

We studied the individual psychological constituents of
understanding—how meaning grows, the central role of
seeing relations, of generalizing, of problem solving and
other kinds of thinking, the significance of value. We noted
the role of impulse and habit in behavior, the dangerous
tendency of people generally to react to the *familiar* and
not to the *significant*. We saw a need to center on *finding
the significant relationship*.

I smile at the glib way in which I dispose in a paragraph
of years of study and organization. From 1923 the psychological studies were being carried on with almost daily discussions with my brilliant associates John Washburne and
Laurence Shaffer, one year with the added stimulation of
Helen Lynd, fresh from the studies she and Bob had just
made in Middletown. Washburne and Shaffer set up elaborate studies in learning, and Chester Mathews[10] worked
in the age and grade placement of material. They designed
and tried out methods and instruments of measurement and
scrutinized the processes. We used the paired-teacher plan
which Ros Clark and I had developed in the mathematics

[10]Vera Washburne and Selma Mathews served also as very able research assistants during several years.

experiment[11] at Chicago some years before. It proved to be signally successful, laying bare the learning process in the school. During the years from 1924 to 1927 the research work of our group was devoted in large part to meticulously detailed analyses of processes of learning. Each day, after watching teacher and pupils in action in the classroom, I would go immediately to my writing laboratory where the next pages of the pamphlets were being prepared. Thus the results of my daily discoveries got directly into the episodes and other learning exercises that the young people were to use in studying the world about them. Sociological studies and psychological studies went on simultaneously—*what to teach about the modern world* and *how to make it intelligible to young people.*

Our work on these educational and psychological frontiers was further analyzed, evaluated, checked and approved or challenged in graduate classes at Teachers College. Once a week throughout eighteen years (I spent two years on other continents studying the "psychology" of peoples and civilizations by other firsthand methods) I have met one or more graduate classes at the college and worked with them on psychological problems.[12] Every week I lectured from documented materials. Actually, then, the orgy of reading and study on the various psychological frontiers has continued almost without interruption throughout the

[11]See our *Scientific Method in the Reconstruction of Ninth Grade Mathematics* and *Fundamentals of High School Mathematics.*

[12]To illustrate: I gave Professor Thorndike's Psychology of the Elementary-School Subjects for some years at the times when he was otherwise engaged, 1920–23; my own Reconstruction of the School Curriculum, 1921–28; Social Psychology, 1928–36; Social Psychology of American Culture, 1936–39; Education and Creative America, 1940–41. In addition, I participated in the course, the Foundations of Education, from 1934 to date, serving as chairman of Section I since 1938. For three years, 1934–37, I served as chairman of an integrated course in the Arts in Education Life, given by the heads of several "arts" departments at the college.

twenty years. And all of it contributed greatly to our own personal understanding and to our ability to reduce the description of the bewildering industrial society to meaningful order.

Consent and Role of the Stereotype

With that side tangent of explanation, I return for a further word on the psychology of consent. Through all the exciting exploratory hours on the psychological frontier nothing was more thrilling or important than our clarification of the concept of the "stereotype" and its significance with regard to understanding and consent—another of those rule-the-world ideas. Our problem, recall, was to discover how understanding could be built in our people. The new literature[13] piling up around me pointed to an important psychological nub—the role of the "stereotype" in the development of individual minds and in the formation of social attitudes and the control of public opinion. Its answer seemed to be: Build *better stereotypes!* To some that may seem to be either superficial nonsense or Fascist reaction. It is neither, as further exploration into the meaning of the "stereotype" will show.

Opinions are formed and beliefs are fixed chiefly in the kaleidoscope of face-to-face groups in the daily current of events. There is the family group with its members practically always in intimate contact, the various clan-family gatherings at holidays, the neighborhood social groups, the church groups and the lodge and club groups. There are the larger heterogeneous groups, attending school, going to exhibitions, concerts and lectures, engaging in open-forum

---

[13]Lippmann's book *Public Opinion* came in 1922 with its fine documentation. (I still think it is his best book.) My friend Kimball Young (see his *Social Psychology*, published in 1930) and scores of research studies by Rice, Chapin, Murphy and others were building a whole new understanding of the process through which social attitudes are formed.

discussions and making group decisions in controversy. There are the groups involved with one's job. All of these personal, face-to-face groups in the ongoing zigzag course of human experience mold a man's character, influence his mind and determine in large part his point of view, his opinions, his beliefs and his general understanding.

In addition there are the less personal agencies—newspapers, books and other publications; the hourly impact of the radio, with its news broadcasts, its political speeches and round tables; the movie features and newsreels; public-relations counsel, supersalesmanship and propaganda of one kind or another; and the government too. These all help to mold the individual and contribute to the culture.

Still less obvious but, nevertheless, powerful and ever present is the force of climate of opinion—the subtle psychological atmosphere which pervades the home, the neighborhood, the social group meetings, the community as a whole and the nation. It presses on the individual constantly, sometimes overtly and sometimes imperceptibly, but always bringing influence to bear.

These, then, are the three principal agencies through which mind and mood, character and personality and opinions and beliefs are molded.

The psychological process itself is interesting and profoundly important to every citizen. Telescoped, the story is this: Every human being grows up in these groups, passing moment by moment from one to another. He is assailed on every side by a bewildering maze of stimuli. Through all the means of emotional and intellectual communication attitudes and meanings are transmitted from person to person; beliefs are altered; convictions are passed on. Each social contact brings some change and modifies the personality to some degree. All day long, all life long, the give-and-take process goes on.

The interaction between the individual and the group is really of twofold nature. On the one hand, the groups are composed of egocentric individuals who are constantly exerting pressures, warping, stamping, labeling and more or less consciously striving to make others over in the pattern of their own image; on the other hand, the reacting individuals are forever in the process of adapting themselves to and defending themselves against the pressures of others and the confusing mental-emotional world in general. There is a kind of endless battle between action and reaction. Thus the culture of the group makes the man; the man constantly contributes his bit to the remaking of the culture. One important outcome of the process is the development of self-centered personalities. As the individual learns to defend himself against the egocentric world around him, as he reacts aggressively as well as self-defensively, he becomes increasingly egocentric himself.[14]

This is all necessary orientation for understanding of the concept of the "stereotype" and its role in human behavior and in social life in general. It leads us to the all-important question: Does the individual react to the whole bombardment of stimuli at once? Not to all of it—either generalized or en masse. He reacts only partially. Instantaneously he picks out a cue aspect here and a cue aspect there—a conspicuous phrase or gesture or event, in a total organic configuration of course—and responds to it. From infancy to adulthood he learns through an elaborate process of trial and error that he can "get along" with others by responding to them in certain selected ways. He learns then to make characteristic responses to the stimuli pressing in upon him. These are called stereotyped ways of behavior,

[14]Even the four-year-old is an aggressive little individual protagonist of self. See Rugg, Krueger and Sondergaard article in *Journal of Educational Psychology*, January–March, 1929.

and certain of the stimuli come, through their development by adult society, to have abbreviated stereotype class names. Let us go into this in more detail.

A realistic analysis of the democratic process in America shows that it is carried on largely through the interplay of many small and large special-interest groups—political parties and machines, self-aggrandizing or social-service groups, powerful business and industrial cliques which together constitute the dominant political force of the community, civic-betterment blocs, chauvinistic-patriotic groups, religious groups, professional groups, racial groups and neighborhood groups. Now in each of these groups are joined together persons who for its purposes hold to approximately the same "views," that is, who react to certain aspects of life—political, economic, social, racial, what not —with approximately the same stereotypes. Thus the community consists of people belonging to and carrying on through in-groups and out-groups—radical against conservative, Southern Baptist against Northern Baptist, worker against owner, Communist against capitalist, Protestant against Catholic, Jew against Gentile, Christian against Moslem, and Nordic against Slav or Latin or Oriental or Negro.

Thus a confused mixture of points of view, opinions, creeds, beliefs, and the like, all organized and stamped and labeled, becomes the psychological base of human culture. And as each mind struggles to comprehend this mixture it gets itself similarly organized. When one individual reacts to another he sees the other not as the mysterious and complex personality that he is; rather he sees him as a composite of traits which he has learned to associate with members of various groups. He pigeonholes and classifies the other under abbreviated, stereotype class names—Jew, Gentile, Christian, Catholic, radical, liberal, conservative, reactionary, Bolshevik, Communist, Negro, Mason, D.A.R., a labor leader, a Harvard man, a professional athlete, a banker, a gangster, a United States' senator, a political agitator, what not. So also with social situations: he reacts to them in the light of the mental pictures, the ·classified and emotionally colored concepts, he has of the points of view and attitudes he associates with the life of the person or group involved. He does not react to the total complex situation but only to those conspicuous phases of it which obtrude at any given moment.

This is where the difficulty in building common understanding among people in a democracy comes in. Rarely, if ever, do two people select exactly the same meaning with which to respond to the same situation. The concepts that people hold and communicate carry great divergencies of meaning. One has only to ask two people to explain their concepts of such words as democracy, capitalism, imperialism or Communism to learn that this is true. Now when any political situation arises involving these or other ideas, each individual concerned responds to it with his own personal meanings. The consequent difficulty of building solidarity of point of view, or securing universal "consent," and of producing joint action then becomes ·clear. And successful democratic action is thwarted without these conditions.

Moreover, the individual tends to select from the world of ideas and beliefs around him those new meanings which accord with the ones he has already formed. He sees new situations in the light of the previously selected and stereotyped meanings with which he viewed past situations. So understanding becomes cumulatively incomplete and more and more lopsided.

This is the concept of the "stereotype" and the process by which it comes to dominate behavior. We do not actually deal with the real world; we deal instead with a pseudo-mental world and respond to it as though it were real, with partial meanings which we have invented for real people, real things, real actions. This helps also to explain the effectiveness of the Forbes-Hart-Rudd name calling, "subversive" . . . "un-American" . . . "poisoning the minds of the young" . . . "treason in the textbooks" . . . what not. These are all stereotypes, and on reading them or hearing them people react to them uncritically and instantaneously—without taking thought, without true understanding.

As our own research and study went on the importance of the role of the stereotype in American life and education stood out clearly. We came to see how effective and constructive democratic action could be hampered, indeed frequently could be made impossible, because of existing stereotypes and stereotyped behaviors. So also we came to see how we and others in education would have to deal with the stereotype and find some solutions for the obstacles it raised in the path of building meaning and understanding among young people in the school.

Ten Distinguished Groups of Creative Americans

What was the vintage we garnered from the creative mind and mood of America?

It was a rich harvest. Every vineyard gave up its fruit: the social frontier, its realistic concepts of the social-economic-political system; the personal frontier, its orientation to the living creature; the psychological frontier, the concepts of thought and feeling; the esthetic frontier, the data of the creative and appreciative acts. Steadily the "good concepts" clarified that would serve as the organizing nucleus for our portrait of man and his changing society. From the validated researches of the workers on five frontiers of creative work they came. A full century had gone into the building of the modern outlook, the scientific, organic and creative climate among students of ideas in America and Europe. Thousands of workers had contributed materials in the form of investigations, measurements, experiments, critical and philosophical studies, works of science, works of art. Slowly as these accumulated, at first unknown, then ignored, some even denied here and there, they came eventually to be accepted as the volume of their chorus of affirmation expanded.

Looking back on the whole thrilling drama, we recognize no less than ten distinguished groups:

First, four groups of scientific students of the living creature:

The students of evolution, who documented the concept of *things growing from small beginnings.*

The laboratory physiologists, who explored the *general behavior of animals and human beings.*

The students of animal learning, who explored behavior and the processes of learning—especially of *generalization and of the perception of relationships.*

The laboratory psychologists, who extended this inquiry to the behavior of human beings.

Second, four groups of "social scientists"—students of the social scene:

The philosophers in their libraries, who laid bare the *organic nature of experience, the generalizing characteristics of thinking and of all progressive living as growing, the experimental method of inquiry* and *the intuitive way of working.*

The sociologists, anthropologists and social psychologists

who developed the concept of *the culture as the process of the interaction of dynamic individuals.*

The regional geographers who revealed the *interactive impact of physical and social environments and human modes of living upon one another.*

The "new historians," "new economists," "new political scientists," who documented the deep-running social trends and clarified the *unified interrelationships of economics, politics and social psychology.*

Third, a vast group of workers on the frontiers of creative arts:

The poets, novelists, literary and social critics, architects, painters, sculptors, men of the theater, dancers, musicians, craftsmen—all of whom came to see man as artist, emphasizing his statement of life as *organic form,* as *integrity of expression,* as *self-cultivation.*

Fourth, a group of creative workers in the schools of our time:

Artist-teachers in laboratory schools, working with children and exploring such concepts as *growth, meaning as active response, integration, purpose, balance, self, integrated personality.*

Ten groups of creative Americans studying their culture, struggling with problems of imagination and documentation, working as intuitive "artists" in the framework of their personal life orientations, working as documenting scientists critically studying man and his culture.

This, then, is the biography of ideas which came to constitute the skeleton of Man and His Changing Society.[15]

[15]The story of the making of the Social-Science Pamphlets into the commercial series of twenty books, 1927-40, is given in Chapter III.

SOME "GOOD CONCEPTS"	SOME "BAD WORDS"
American life—a high standard of living.	America, highest standard of living the world and potentially a land plenty, is a depressed society.
The individual should have full liberty of action to make the most of himself.	"My freedom stops where my neig bor's, or the public's, good begins."
America—a land of opportunity with a ladder of opportunity for those who compete, work hard and persist.	America—a land of great opportunity many, but today not of equal oppe tunity for all.
The American system of free enterprise.	Free competition balanced by gove ment controls over economic enterpr for the general welfare.
The Founding Fathers—brilliant and devout patriots.	The Founding Fathers, brilliant and vout patriots—men of property w made a constitution difficult to change
The free play of private ownership.	Private ownership except where pub ownership is necessary to guarantee p lic welfare.
Unrestricted freedom to develop natural resources.	In parts of America land and peo were exploited, eroded and wasted uncontrolled freedom.
Scientific management in industry.	Accelerating technological unempl ment.
The American Constitution, one of the world's greatest state papers of democratic government.	The "economic determination of Constitution."
Democracy as the American way of life.	The characteristics of Socialism, Co munism and Fascism compared w those of democracy.
Initial swift development of the continent, a magnificent physical achievement but necessarily not planned.	To prevent the recurring breakdo of the economic system it must planned.
Resourceful people, each looking out for himself. . . . A sense of equality, absence of class lines among the people— "I'm as good as you."	Our people exhibit vast individual d ferences, energy, intelligence, ambiti and other traits.

Chapter XII

GOOD CONCEPTS AND BAD WORDS

Almost from the beginning of my work in preparing school materials it was evident that to get a sound and clear description of society into the school required more than my own capacity to understand that society myself and to write it clearly and with the greatest possible objectivity. It required parents' co-operation in helping to build understanding in our young people. Would they give it? Would other citizens, especially those of the community who have prestige and leadership, go along with us on the idea? Could they be brought to see the importance of young people confronting social conditions and issues squarely and digging to the very roots of our changing culture?

As the years passed I became more and more convinced that democracy could not survive the attacks upon it unless young Americans came to a thorough understanding of the world in which they were living. The democratic process in America, I was sure, could not be guaranteed unless our youth were introduced to the full story—the deficiencies as well as the achievements of our society, the problems and issues as well as the narrative of adventure. Would adults in the community share this view?

It was not long before we found out. Throughout the years thousands of parents have read the books along with their children. Reports from them have come continuously, and these show that they themselves have become aware of the urgency of having a real description of society in the schools. It is not these who have voiced the protest against the ideas presented. A small group of self-appointed censors entered the scene. They took it upon themselves to criticize the content, approving some ideas and some words and condemning others, all in terms of their own interests, prejudices and philosophy. Increasingly we saw that certain indispensable ideas came to be the nub of the attack. These ideas I have called the "good concepts" and the "bad words." The frontispiece of this chapter serves as illustration for some of them.

Were these ideas, these concepts, dangerous to our youth, as the critics said? In the light of twenty years of documentation these are my conclusions concerning them:

First, every concept in both lists is indispensable to a real understanding of American life—the country's magnificent achievements, its vast potentiality for an abundant physical and spiritual life, certainly, but also its deficiencies and problems. All are needed that men may understand.

Second, the ideas listed on the left, called "good concepts," arouse no opposition at all. The patrioteers as well as the merchants of conflict think they are grand; in fact, they constitute the bulk of their own verbal stock in trade. America to them is portrayed only in these terms.

Third, the concepts listed on the right, called "bad words," simply cannot be introduced into the school in any form without arousing the bitter opposition of certain special-interest groups—persons like Miller of the 1921–26 witch-hunt and the Forbes-Hart-Rudd-West combination of today. It can be seen from my story that although these persons are very few in number they are powerful in influence. They can and do try to prevent materials that speak the "bad words" from being used. Furthermore, the ideas are such that they cannot be camouflaged with "good words." The ideas must be made clear, and as soon as they are, no matter how phrased, they become "bad"—"subversive," "un-American," "poisonous," "treason," what not.

Fourth, the evidence is clear that the preponderance of our thinking citizens who do not have personal axes to grind by censoring the schools are actually well disposed toward having all of the indispensable ideas for understanding presented to their children. Indeed, after studying the problem they welcome—no, insist on—it. I draw a clear line, therefore, between the vast body of reasonable and well-intentioned citizens and the little corporal's guard of self-appointed censors of the schools.

"You Can't Say That!"

The lists deserve careful study. Note that one can talk about the "free play of private enterprise" but not about "controlling the free play of private enterprise in the public interest."

One can describe the Founding Fathers as "brilliant and devout patriots" but not as the "Founding Fathers, brilliant and devout patriots, men of property who made the Constitution difficult to change."

One can praise the Constitution as "one of the world's greatest state papers," but one cannot say or imply any "economic determination of the Constitution," even though the monographs of Charles A. Beard and others are now accepted as valid documentary evidence.

One can teach "America—a land of opportunity" but not

"America—a land of opportunity for many, but not a land of equal opportunity for all"—even though proof that it isn't glares at us from ten thousand communities and ten million families.

One can speak of "scientific management in industry"; but "technological unemployment"—that's bad! I need not go on; the reader can multiply the examples manyfold.

It becomes clearer and clearer, then, just what the liberal baiters will not have in the schools. They will not have: (1) anything that even approaches a questioning of the complete purity of motives and behavior of the founders of our country or the leaders of the past, (2) anything that questions contemporary American life, (3) anything that presents negative aspects of American history or development, (4) anything that portrays social change, and (5) anything that deals with controversy. "Such things must not be brought into the school!" they say. These guardians of "everything rosy" know well, of course, that our young people are confronted with striking examples of social change every day of their lives. The children themselves engage in the discussion of matters of controversy in public and private life. (What boy or girl of eleven or over does not have an opinion on how and why people made their choices in the recent presidential election?) As for the deficiencies in American life, it is hardly necessary to remind ourselves of the fact that youth's eyes and minds are open to evidences of them on every side—in their homes, on the streets, in the playgrounds, in the movies, where not; they read and hear about them in the newspapers and magazines and over the radio. But, say the attackers, our young people may not talk about such things in the classroom, shouldn't even think about them. They must not question American life, its heroes of the past or present. The function of education is to build in youth an admiration for things as they are. The school is to be used to buttress the *status quo*. A. E. Stevenson says, for example:

. . . our system of public education has been set up to teach our children those rules so that they may become useful, self-reliant and law-abiding citizens of the state as it *now exists*.[1]

The first lesson that I learned, then, from the self-appointed censors in our schools was that in dealing with the materials of education one must distinguish sharply between the "Good Concepts" and the "Bad Words."

How to Introduce the "Bad Words"

The second lesson deals with the question: How shall we handle the ideas called the "bad words"? They cannot be camouflaged; they must be clarified. One step in this direction is the launching of a vigorous campaign of adult education. The local community leaders, along with superintendents, principals and teachers, must take the chief responsibility and carry the community along in advance of the use of the controversial issues in the schools. If the study of the ideas underlying the culture is undertaken by the adult population there will be no fears about them or rebellion against them, because the people will have come to understand.

The other step must be taken by the organizers and writers of the materials. They must make meticulous distinction between "history" and "hypothesis." Some concepts are so firmly established and so fully documented by research data that they can be taught as history. On the soundness of these the total body of historians stand, a solid phalanx of support. Other concepts and generalizations,

[1]"Background and Philosophy of the Rugg Social Science Textbooks," by Archibald E. Stevenson; a transcript of a radio address printed in M. K. Hart's *Revolution through "Social Science" in the Schools*. American Parents Committee on Education, New York.

while confirmed by some buttressing evidence, still do not
command the full support of all the competent students of
society. Where there is still some doubt about their validity
the tentative conclusions must be recognized and deliberately pointed out in the text of the materials. Those which
have been established by history should have all the supporting evidence in place.[2]

With regard to the hypothetical concepts, they, too,
must be brought into the school but must be presented as
hypotheses, with all evidence for and against included.
They must be introduced as questions and treated as problems for investigation and thorough discussion of all sides.
These are the concepts which frighten the timid soul and
enrage the representatives of special-interest groups which
feel that they are being attacked.

Thus it seems to us that the distinction between fact and
theory, history and hypothesis, becomes increasingly clear
to young people if so presented in the materials for study.

Shall We Have Controversial Issues in the Schools?

Another example of the "out" content reveals the fear
of controversy about the issues and problems of our day.
It is my thesis that if we are to have consent in a democratic people it must be built upon the study of controversial issues, because such study is the intellectual foundation of the schools. One of the chief planks of my program
is that the young people shall be urged constantly to *take
thought before they take sides,* but it is obvious that to
"take thought" to make choices, they must confront the
alternatives set out clearly before them. How else can

---

[2] This point is of great importance and needs to be illustrated very
carefully. I shall do that in the next chapter where I deal with the problem of teaching such concepts as "social control," "socialization of
property," and "free enterprise."

human beings practice decision making than by confronting issues? *To keep issues out of the school program is to keep thought out of it.* Issues are the very nub of the psychology of consent. Indeed, the psychology of learning inevitably leads to the conclusion that the whole intellectual program of the school must be organized around issues if the school itself is to be a practicing democracy.

This approach does not imply, as the self-appointed censors say, that we propose a "plan for a new social order" with which to "indoctrinate American youth." These patrioteers accuse us of "indoctrinating a new social order," "selling a collectivistic society." This we do not do; this we would not even wish to do, for so long as the concepts are hypothetical and controversial, we ourselves reserve our own decisions until historical documentation gives them unquestioned validity.

Who then are the real indoctrinators? The liberal baiters themselves! Stevenson, et al., say straight out that the schools shall be used to "teach" the *status quo*—despite the fact that the world is changing at such a pace that one cannot predict the course of events from one month to another! If their version of the *status quo* shall be taught—then all thinking people must be unalterably opposed to it. Acceptance of that point of view is totally inconsistent with belief in democracy, for such a procedure is sheer "imposition." It negates freedom of speech and equal opportunity to impart all opinions (minority or otherwise). It serves in the long run to limit the intellectual heritage to that tiny minority who will have dictatorial control over the lives of all of us. All-round development of either individual or group is impossible under such imposition.

So if Americans are to continue the tradition of consent,

controversial issues *must* be presented in the schools. We who prepare the materials must give all the data about every reach of American life and the modern world that we can get from the best public and private fact-finding institutions. No documented fact shall be excluded—*no documented fact, I say*—even if it presents a view contrary to the conventionally accepted one. Moreover, we shall pass on to the young people the "interpretations" the scholars of the social scene have made of the documented "facts," being careful always to seek to include all points of view. All sides shall be heard in the school.

Censorship and Social Danger

We come now directly to the question of censorship, and I trust that this book has offered sufficient proof that public education is being censored today. It is being censored by a small minority of persons, some in certain national organizations without even the informed backing of their membership. And since the problem of censorship in education is extremely important its foundations should be examined.

Let us begin by discriminating clearly between censorship and the proper expression of the opinions of any group of our people concerning what shall be taught in the schools. There is no opposition to the latter; in fact, active interest and expression on the part of all citizens in the education of their children should be encouraged. I hold that true democracy cannot be carried on unless such expression is actually heard from all sectors of the population. From *all sectors*, I repeat. Throughout twenty years of making new social-science materials for the schools this has been my guiding principle.

But to censor is to withhold. It is for one sector of the population, by virtue of its prestige and power and hence its control over the agencies of communication, to withhold data needed for the total group to carry on social life efficiently and co-operatively. Whereas to propagandize is positively to *distort* the data that are necessary for group decisions and the enhancement of social welfare, to censor is to withhold such data altogether. As Lippmann has well phrased it: it is to erect a barrier between the event and the public. It is to transform a public event into a private one. It is the artificial creation of privacy.

Of course I am not unmindful of the fact that most human events are to a certain extent episodes in censorship. The very nature of the development of personality in social groups tends to bring that about. The culture itself, by virtue of the child's membership in certain face-to-face groups (such as being born into a family of given political-economic-social-religious orientation and growing up in similarly "censored" play groups, school and church groups, what not)—the culture itself, I say, presents to him a definitely censored world. But this is naïve censorship, the kind of limitation which is inherent in heterogeneous groups of multitudinous and varied pressures. We do live in a censored world, a pseudo-mental world of ideas and beliefs, but we behave in it and toward it as if it were a "real" world. We respond with the very meanings which the culture has "selected" and organized for us. All this we grant in the naïve censorship of the culture itself.

We recognize also that there is a kind of conscious, deliberate censorship in times of crisis, which can be justified as being "in the public interest." In times of war democracy may have to be set aside for the time being, and censorship by properly delegated officials may be necessary. Witness: an army headquarters—"a literary council of war"—preparing the daily communiqué to be read around the world by hundreds of millions of people. To prevent panic and the turning of military defeats into disasters it may be necessary to "prepare the attitudes" of the people. It may be necessary to build a pseudo environment to which the people can react in place of the real environment. This is censorship imposed for the public good by officials elected for the purpose. They are subject to recall by the general body of electors whenever the need disappears. This kind of deliberate censorship is not opposed to democratic government in action, though its constructive usefulness does depend upon the wisdom, competence, honesty and personal disinterestedness of the censors.

The Truly Subversive Enemies of Democracy

But for minority groups to attempt to censor the citizen's world in a democratic society, and particularly in a time of crisis, is a matter fraught with great danger. It is to destroy the only instrument which can make democracy work. So I say to the self-appointed censors of education: Censor the schools and you convict yourself by your very acts as the most subversive enemies of democracy. Censor education and you destroy understanding . . . you instate bias . . . you give free reign to prejudice . . . finally, you create Fascism. Nothing but an education in the whole of American life will build tolerant understanding in our people and guarantee the perpetuation of democracy.

★   ★   ★

Perhaps no nucleus of concepts turns so quickly into "bad words" as that of "free enterprise." The current press and rostrum resound with many versions of it. No sooner are the words "free enterprise" uttered than people, even intelligent people, are frozen into one of two antagonistic attitudes. To one it brings in its train *rugged individualism*—fine! To the other, *ragged individualism*—horrible! One group says "hamstringing of business"; the other, "government control." Both are emotional, unreasoned responses.

Because it is such a perfect example of the "good concepts" and "bad words" problem, I have devoted the entire next chapter to a concept which demands the most serious and objective study. It must lose its connotation of "bad word" and become a "good concept" to be explored and understood by all our people.

And because it has often become the nub of the conflict over the social sciences in the schools, I wish for that reason also to discuss it further.

Chapter XIII

THE CRUX: "I" AND "WE"

W<small>E HAVE COME</small> to the crux—to the problem that torments men's souls. For many centuries, but especially within the past three, it is the problem that has baffled the ingenuity of mankind. It may be said, I think, that man's failure to solve it is the chief cause of the current fighting on the battlefields of Eurasia and the chief reason for the present deadlock between government and business in America.

And so I give it its proper name—the crux. The concepts involved in it can be juxtaposed in many different ways:

The Individual	and	The Culture
Freedom	and	Control
Self	and	Society
Expression	and	Control
Private Enterprise	and	Government Enterprise
Individualism	and	Co-operation
Private Capital	and	State Capital

In these and in many other ways the impasse can be indicated, but irrespective of the phraseology, they all pivot around the agelong crux: the relation of "I" and "We."

★   ★   ★

To .let the individual state himself for his own soul's sake as well as for the good of his neighbors and yet not encroach upon those neighbors.

To let the group foster the individual's growth and encourage his statement to the uttermost limits within their proper spheres but never blighting them by unwarranted restraint.

With Robert Frost I'd say:

Keep off each other and keep each other off.

But I'd add with Whitman:

There is something in staying close to men and women and looking on them, and in the contact and odor of them, that pleases the soul well.

★   ★   ★

The reconciliation of "I" and "We" poses the double task of the twentieth century: one, to maintain a Bill of Rights and, two, to formulate a Bill of Duties—both of which will give energy to our people and guide them in a strange new world. We already have a Bill of Rights, grown out of a thousand years of agrarian culture history which has been the chief propulsive power in the clearance of the continents of the earth after 1600 A.D. A parallel Bill of Duties, not so seriously needed in a first day of expanding culture, has become an absolute imperative in our present culture period of swift transformation.

Our Special Contemporary Crux

Broadly put, the nub of our special conflict today is: What interpretation of "the American way of life" shall guide the study of civilization in the schools? More specifically, in the terms of Hart, Rudd and company, it is: *Which Brand of the American system of free enterprise shall be taught?* They have one emphatic answer: It shall be that concept which guarantees government's hands off all business, old-fashioned laissez faire, freedom of the individual from any regulation or control by the people generally. My colleagues and I have a different answer, hence the irreconcilable conflict between us.[1]

Their argument on this point is illustrated by Merwin K. Hart, speaking of the individuals who built up the American system. He says:

Without such men, each free to strive to the full extent of his ability, unhindered by government bureaucracy, it [the American system] never would have been possible. And only through such men as these, free enough to exert their full abilities, will private enterprise be perpetuated. Clearly, the author of the Rugg books would have government bureaucratic control substituted for the liberty of private individuals. Some of the views set forth in these books have prevailed the past seven years in the hamstringing of private enterprise by control from Washington and the state capitals.[2]

Another puts it thus:

Let us stop passing new laws and regulations every minute, so that the successful, industrious man may again prosper, and as soon as our industrious, frugal businessman finds that the fundamental theory of hard work without stint and saving is again worth while, then and only then will business again become normal.[3]

[1] An important caution at this point: The conflict with the merchants of controversy is irreconcilable, but we have no such conflict with the bulk of the American people. Their own voice in elections and the acts of their chosen representatives are proof of the side on which they stand.

[2] Merwin K. Hart, *Revolution through "Social Science" in the Schools.* American Parents Committee on Education, New York, p. 13.

[3] Letter to the New York *Times*, February 28, 1935.

Quotations could be multiplied n-fold from pronouncements made by the rugged individualists during the past
decade, but these are characteristic of the position. Three
times in one paragraph Hart voices the concept of freedom.
Witness, "free enough to exert their full abilities" . . .
"free to strive to the full extent of his ability" . . . "the
liberty of private individuals." I pick them out for
emphasis because they are characteristic of any man speaking—not merely the American. All men wish to be free to
follow their own bent. Who is there among us who does
not?

Aren't We All Individualists?

The purpose of this discussion of freedom and control
will be well served if we grant at the very start the deeply
ingrained nature of the "I" traits in all of us. We Americans
crave and demand freedom, perhaps more than any people
in the world. Every one of us is a rank individualist. Each
wishes to have his own way; each one is irked by restrictions. Each person wants privacy—a house for his family,
a room to himself, his most personal possessions unused by
others. He wants freedom in his job to work his way.

Aren't we all individualists? Aren't the social reformers
as well as the economic royalists irked by restrictions? Of
all the meanings of freedom, this one—the absence of restraint—is most prevalent among our people. Throughout
history it has sent restless men a-packing and a-moving
when, as Daniel Boone put it, they "could hear their neighbor's shotgun."

Each Individual Wants to State Himself

In a less clear way, perhaps, every man feels deeply the
urge to get himself stated. Examples from the homely and

naïve as well as the self-conscious and sophisticated abound
on every hand. The young mechanic wishes to have his
own garage; the young librarian, her own little bookstore;
the barber, his shop; the artist-craftsman in wood or iron or
stone, his own studio; the housewife, her own personally
designed, planned and equipped home. With Whitman
again:

Each singing what belongs to him or to her and to none
else.

Each human being has the urge to put into some objective form what he feels and thinks, indeed what he is at
a given moment. With dogged persistence the man, the
actor, the painter, the composer of music, the writer of
words, the dancer, the carver in wood, the architect of a
house, the statesman of a nation, the creator of a great
business, the goodly judge of a court, the philosopher of a
society—each strives to objectify what he feels and is. And
he craves to do it in his own unique way—to make his utterance a replica of himself. Moreover, if his personal philosophy constitutes an honest program of life, and if he has
mastered technical competence in the medium he chooses,
his statement will be an honest statement of himself.

"All my life," said Isadora Duncan, dancer, "I've struggled to make one authentic gesture."

And Allan Abbott, literary man: "The creative artist
. . . creates a world that in actuality is his view."

And Albert Einstein, distinguished mathematician: "Man
tries to make for himself in the fashion that suits him best
a simplified and intelligible picture of the world."

Freedom of the individual to make of his life what he will
and freedom to get himself stated—these are the desires of
every man.

★   ★   ★

The corresponding social aspiration of our times is so to arrange the social scene that both of these desires of the individual can be satisfied. James T. Adams saw the ideal arrangement as: "that social order in which each man and each woman can rise to the highest stature of which he is innately capable." Society is conceived as a "multitude of individuals," and the social scene is looked upon as a stage so set that each man is able to advance steadily toward the goal of being the person that he is potentially.

These goals cannot be reached except through the reconciliation and collaboration of "I" and "We." The individual must take on a Bill of Duties as well as enjoy a Bill of Rights. He must make himself a co-operative person of responsibility and competence. Society in its turn must collaborate in helping to guarantee the individual economic security and maintain a climate of opinion marked by spiritual freedom.

What a problem! Well named—the crux!

And it is a problem that no significant program of education can ignore. For this reason I did not ignore it in my books but stated it as clearly as I could, relying always upon the documentation of history. Throughout the organization and preparation of the materials of Man and His Changing Society the world-shaking impasse between the "I" and "We" served as a constant guide. In book after book its history is traced, its contemporary status presented.[4]

[4]See, for example, *Changing Governments and Changing Cultures: Dictatorships vs. Democracy, America's March toward Democracy, Citizenship and Civic Affairs.*

"I" and "We" in History

Each epoch and each people, so far as I have been able to find out, has in one form or another confronted the problem of "I" and "We." I think it has always been a tormenting issue; men have fought over it.

In the new educational program it is studied in the background of the fragile world-wide mechanism which has been built in a thousand and more years of history. In the pageant of history scene after scene portrays the peoples of the world trying to carry on economic, political and social life. Simple frontier societies are shown being transformed into complex urban ones. The outcome of it all, the contemporary scene, reveals two billion people in seventy-odd nations (not to mention two thousand tribes) trying to manage a bewilderingly complex and interdependent scheme of production, distribution, government, creative expression, what not.

The Historic "Law" of Individual Differences

In the center of every scene has been the individual. No matter in what age or geographic setting, society has been, to use Whitman's phrase, but "a multitude of individuals," egocentric, competing individuals, each governed by drives for economic security, drives for personal power, drives for social prestige, what not; each feeling, if he did not say, "That's mine! I invented it! I copyrighted it! I organized it! I built it! I saw it first and staked it out! Or, at any rate, my father did! So it's mine! You can't tax it! You can't encroach on it!"

Through the pageant of history the individual has tried to deal with his fellow individuals. During part of the time, in fact throughout much of it, he dealt with them on the basis of competitive violence and shrewdness, often with resultant exploitation. The strong individual tended to exploit the weak.

Even in the distant past the "law of individual differences" seemed to hold true. Everywhere people appear to have varied widely in energy, in ambition, in intelligence, in resources. They revealed the long and the short, the strong and the weak, the domineering and the submissive, the dynamic and the inert, the adventurous and the timid. For every trait a vast mediocrity bulked large between the extremes.

The implications of this "law of individual differences" seem always to have been at the very heart of the problem of the "I" and "We" and of man's struggle to build a more co-operative commonwealth with egocentric, competing individuals. All history, I say, seems to reveal this. The more I came to understand this "law" as well as the egocentrism of men, the more I became convinced that here was a cue to be given to American youth, that it might add a tiny increment of understanding to their knowledge of man.

WHAT HAPPENED WHEN MEN WERE LEFT FREE TO PRE-EMPT AND DEVELOP WITHOUT LET AND HINDRANCE?

Another recurrence of history was of striking significance. From epoch to epoch, century to century, men moved about in great human migrations, hunting the "better land over yonder." At the dawn of recorded history they were doing it in China's Yellow River valley, in the Nile River valley, in the Tigris-Euphrates river valley. The Indo-Europeans were doing it in 2000 B.C., moving east and west from the Caspian, settling around the northeast end of the Mediterranean and into Europe, carrying with them the roots of the languages and culture forms of fifty modern nations. When the west Europeans, their children, started on world-wide treks after 1600, they Europeanized every continent to which they came. In 1600 A.D. they numbered only about a hundred million, and relatively all were living on the European continent; in 1940 their descendants number 650,000,000 with over 200,000,000 living in other parts of the earth. Thus wave after wave of moving people created cycles of human migration, clearance and settlement, the conquest of North America being merely the latest.

Man's Violation of the Sustained-Yield Principle

Taken in the background of world history, what the Americans did is enlightening. In a two-century-long orgy of construction they built the structure of our industrial-democratic civilization. On the credit side of the culture ledger is recorded a spectacular physical achievement, most of it accomplished in a century. On the debit side is the red record of costs, the vicious debilitation of the land and many of the people. In the restless haste to get immediate profits the earth was mined: the topsoil, the forests, the grasses, the coal and the oil, the iron, the copper and other metals. The people, too, were mined—their security in the land, in neighborliness, in sanity, in confidence, in human integrity. Everything in and on the earth was taken in a swift, unrestricted race for gain. As a result many phases of the culture were *eroded*—men as well as land. Studies show that our giant economic system, as well as the other major industrial systems of the world, stands pitifully stalled in these depression years primarily because of the excessive violation of the sustained-yield principle.

Here, then, is another of the great ideas that rule the world—or throw it into chaos. On the destructive side it is erosion and waste of the gifts of nature and human beings;

on the constructive side: build the soil, sustain the yield and enrich the human race! As Frost stated it so beautifully:

> Build soil. Turn the farm in upon itself
> Until it can contain itself no more,
> But sweating-full, drips wine and oil a little.
> I will go to my run-out social mind
> And be as unsocial with it as I can.
> The thought I have, and my first impulse is
> To take to market—I will turn it under.
> The thought from that thought—I will turn it under.
> And so on to the limit of my nature.[5]

Thus either from the scientific agronomist or from the poet-agronomist we learn the important lesson: *Whether it is land or people or minds you are growing, provide for a sustained yield. Build soil!*

Is the Individual Competent to Cope with Nature and His Fellow Man?

The idea of sustaining the yield is not a new one to the practical farmers of fifty centuries. But it is a lesson of history that man in general has never taken very seriously. The record of agrarian civilizations is an example. A people, a "multitude of individuals," settles on subhumid land . . . they overcut and overburn the trees . . . they overplow and overplant the soil . . . their cows and sheep overgraze and overbrowse the grasses. The floods wash off the topsoil, and the rivers push it into the oceans . . . the rains cease and the winds blow the soil off a continent . . . the civilization declines.

Sometimes the people rouse themselves and begin again. Sometimes they do not. If the awakening comes too late the

[5]Robert Frost. *A Further Range*. Henry Holt and Company, New York, 1936, pp. 93-94.

civilization actually dies. In any event the people pay a terrible penalty.

So it was with China . . . with Mesopotamia . . . with Persia . . . with India . . . with Amerindia. The sustained-yield principle was violated . . . the civilizations all declined . . . some died.

In later civilizations, too, the great principle was violated. There was waste of metals, fuels, fibers and other natural resources. Under the rule of laissez faire, an old formula in a new world, the shrewd ones among the people cornered the things which others needed; in many cases they came actually to own the others. The society became stratified in a hierarchy of social classes. The masters came to dominate over and exploit the workers. Exploitation of workers and resources frequently led to closed markets and stalled production systems. And because here again there was violation of the sustained-yield principle, civilizations declined and passed away.

So, we are led to believe, it was with the Egyptians . . . with the Phoenicians . . . with the Greeks . . . with the Romans—to name only a few.

History seems to document the general thesis that thus far *all civilized people have denied the sustained-yield principle*, and thorough study reveals why they did it, including why even the Americans have done it. Our old friend, "the law of individual differences," taken in conjunction with laissez faire—every man for himself and the devil take the hindmost—accounts for it in very large measure. The strong, the shrewd and the ambitious, deliberately or inadvertently, exploited the land and their neighbors. Actually each individual felt that he could cope with Nature—alone. Anyway, the general feeling was that Nature was boundless and could easily and quickly replenish herself; hence, "I need not take thought for the morrow." The lure of better living as well as the power and the glory was very strong, and one did not think, or did not choose to think, of foregoing immediate profits for a deferred social security. *One did not spread the fat year's surplus over the lean year's deficit.*

Throughout history peoples have invented and discovered many ways to get rich quick, but careful investigation proves that nearly every one of them violated the sustained-yield principle. It cannot be denied that this accounts for many of the great American family fortunes accumulated during the first stage of industrialism. The personal rewards were enormous, but in many cases the compensatory impoverishment of both man and nature was the ultimate social outcome.

This is the lesson of history.

This is the lesson our people must learn now.

Another Lesson from History

There is still another lesson of erosion and sustained yield to be learned from the history of "I" and "We." It is the lesson which will help to clarify the crucial problem: How "free" should the free-enterprise system of America be?

This takes us back to the historical drama of the race for land and wealth, for power and prestige, by men of every migration and every frontier—our American episode being again merely the latest and, to us, the most dramatic of the long procession.

History proves that if a number of people start on an equal basis in any enterprise and are left free to compete— for honors, jobs, land, money, power, prestige, what not— within a short time the few who are shrewder and more vigorous, ambitious and more intelligent, will come out on top with the best jobs, the best land, most of the money and control over their fellows—in short, more of the world's goods and most of the power and the glory. It is also true that some persons combine more effectively than others the traits needed for success in a competitive world. They arrive naturally at the top of the society, becoming the leaders, while the others remain the followers, the men on the street. Throughout the history of civilization—in the case of every tribe, clan, family and nation of which there is any record—this has been true. So we speak of a second "law" in social psychology to accompany the "law" of individual differences; indeed, the first is a corollary of the second.

But the fact of the law, while interesting, is not as important as the effects it brings in its train. Unless society— the "multitude of individuals"—is vigilant and sets up controls on the individual the whole system is likely to be disrupted and millions of people exploited. At least this is what has happened time after time in history. The fundamental problem arises, then, of how to operate an interdependent society of free individuals on the basis of sustaining the yield for a large number. This involves the extent to which the individual submits to control.

The Problem of Control

Throughout history there have always been certain individuals who have fought for control over other individuals. Some fought for wealth and prestige, but it was the control that went with them that was the real prize.

The routes to control were various. For a long time physical prowess or leadership in conquest and empire building or cleverness in the market place or on the rostrum was the chief route. Strength or shrewdness or skill in physical combat, in military maneuvers, in bargaining, in oratory, enabled the individual to gain *political* power and to be elected or to seize the seat of government and govern.

In the long run, governing power went with economic power. For evidence of this one needs only to study the well-documented history of the business families[6] who ruled in Europe from the twelfth century as the doges, counts, kings, queens and cardinals.

The securing of ownership—"That's mine!"—was another principal route to control, especially ownership of vital needs of society—such as the critically indispensable financing power, credit, natural resources, transport or communication agencies. Throughout history there has been a parallelism between the control of government and the ownership of a strategic mountain pass or island, river valley or river junction, a merchant marine, harbors and docks, banks and other credit agencies, mines, indispensable metals, factories with skilled workers, a far-flung system of banks and trading enterprises. As Edward Bellamy put it: "He that owns the things that men must have own the men that must have them."

With the rise of interdependent industrial civilizations came critical changes in the story of "I" and "We." Economic society became more and more one of a money economy. The chief leverage on social control became the financing mechanism—the government treasury (national, state and local) and the private banks and credit agencies. More and more economic society became a complex of corporate enterprises. With the growth of the modern corporation and its wide dissemination of small units of ownership, control became increasingly separated from owner-

---

[6]Two conspicuously important assemblies of the data are in R. H. Tawney's *Religion and the Rise of Capitalism*, Harcourt, Brace and Company, New York, 1926, and Miriam Beard's *A History of the Business Man*, Macmillan, New York, 1938.

ship. All of this resulted in a drastic shift in the sources of and the routes of control and a corresponding shift in the prizes over which men fought in economic and political life.

Perhaps the best way to get at this question of control is to resort again to history, contrasting sharply the characteristics of the simple life of the self-sufficient frontier home with the complex life of the interdependent urban one. For one characteristic after another the contrast is sharp and clear and illuminating to our problem.

The Agrarian Community

The life of the frontier family was simple and only very roughly planned. So far as nature permitted, all crops, animals, textiles, tools, and the like, were produced and consumed on the spot. Providence favoring, there was little overproduction or underconsumption.

All human relations were personal, direct. Decisions were arrived at by face-to-face discussion. There was no unemployment. Owners "worked for" themselves; no intermediary agencies came between the actual production of goods and their consumption. Exchange was chiefly by barter: with "prices" decided upon by face-to-face agreement. There was no interest to pay or other "fixed charges"; there were no mortgages or bonds. Each family had direct control over bargaining power, work and craftsmanship.

On the whole the standard of life was meager, but within the limits of natural bounty it was secure—largely because it was personally planned, operated and controlled.

The Urban Family

All of this was changed drastically during the industrial expansion in the nineteenth century, chiefly by the rise of cities and with them the urban family. Life today has become impersonal, anonymous and hence is unresponsible. The individual is largely ignorant of and indifferent to social problems, except as they seriously encroach upon his personal life. Many decisions on public problems are made by proxy.

From a population of owners and owner-workers we have become largely a population of wage-earning, specialized workers, producing things or parts of things designed by others and to be sold and used at a remote time and place. There is constantly recurring unemployment because of the breakdown of parts of the complex scheme of production and distribution.

But the most drastic change of all has come about in control. In the agrarian economy the farmer and his family exercised, within the limits set by nature, direct and complete control over their work, their physical possessions, their personal and social activities. Today for the preponderance of the people the situation is utterly changed. Unless the individual has an impregnable financial status he exercises very little direct control over his economic security.

Most of the millions who work in power-machine, automatic factories producing quantity goods are machine-tending wage earners, lacking assurance of steady employment. Increasingly, and especially during the past half century, countless new types of agents have come between the worker and his job, his purchasing power, his craft skill. Thus to a considerable degree the owner-worker world has become a wage-employee world, and the era of worker-owners and small business partnerships has given way in large degree to an era of vast integrated corporations. Steadily control shifted from the owner-worker to owner-manufacturer, to promoters of corporations and financing agents with headquarters in a few large cities utterly remote from the industrial production plant.

The dramatic change then has brought two important consequences in its train. The first is that the livelihood of most of the people now depends upon the uninterrupted operation of a fragile interdependent scheme of production, distribution, money and credit. The second is that the individual's direct control over his livelihood has been lost.

The Free Enterpriser's View of It

It is an historical fact that as our simple agrarian community world became a complex industrial one the interpretation given of "freedom" by those we call the "free enterprisers" remained the same. From their own pronouncements, "freedom" to them means essentially what it meant to their fathers in 1870—freedom to invent a new idea, to build a practicable machine or instrument with which to produce man's goods and services, to patent it, to pre-empt it and its emoluments, to manufacture it and put it on the market—but all *without let or hindrance.* This is the American system of free enterprise as they see it—*without let or hindrance.* The ninety and nine among us agree with them so far as all the processes of invention, organization, production and distribution carried on by the individual are concerned. "Leave each individual as free as possible to carry out his own chosen work" is still the platform of most of us. It is mine. Disagreement enters over the "without let or hindrance" provision.

Two real difficulties are encountered. The first is that the glacierlike corporate trend and our mass-production economy have already made it well-nigh impossible for the individual to do these things. Even those so inclined find themselves limited on all sides by technical restrictions and demands. The processes of invention, patenting, manufacturing and marketing are all subjected to mass production and standardization. Moreover, the individual, *as an individual working alone*, can do little or nothing about dissipating the trend or diverting it or directing it.

The second difficulty arises from the lag of social invention behind economic productivity. The fragile economic system does stall badly from time to time, with resultant erosion and wastage of lives—the present cycle of "depression" is the clearest exhibit of it. And thus far neither those who would perpetuate the old form of "free enterprise" nor government leaders have been successful in finding a solution.

How Free Shall Private Enterprise Be Today?

This is the real question before us.

Neither the "free enterprisers" nor the new historians have the answer. The "free enterprisers" merely demand that we continue the old definition of freedom—namely, absence of restraint—and they fight all proposals for social control. They reiterate that freedom means:

Freedom to develop new coal mines, new oil fields, to build and operate new factories, new power stations, dams, what not, irrespective of effects—effects upon the operation of existing plants, upon the employment of workers, upon the national resources.

Freedom to close mines or oil fields, factories, mills, power stations, what not, irrespective of how many human beings are deprived of work and money and life.

Freedom to hire and fire at will.

Freedom to fix wages and determine other economic conditions of labor.

These are but a few examples, but they will serve to illustrate the position: It is freedom without restraint. It is the ancient doctrine of "It's mine! I can do with it as I will!" It is the old view that to keep the American system of "free enterprise" running uninterruptedly we must free it, as Hart puts it, "from hamstringing limitations by government." Thus they give no answer, offer no solution to the tragic recurrences of economic stalemates.

The new historians have no solution either, but they maintain that one will come only if it is based upon a new definition of freedom, one to fit the new conditions of interdependent life. The whole mechanism of national and world production and exchange has changed so drastically, they insist, that new controls must be instituted. They see society not only as complex and technically efficient, but see it on the one hand as potentially abundant and on the other as one in which a third of the existing coal mines could supply all the coal needed by our people, in which there are more oil wells under development than are needed, in which there are more grain fields, cotton fields, fruit fields, citrus-fruit farms, and the like, than are needed even if all our people were supplied with a high standard of living. For such a society, they say, the bounds of freedom and the extents of control must be readjusted.

They do not pretend to know the answer. And they do not indoctrinate young Americans with any special solution. They do, however, insist on presenting the problem to adults and young men and women as one of the critical problems of our day. And they do it by incorporating in the educational program (1) the clear statement of the problem itself, (2) various views which are held about it and (3) the history of recent social trends which will show the directions in which solutions are being worked out.

I have said that they emphatically do not propose to indoctrinate American youth with any particular pet scheme of social control; they have no such scheme. They positively have no "new collective society" to teach. But their stock in trade is the *trends of history*, and they intend to fight to teach these trends in the school—the "free enterprisers" to the contrary notwithstanding.

What "History" Do the New Historians Propose to Teach?

The new historians propose to give the recent history of "I" and "We"—the story of how the American people have actually redefined freedom of enterprise in the past few generations and particularly since 1900. This story of actual social redefinition is the content of their studies. The new history traces for youth the actual story of how controls over "free enterprise" have been developing; they give the facts of community water supplies, fire and health protection, highways and bridges, schools and docks, rivers and harbors, flood control and drought.

The treatment of water supplies will illustrate the data used and the method. They show that in 1800 there was only one publicly owned municipal water supply in the country, two thousand in 1900, and today practically universal ownership and operation of waterworks by American towns and cities. They explain this drastic change from "free enterprise" to actual public ownership and operation—the proved dangers to the public good under the private systems: the long list of fires and epidemics, the interrupted flow of pure and high-pressured water in quantities large enough for great populations, the inability of private agencies to manage the enormous financial and technical requirements of maintenance.

The history of the "socialization" of other community

enterprises is given. Schools are an example. These were formerly all private. Today they are both private and public but predominantly public. I myself favor "freedom of enterprise" in education where it is possible—on the grounds that under it there is greater promise of variation in the life and program of the school; there can be greater experimental trial of new plans; and the varied interests and needs of diverse sectors of the population can be dealt with better. But I welcome the fact that the principle of publicly supported and operated education has been established.

Witness the change in the ownership of power utilities: In the year 1927, of the 4300 municipal power plants 2137 were privately owned and 2198 were publicly owned. Fifty years earlier all were privately owned.

A host of other enterprises, formerly left entirely to private initiative but now either entirely or partly publicly supported and operated, suggest themselves—highways, bridges, parks, recreation grounds, streets, docks, dams, reservoirs, flood control, navigation, irrigation, research and public information and other services in agriculture, industry, health, and the like. A century and a half ago most of these were left to private initiative; today they are chiefly managed by government.

Economists estimate that 30 to 40 per cent of our group life is now socially managed—most of it without objection from individual citizens on the ground that it encroaches on their freedom. Indeed, most of the people recognize that such social control in the long run really gives them greater freedom.

In the new social sciences we give the historical facts of these shifts. Does this mean that we advocate "Communism" . . . that we are "subversive" . . . that we undermine the American system of "free enterprise"? The

American people *actually did these things in a hundred years of history.*[7] Are we not to be allowed to teach history?

There were many activities in which "We"—the people —have attempted to deal with the "rugged individual"— "I"—on a co-operative nonpublic-ownership basis. We discuss these in the school also. For example, we give the century-long history of the labor movement, how workers organized to hold some control over their personal economic bargaining power, wages, hours and conditions of work; how farmers and other groups formed "co-operatives for the production and distribution of their products; how they all went to local, state and national government, asking for help and redress for their grievances; how citizens in towns and cities formed co-operatives to serve as price yardsticks for the buying and selling of consumers' goods; and there were other examples. Is it "subversive to the American way" to tell young people about these things?

We do teach these concepts and historical developments in the new social sciences and are convinced that all who

[7]A fuller treatment of the extension of control by the people over the individual would cite the documented facts of taxation by government and the widening areas of governmental activities. It would give the history of the creation of new departments of government, from the Federal Reserve Board in 1914 to the Farm Board in 1928. It would show how with the coming of the Great Depression the Hoover administration used the office of the national government to do something about prices, maintaining and developing credit, and about giving relief through shoring up private banks, railroads, private businesses, insurance companies, and the like, and how the Roosevelt government continued and extended this policy. The discussion of these and other matters are anathema to many of the "free enterprisers," even though much of the relief given actually helped save and revive their own enterprises and ownership.

prepare educational materials must do so if their program is to be an honest one which will make for intelligent understanding of American life by young Americans.

Is the Story of Advancing Social Control Indoctrination?

In any discussion and controversy over the treatment of these trends in the school the following questions inevitably come up: How far will the advance of "We" over "I" extend? Do you "teach" the answer?

To the first question my answer is: "I don't know—and no one else knows." I so teach in Man and His Changing Society. But I do not ignore the partial answer that the American people have given throughout the years of their history. They have shown clearly that they believe in utilizing both public and private enterprises. They have shown, for example, that they believe in both private and public hospitals, clinics and institutes. In my books I give the historical facts. But note, I do not merely say that the cities and larger towns have a good distribution of public health institutions. I give an all-round total picture of the situation in the whole country, including the fact, for example, that in more than half of the counties of the United States there is no hospital at all and no likelihood of developing a privately owned and administered one because of the lack of financial support. How far will this combination of private and social enterprise in health be extended? I don't know, but I present "the problem"—giving the facts concerning the health of our people, their financial resources, the inequalities of financial support throughout the country, the needs of the people, the new governmental services available, the description of experiments being made to attempt to solve the problem. This is not teaching or preaching the socialization of medicine. It's merely posing a pressing American problem and supplying historical data which may be helpful in leading to a solution.

This kind of issue ramifies into every aspect of our culture—transport, communication, power, merchandising, what not. How far, if at all, should the public, "We," go into these areas? I don't know and so teach in Man and His Changing Society. I urge careful study of the basic trends, movements and factors of American life, both the deep-running, long-time trends as well as the recent current ones. I urge the study of the present conditions and needs of the people. And I go so far as to say that from all these data the American people, through their leaders, can design workable plans for the future. They can carry out those plans, revise them in terms of needs and in the light of experience, even make new plans through the years, trying each one out, testing its effectiveness and readjusting phases of it to accord with changing circumstances.

This is the American way of progress; this is our surest recourse. I teach in the schools that only the cumulation of community and national experience—of co-operative thinking and discussion—can determine to what extent the American system of free enterprise will be "socialized" and into what areas of endeavor government or "We" will not enter.

"MINE EYES HAVE SEEN THE GLORY"

Chapter XIV

THE NEW EDUCATION: IMPLEMENTING DEMOCRACY

*The Focus of the New Education: Young Americans
Working at the American Problem*

As the twenty years have passed I have become convinced that the life and program of the school, like life in the American democracy itself, must be focused and given motive power by a great purpose. Professor Bode said to me recently: "To make democracy work we must make a religion of it!" I feel the same way about making education work. We must give it a driving purpose, so clear and magnetic that thousands of teachers and millions of parents and youth will be energized by it.

I have tried many leads, but none has been so helpful in my own practice as the vision of millions of young Americans working at the American problem. Not a hundred problems, not fifty, not twenty—but one! The American problem! What is it? It is to bring forth on this continent the civilization of abundance, democratic behavior, integrity of expression and appreciation which is now potentially possible.

Throughout the years I have tried to emphasize education's strategic and imperative role in the realization of this potentiality. In the center I see American youth at the task of understanding the American problem, scrutinizing and appraising, year by year, the giant capacity of our continent and the ways and means of making the yield commensurate with the capacity. I see them courageously confronting life as it is actually lived in America, its tragic wastes as well as its splendid achievements. But above all else I see them building enthusiasm for the economic and spiritual abundance which lies across the threshold of the new epoch of modern history now being ushered in.

It is my belief that the hope of making the American way work lies in educating a large body of citizens to understand the forces obstructing the solution of the American problem and to do something about them. This is not to imply that public and private schools of America can do this alone. Education includes far more than the facilities of the schools. The changing climate of opinion is a far more potent instrumentality for learning. But its agencies are partisan in character; they create propagandists, form gangs, parties, marching bands. They do not produce the students of society who are now needed. But the school can provide real leadership in the study of society and society's problems. Indeed, its function is the development of sensitive, clearheaded, fearless and confident young men and women who will understand American life and be determined to build a magnificent civilization for themselves and their children.

What does this mean? It means building a new kind of "school" for human beings of all ages, dedicated to the democratic way of life.

EDUCATION TO IMPLEMENT DEMOCRACY

Two Sovereignties

Democracy! our greatest resource and possession. Just what is democracy? Certainly at the very center of it is the individual we have been talking so much about. Perhaps it would be more correct to say that it is, in essence, two individuals living together as equals. Not as equals in strength, energy, height or other anthropometric traits. Not as equals in intelligence—verbal, mechanical, social or any other variety. Not as equals in esthetic sensitivity or creativeness. But as two equal sovereign personalities in the confederation known as society.

Two sovereign personalities:

Each insisting on the integrity of his own self but implicitly accepting the integrity of his neighbor.

Each a believer in the validity of his own philosophy but deeply admiring the authentic inner truth in every other one.

Each inflexibly determined to be happy, to prevent intrusion upon the sacred continuity of his own inner life, convinced that nothing outside himself can destroy his belief in the worth of his own life.

Each possessing deep-rooted belief in the necessity of frequent communion with others and recognizing the necessity for frank, glad compromise, sufficient to maintain happy relations with others.

Each prizing his freedoms but not infringing upon those of his neighbor.

Each using creative imagination and stating himself in his own unique way.

Each fostering a way of living in which each man, woman and child is free to grow to the finest possibilities that are in him.

Each having a profound interest in his neighbor and developing skill in collaborating with him on the basis of reason and understanding.

Each building habits of self-control and moderation in all phases of life.

Each singing and believing that "a man's a man for a' that"—

no matter what his property, his skin color, his race, his nationality, his religion.

Each a person of responsibility, of moral courage, of honesty and fair play.

These are to me important criteria of democracy. They can be summed up in one concept—sovereign personalities binding themselves together in that union which will preserve the greatest personal sovereignty of each. But this is really the crux again! It is the reconciliation of "I" and "We."

Education's implementation of democracy requires that youth be practiced in living in these ways. Is it possible today?

Yes, if we lift ourselves out of the lethargy either of indifference or defeatism! No, if we appease or drift!

But heroic measures will be required to achieve this, for education confronts a battle.

Resources with Which Education Can Implement Democracy and Help Build a New Day

In order that education may be molded into a powerful instrument to implement democracy no less than three resources are needed: dynamic motive power, that is, a religious fervor for the battle; intellectual and emotional weapons—the "stuff" with which to fight; creative outlook and technical competence.

These are the makings of educational reconstruction. Do we have them? Yes! Thank heaven we need not fight with awkward hands and empty heads. There are weapons—powerful ones, tempered in the white heat of the forge of our times.

The Motive Power

As for the motive power, it springs first from our deep-seated "I" traits, fostered through three hundred years of practice. Perhaps no other people in the world have the "Let-me-be-the-one-to-do-what-is-done" idea ingrained in them so deeply and dynamically as the Americans. Our people have experienced our own kind of democracy so deeply that the defense of "keep off each other and keep each other off" has, for all practical purposes, become "socially instinctive." That, indeed, is what we mean when we say "the 'instincts' of the Americans are for democracy, and they'll fight to defend it." They feel it deeply, though most of them could not expound the abstract concept in words. As Morris used to put it, "they know by their feelings what they want." That they want their American brand of freedom and that they will fight to keep it have been clearly shown by the nationwide shift in temper within two weeks after the fall of France in June 1940, from an "isolationist" mood to hearty approval of total defense preparation. They were not thinking merely of bombs dropping on their homes when they sanctioned the new armament budget. They could picture America a world of slaves stripped of their freedom. They could see *gleischaltung* and the terror sweeping through the land. In the offices of newspapers all over the country, from the metropolitan daily to the village and county weekly, the editors' pens proclaimed the preciousness of American democracy.

Certain it is that the American people are developing a fervor that gives promise of enabling them to battle for the preservation of democracy.

Three Weapons with Which to Fight

Equally certain it is that we don't have to start from scratch. Powerful intellectual and emotional weapons abound on every hand. Expressed in the terms of the academy, they are: (1) a new sociology, (2) a new psychology, (3) a new creative outlook and way of working.

1. A New Knowledge of Society

As for the intellectual and emotional stuff with which to build a new education, we have the knowledge which has cumulated in a half century of research on several frontiers of thought and feeling. The social frontier provides us with the realistic concepts of the economic-social-political system; the personal frontier, with the biological and psychological orientation to the living creature, and from the esthetic frontier we get the data of the creative and appreciative acts. With all of these resources we can begin to build a magnificent school, one that will really implement democracy.

My story has already shown that a new sociology of American life and world cultures is now available. No more need be said here than that we must take this knowledge of society and build new understanding with it. But we must do it quickly. We shall be delinquent if we fail to turn this knowledge and mood into a powerful democratic instrument. We shall be denying Veblen, Turner, Thomas, Robinson, Beard, Dewey, Boas and their brilliant and profound company if we fail to meet this imperative need! Now is the time to build, not a classics-centered school, but a truly society-centered as well as a child-centered school. If we succeed we shall produce a generation of young

Americans who can proudly and confidently contribute to the building of a great culture.

2. A New Psychology of the Living Creature

From time to time I have referred to the revolutionary changes in the life and outlook of our people during the past fifty years, applicable both to our more cultivated people and to the so-called men on the street. Perhaps no change was more far-reaching than that in their outlook concerning man's nature and behavior. In academic parlance we say that a new "psychology" developed. It was the fused results of the brilliant work of intuition and dogged scientific documentation of several thousand creative workers on all of the frontiers: the scientific students in the natural sciences—the students of evolution; the laboratory physiologists; the students of animal learning; the laboratory psychologists; the students of the social scene, including philosophers, sociologists, anthropologists, social psychologists, human geographers, historians, economists and political scientists, and finally, profound and creative artists and artist-teachers.

The seeds of this new orientation to living creatures—human beings, animals and plants—had originally been sowed before the turn into the nineteenth century; its soil was nourished in a century of exploration by all these trail blazers; it flowered and came to fruition in our imaginative and creative period of the Great Transition. Today an intelligent and intelligible program of education can be founded on it, for its validity has been tested and proved.

The shift in mood and outlook constituted nothing less than a revolution in orientation toward living beings. Throughout most of the nineteenth century a mechanical and "atomistic" view of human nature and behavior gripped most "educated" men—those who studied human and other living beings as well as those who worked with "the rocks." Indeed, by the close of the nineteenth century the primary concepts of the physical sciences, with a complete adherence to a mechanical outlook, were generally accepted and increasingly were being carried over into the natural and social sciences. The scientific outlook and method of work, with its systematic assembling and classifying of quantitatively measured data, had developed through several hundred years of analysis in astronomy, physics and chemistry and steadily extended further and further into the field of natural traits. Thus the psychologists, as they built their "science" after 1890, surrendered to the mechanistic outlook; so did the educationists as they built their technology after 1905. Speaking as one who lived in the technological matrix and for ten years was one of the most active exponents of the point of view, I believe that as late as the beginning of the Long Armistice most of the educationists were still basing their work on it. In doing so they made implicitly two assumptions:

That human nature is mechanical and not organic; that human personality can be thought of as an "assembly" of parts —bony frame, muscles, nervous system, and the like.

That these personality "traits" can be taken apart one from another and measured and evaluated by the statistical methods of averages, dispersion and correlation; that, separated, they can be trained (that is, educated), remeasured, retrained, and the like, and by some (unknown) process put together again into a complex human being. The school and college program of the entire literate world has been developed on the basis of this conception.

This brief statement of assumptions is enough to indicate the character of the point of view taken toward human nature—namely, that it was "mechanism" rather than "organism." Throughout the nineteenth century and in the early years of our twentieth century mechanism was the popular god.

The development of sound insight concerning growing living things was further retarded because these concepts of mechanistic science were fused with those of an animistic theology. As Thorstein Veblen said of the outlook that gripped the whole intellectual world as late as 1880, the central axiom of the "conjectural history" of the times was an "uncritical natural law . . . which coerces the course of events." The statements of natural law by the college professors of "natural" philosophy were marked by an obsession in "order," in predestined forms. The uniformities of nature were seen as "final causes," a natural or normal order, a teleological order arranged by an unseen hand. This, as Veblen described what was going on around him in the universities, was the "received tradition."

Thus social scientists and artists, as well as psychologists and biologists, were unable to break away from the deeply rooted mechanistic and theological concepts and get down to the very organic foundations of human living and of the new industrial society.

The Transition from Mechanism to Organism

Nevertheless, throughout the nineteenth century pioneers in the infant "organic" sciences were doggedly but quietly assembling the makings of a totally different outlook. By the 1850s important but relatively unnoticed events were reported in the medical press of Europe. Even at the moment of the publication of Darwin's *Origin of the Species* word was spreading of new discoveries and theories concerning the generalizing functions of the endocrine glands. In the next half century and especially after 1900,

largely owing to the work of a growing group of physiologists—of which the Russian Pavlov, the British Sherrington and the American Cannon were later leaders—a body
of scientific evidence was cumulating to establish what is
generally known now as the "integration principle"—that
"the organism responds as a unitary whole." It was established, to name single examples, that changes in the
ductless glands produced corresponding alterations in the
organism as a whole; that under certain drastic changes in
glandular material death resulted and that under others
debilitation or marked alterations in the body ensued. Cannon's group documented the inextricable fusion of the
human being's emotions and his physiology and showed
that direct relations exist, for example, between man's states
of anger, rage, fear, pain, what not, and the action of his
digestive system. The integrative action of the nervous
system, the "mass action" of the total individual, was established by the work of Sherrington, Coghill and others.
Increasingly after 1910 physiologists came to adopt the
concept of integration as the very basis of their interpretation of human behavior.

As Professor Haldane described the shift in outlook, such
processes as "secretion, absorption, growth, nervous excita-
tion, muscular contraction, were treated formally as if
each were an isolable, physical or chemical process, instead
of being what it is, one side of a many-sided metabolic activity of which the different sides are indissolubly associated." Thus the new view was organic, "organismic,"
in contradistinction to the mechanistic view of our fathers.
It held that both in structure and in behavior the human
being is a whole, an integrated organism making unified
integrated responses.

Slowly after 1900 and quickly in the years of the Long
Armistice the shift in mood and method came into the work

of all the "organic" sciences. Mechanistic views steadily
gave way to organic ones; "organism" ousted "mechanism"
in the study and interpretation of living creatures. The concept of the new "integration principle" was firmly established. The mechanical, "specific" view was supplanted by
a view of the human being as a generalizing being.

It can fairly be said that today the organic outlook has
come to pervade the whole creative mind of America—
gripping the social scientists, the philosophers, the students
of animal learning and the leaders of all "schools" of
thought in psychology—including the Gestaltists, the Behaviorists, Dewey and his followers, Woodworth and the
dynamic psychologists, the social psychologists and others.

This, then, is the first great psychological idea:

1. Each human act is integrative, not additive, the organism
acting and growing as a whole . . . *the scientific principle
of integration.*

Other Great Psychological Ideas

Meanwhile other "ideas that rule the world" had been
intriguing the minds of those who were breaking away
from the old mechanistic, formal education. One was the
concept of "growth." Formerly, as Dewey pointed out,
growing was thought of as something "completed in odd
moments"; the new view held that all organisms, all living
creatures—children, plants, animals, as well as the communities of men—must be thought of as growing, as the
physiologists said, "from small but whole beginnings."
And, quoting Dewey again: "Since growth is characteristic
of life, education is all one with growing." Slowly sensing
this principle after the beginning of the twentieth century,
thousands of artist-teachers developed new programs of
study based upon it. They created new free-lance "Schools
of Living."

If the "organic" principle is the first foundational idea for a new education, here, then, was another:

2. The living creature seen as a growing organism, evolving, maturing from small but whole beginnings . . . *the concept of growth.*

In the half century just past a third important idea took root in the minds of imaginative psychologists and teachers carrying on laboratory and classroom investigations and making day-by-day observations of human behavior. This is the concept that meanings are built up through active experience, not through some hocus-pocus of passive absorption, and that knowing comes through the active response of the individual. James said in his great *Principles of Psychology* in 1890: "Experience is never yours merely as it comes to you; facts are never mere data; they are data to which you *respond;* your experience is constantly transformed by your *deeds.*" James had the concept, but it is largely because of Dewey's study and writing, the "intuitive" insight of countless artist-teachers and the "scientific" analyses of laboratory workers that we can state today a whole new conception of how the human mind "gets meaning":

3. The living creature is dynamic, always characterized by active movement, thus learning is reacting, making responses (as likewise is the building of meaning, of intelligence, of skill, what not) . . . *the concept of dynamic response.*

During the same years several "schools" of new psychology, aided by the theories and logic of the philosophers

in their libraries and their perception of the foundational
role of the scientific method, built a new conception of
thinking, especially that type called problem solving and
generalization:

4. Man thoughtfully is a generalizing being . . . that central
to every response is the perception of the relationships between parts of the whole situation . . . that the meaning
of any phase is determined by such relations . . . hence
that continuous education in seeing relations, in generalization, in problem solving, is basic . . . *the concept of
generalization.*

This is, of course, the corollary of the idea that the organism responds as a whole; a mechanism cannot generalize.
Thus another foundation idea was added to the intellectual
structure of the new education.

The four ideas just stated constitute less than half of
the total discovery of concepts on the psychological and
other frontiers during the past fifty years of research. I outline a few of the others briefly and remind the reader that
in the building of our new education they are equal to the
others in foundational importance.

There is, for example, the concept of purpose which
serves as the individual's primary drive to bring about the
appropriate organization of his meanings, attitudes and
habits. Summed up, it is:

5. The living creature is primarily a goal-seeking organism,
his behavior determined by his purposes, by his attempt to
satisfy his needs . . . ends and means are continuous,
unified . . . *the concept of purpose.*

Two others we have already referred to in the treatment of the psychology of consent[1]—self and personality and the stereotype. Put briefly again, they are:

6. By the process of interaction between the individual and his environment the self is formed, egocentric and defensive, the product of learning . . . *the concept of self and personality*.

7. The individual learns to adjust to his world by patterns of behavior which have been selected and stereotyped for him by the culture . . . *the concept of the stereotype*.

The role of habit has long been in the center of the psychologist's thinking; indeed, it domineered over the ideas of the mechanists of the nineteenth century. But as the organic point of view obtained wider and wider acceptance, habit forming came into a new and different perspective, dull, verbatim repetition giving way to purposeful, planned recurrence. Thus the eighth idea can be stated:

8. Indispensable technical competence in behavior (intellectual, social, manual and other physical skills) is furthered by recurrence of learning situations in which settings are varied and marked by purposive intention to learn . . . *the new concept of habit*.

Another idea central to the ways scientists and speculative philosophers as well as artists work will be discussed at great length in the final chapter of this book. It is the concept of the creative act. Briefly stated, it is:

9. Integrity of expression requires: originally imagined con-

[1]See pp. 224–239.

ceptions, "clarity of perception" and technically competent objectifying of imagined conceptions . . . *the concept of the creative act.*

★ ★ ★

Perhaps the one great idea running through the whole changing psychology is the new concept of self-balance:

10. The delicate, highly differentiated living creature, continuously beset by the danger of instability, is equipped with sensitive means of self-regulation . . . *the concept of self-balancing.*

So much for the key concepts of the new outlook. Still others could be stated, and these could be phrased in other ways. But the ten here given constitute in large measure the intellectual framework of the organic approach to the problem of educating personality.

3. *The Creative Outlook and Way of Working*

Because of the ominous nature of the world drama and our own bewildering domestic problems, never before have we had a more imminent need for social invention and a new strategy of social action than in the 1940s. From the standpoint of the creative effort demanded of us today, we can truly say that this is Armageddon.

Have we resources in imagination and power of original design to meet the demands on us? We have! The half century we have called the Great Transition constitutes the most creative period in American history. The swift change in every phase of the culture, the periodic stalling of the economic system, the menacing threats from authoritarians within our midst and the recent danger of frontal attacks by bullies from abroad—all have served as compelling stimuli to the tense gathering of ourselves together for creative and vigorous effort. In this case necessity actually has been the mother of invention. We live in the midst of a great conflict in ideas and a warring climate of opinions as well as a brutal clash of arms, but our social atmosphere is hospitable to imagination.

Again I say we are not starting from scratch, as will be shown clearly in the next chapter. Creative workers are vigorously active on new frontiers in every section of our country and in every medium of expression: social engineers, scientists, architects, industrial designers, artists in community reconstruction, novelists, poets, essayists, painters, dancers, sculptors, photographers, artist-teachers, experts in government, in industry and agriculture, in forestry and mining. Moreover, our creative resources include the great research and planning institutions and services—schools, colleges and universities, art institutes and institutes of research in such fields as economics, social welfare, education, medicine, public health and housing.

With such resources in spirit and ability America can now build a great civilization.

A New Education Was Bound to Come in Our Times

Given the brave brigade of thousands of scientific and poetic workers of the past seventy-five years great reconstructive changes in American life were inevitable. Given the new frontiers—technological and social, psychological and philosophical, cultural and esthetic—dynamic human beings were bound to emerge who would create a hunger for a new world which would guarantee America's aspirations for the good life.

And—just as the workers on all these fronts are now showing that they will not permit America to become a vassal state to totalitarianism, just as the ten great army

corps of brilliant and dogged frontier students and artists
are proclaiming that they are not and will not be content
to live in a niggardly poverty while surrounded with the
makings of an abundant civilization—so, too, the collective
voice of the students of the new sociology, the new bi-
ology, the new psychology and the new esthetics has already begun to shake the old and inadequate out of our
educational system and to lead to the building of a new
school to implement democracy. Nothing save a major cultural catastrophe can now stop its progressive advance. It
was utterly inevitable that workers in education would find
the vast library of documented data produced on the other
frontiers and use it in the systematic reconstruction of the
schools.

Schools of Formal Literacy

In fact, throughout the entire period of swift expansion,
1850 to 1900, the building of the physical structure of a
national regimented school system paralleled the spectacular development of such other parts of the culture as the
corporate industries and great cities. America and the
Western world was actually made 95 per cent literate in
less than a century of school building. Mass schooling for
literacy actually kept pace with industrialization and ur-
banization; whereas in 1870 there were only twenty-six
organized city systems with superintendents of schools, in
1890 the United States Commission of Education reported
twenty-nine hundred! It was a breath-taking achievement,
considering all the parallel tasks of designing and erecting
new schoolhouses, of finding and training teachers, and
the like.

Bearing these difficulties in mind and the actual achievement of almost universal literacy, one becomes less ready to
condemn our fathers for setting up a formal regimented

scheme of education, with children herded into huge classes and taught by *memoriter*-recitational methods. But the fact is that from the factory education of Lancaster's monitorial schools of 1805 and the Quincy type of central community graded school of 1847, straight through the standardized graded school scheme of the 1890s and early 1900s, mass education took form. For over a hundred years in the towns behind the moving frontier, twenty, forty, sixty, children were taught in grade groups by a single teacher.

The subject matter of education was a patchwork of school subjects—reading, writing, arithmetic, history, geography, science, algebra, geometry, Latin, Greek, what not; and the textbooks—readers, arithmetics, language books, spellers, geographies, histories—were all designed, numbered and catalogued to fit the compartments of age and grade. The books themselves were prepared by university professors and their younger assistants—the only ones equipped to undertake the task—and their organization of content followed closely the compartments and ideas of the academic research in which they happened to be engaged. Because they knew little of child interests and needs and capacities, the program of studies was, when measured in terms of child growth and the development of understanding, one of narrow and relatively nonuseful school subjects.

A "rigid procrustean bed of grades" was set up in which four conceptions of education ruled the minds of teachers and administrators:

That education is what takes place in the school five hours a day, aloof from the community and national life which created it; being educated and going to school are synonymous.

That education is something you do before entering your life's work. It is preparation for life. For some children this preparation lasts only six or eight years; for others, twelve; for

the select few, from sixteen to eighteen or more. For all it is a
getting ready, not a doing now.

That education is the acquisition of skill in the use of words,
mathematical signs, and the like.

That the curriculum—the life and program of the school—
consists of a body of facts and principles which man has discovered and which his children will learn in the formal school.

Administrators Tried to Reform the School by Tinkering with the Subject Curriculum

By 1890 school administrators were recognizing that the
graded system was not working well. It was getting out
of hand, becoming a complicated machine difficult to manage. Classes were too large. Financial support for the maintenance of the schools was inadequate. The classification
of children by chronological age with promotions once or
twice a year was proving unsound.

Confronting these and other difficult conditions and
sensing the need for taking into account differences in
ability to learn, superintendents tried to solve the problem
by tinkering with administrative rearrangements. Efforts
were made to discover better ways to classify the pupils.
Children of approximate ability were placed in the same
study groups, with adjustments of curriculum materials
made in terms of individual ability—richer content for the
brighter pupils and simpler for the more limited. From
Preston Search in the 1880s and Frederick L. Burk in the
1890s to Carleton Washburne after 1919 attempts were
made to individualize the school subjects. New grade organizations were tried—6-6, 6-3-3 or another plan instead
of the standard 8-4 division. Children were promoted from
one grade to another more frequently. Marking and testing systems were revised. The school housing problem was
worked at. More attention was paid to building incentives

for better work. Better supervision of study was provided.

But even with these hectic efforts the total accomplishment was little more than tinkering at rearrangement. Not once did the schools catch up with the content of the social scene. A disheartening twofold gap between the program of the school and adult society on the one hand, and between the program and the needs of the children on the other, remained. Even in our own times only a few new schools have succeeded in partly closing this gap.

But—a New Education Was in the Making

During the very years when the administrators were thus rearranging the superficies of the graded school a few scattered scientifically minded technologists were working in their laboratories and a few equally isolated pioneer artists of education were carrying on thrilling adventures with children in new types of schools. In fact, their work illustrates well the rebellious and improvising nature of the whole of our times. Some of them were definitely influenced in the later 1800s by the Europeans; Pestalozzian, Froebelian and Herbartian ideas were discussed, and some applications of their theories were brought into American schools. As a consequence of the administrators' tinkering and the improvisation of these pioneers in education we know much about what to do and what not to do in building a great democratic program of education out of the new resources.

But there were two groups of researchers and experimenters which affected today's education more than all the others; these were the two I mentioned in the account of the Lincoln School—the society-centered and child-centered workers. Each has a history of more than thirty years in practical work, and each has antecedents covering a period of a generation before that.

1. The Society-Centered Schools

The trend known as the scientific movement in education began in the work of such men as Edward L. Thorndike shortly after 1900 at Teachers College and Charles H. Judd at the University of Chicago after 1909. In those days education was merely the latest infant of the technologies into which the elements of the scientific method were spreading. While aspiring to be considered a science, education was in reality no more than an art and a technology, making use of the primary concepts of the psychological and sociological sciences as these were developed.

The philosophy and method of the "scientific methodists," a name I gave them at Lincoln, can be seen from the twofold nature of their work—the making of quantitative studies of school subjects in the standard curriculum (while accepting the basic philosophy underlying it) and the making of job analyses of the facts, principles and skills more needed and used by human beings in everyday life. These tasks were done through measurement, tabular classification and statistical methods.[2]

A broad range of facts were tabulated; for example, those dealing with the community and the school population, age-grade census, attendance, size and grouping of classes, promotion, the record of success and failure, costs, operational management, buildings, what not. During the

[2] Fifteen years ago while in the midst of the intellectual somersaults which pushed me out from the technological frontier to the other, I prepared quite a full history of this movement. See Part I, "Foundations of Curriculum Making," of the twenty-sixth yearbook of the National Society for the Study of Education; also my later statement in Chapter X, "Curriculum Construction and the Scientific Study of Education" in *American Life and the School Curriculum.*

1910s efforts were spent largely on the design and use of standardized tests and the statistical scrutiny of the content of textbooks and courses of study. Slowly the measurers extended their techniques from an analysis of what is taught in the school to what should be taught, using primarily the criterion of social use. The general basic theory was that those facts, ideas and skills which are actually used by a considerable part of the general population were the ones to be taught in the schools. Meager beginnings were made toward determining the problems of American life, but this work did not get beyond the tabulation of formal areas of study into which college and school textbooks in government, economics, sociology, and the like, were divided.

My own group at Lincoln in the 1920s departed somewhat from the limited practices of these "scientific methodists." We used analysis but carried it into the study of the entire culture and set ourselves to the tasks of preparing a comprehensive portrait of American and world industrial civilization and introducing it into American schools on a large scale. The general testing movement advanced; a comprehensive study of school administration developed, and a host of scientific curriculum and learning studies made in the sciences, humanities, arts, languages and mathematics. That these brought greatly improved study materials into elementary and secondary schools cannot be doubted. But actually the bulk of our schools continued to be formal and subject centered; the high schools remained classics centered (linguistics and mathematics took two thirds of the entire curriculum). Democracy was given lip service, but the institution of American education generally was authoritarian in character.

I link the so-called scientific group of educationists with those who led and carried on the conventional classical

program, though I know that there were important differences between them. I do so because, until the past few
years, they were essentially one in general spirit and outlook and methods of work. They both centered attention
on some phase of society rather than on the child—the
measurers by tabulating man's more superficial social activities directly, the classicists by sticking to the book
record of man's social heritage and insisting on getting it
learned in the school. Both reflected a fairly mechanistic
psychology, tending to neglect the creative process and to
build appreciation solely by listening and observing. Both
gave a large amount of time in the school to memorizing
facts and mastering minimum essential skills. Both tended
to concentrate on linguistics, mathematics and physical
sciences and to neglect the social sciences and the arts.

I worked twelve to fourteen years of the past thirty with
the tabulating wing of the social-centered group. And
through practically all of the time up to 1925 (for most
of these workers through most of the next decade) we
made very little use of the magnificent new materials developing on other creative frontiers. Certainly the workers
in the mass schools made little use of the foundations of
the new sociology; the creative arts were almost totally
ignored. As for psychology, they failed definitely to in-
corporate most of the ten foundational concepts to which
I have just referred. The purposes and interests of the
young people and the concepts of personality, growth,
balance and integration were minimized. The spirit of the
"recitation" was verbatim habit formation and was marked
by passive acquisition rather than activity and problem
solving. And, I am confident, the educational conceptions
which gripped the administrators and teachers in these
mass schools greatly enslaved the scientific, society-centered group as well.

Yet those who are trying to build a new education today are profiting greatly from the studies made by the whole generation of these workers. The development of the new school is enhanced especially by four contributions they made:

1. The idea that the curriculum should be built from the findings of careful analysis of social activities and needs.
2. New types of programs of study and new organizations of materials.
3. New textbooks based directly upon the results of social analysis.
4. A few practicable tests and scales with which to diagnose and improve the learning situations and procedures of the schools.

2. The Child-Centered Schools

The chief impetus to the building of a new education, however, came from outside the formal schools altogether. It was the efforts of intelligent "upper-middle-class" parents in various parts of the country to provide good schools for their children. Indeed, the public-school systems had barely been set up when groups of sensitive parents were organizing and collaborating with creative schoolmasters and -mistresses in starting scattered schools of their own. The first really historic instance of educational reconstruction took place in the little Massachusetts town of Quincy, home of the Adams family. There for five years, 1875 to 1880, a far-seeing president of the school board, Charles Francis Adams, sponsored and encouraged America's first experimentalist to build child-centered schools. This was Colonel Francis W. Parker, distinguished federal army officer, graduate of the University of Berlin, superintendent of schools at Quincy from 1875 to 1880 and builder of the (Chicago) Cook County Normal School, 1883–1901.

At the Quincy and the Chicago institutions his educational program was centered on the active lives of young people; there was less emphasis on memorization of isolated facts and more study of actual life through direct, firsthand observation and experience. Colonel Parker's were the first truly child-centered schools.

Although there was a good deal of educational ferment under the leadership of a few scattered administrators and such college leaders as Charles W. Eliot of Harvard and William Rainey Harper of Chicago, it was not until 1896 that another really important child-centered school came into existence. A group of Chicago parents, lay citizens as well as professors in the University of Chicago, started a little laboratory school in the home of and under the direction of John Dewey and his wife, Alice Chipman Dewey. In 1901 this little school was merged with another to form the Laboratory School of the University of Chicago's School of Education. Colonel Parker became its first director, but after his death the same year Dewey took over until 1904, when he left for Columbia University, never again to take active part in the operation of a school.

The theory behind the life and program of the Laboratory School was very unlike that of the mass school. Dewey himself wrote[3] that he was guided by children's "full spontaneous interests and intentions." He urged that school subjects, like reading, writing and arithmetic, should develop out of children's "life activities" and methods of living and learning, not out of "distinct studies." He maintained that the life of the school should be active, not passive; that the children were to work, not merely to

[3]Dewey's early theories are made clear in such of his books as *The School and Society* (1899), *The Child and the Curriculum* (1902) and many other publications in later years—conspicuously *How We Think* (1909), *Interest and Effort in Education* (1913), his classic *Democracy and Education* (1916) and *Human Nature and Conduct* (1922).

listen. He organized the curriculum around four chief impulses: "the social instinct of the children," "the instinct of making—the constructive impulse," "the expressive instinct—the art instinct" and the "impulse toward inquiry, or finding out things."

At the turn of the century also, in 1901, another group of Chicago citizens, led by Mrs Emmons Blaine, now long regarded as the city's famous benefactor of education, organized the Francis W. Parker School. Flora Cooke, one of Parker's teachers, was made director, and the school enjoyed her splendid leadership until 1936. From the day of its opening the Parker School has been known as one of the pioneering "new" schools.

Up to the World War only a few other "new" schools made their appearance. There were Professor J. L. Meriam's[4] laboratory school at the University of Missouri in 1904 and Mrs Marietta Johnson's Organic School (1907 at Fairhope, Ala.) and her Edgewood School (1913) at Greenwich, Conn.

Beginning in 1912, several new free-lance schools were started—the Play School (1913), later the City and Country School, under Miss Caroline Pratt; Margaret Naumburg's Walden in 1915 and Shady Hill (1915), organized by a group of Harvard professors and Cambridge citizens. Several "Park" schools were opened in various cities.[5] In 1917 Mrs Cora Williams' Institute of Creative Education and the Lincoln School of Teachers College were opened. After that date a dozen or more others appeared.[6]

[4]Then one of the first doctors of philosophy in education from the new Teachers College, Columbia University.

[5]There was the Park School of Baltimore (1912), that of the Moraine Park School of Dayton (1917), started by Arthur E. Morgan and his neighbors.

[6]Stanwood Cobb's Chevy Chase in Washington, D.C. (1919); Sunset Hill, in Kansas City; the Downers Grove (later the Avery Coonley

All were child centered; not one was of the society-centered stamp; not one was a part of a public school system or of a professional college department of education. They were truly "free-lance" schools.

The Progressive Education Association, 1918

In 1918 the leaders of a number of these new schools came together in Washington, D.C., to talk over their mutual interests and to form some kind of union,[1] and out of their discussions came the Progressive Education Association.

For some years this group constituted almost the only clearing house for the interchange of new educational ideas. They met in annual meetings and corresponded vigorously with one another throughout the year. But it was a struggle to keep the association going financially. Had it not been for the untiring efforts of Mr Cobb, Mrs Coonley, Miss Morse and a few others, the young organization, no doubt, would have died. But Mrs Coonley gave liberal grants, and others served without financial reward.

School), near Chicago; Scarborough, near New York; Tower Hill, in Wilmington, Del.; Beaver Country Day (1922), near Boston—to name only a few.

[1] There was Stanwood Cobb, founder of the Chevy Chase School, who became the first president of the little group and who for ten years played a leading part in it; Mrs Marietta Johnson and Miss Lucia Morse; Mrs Avery Coonley, to whom we have referred; Mr Arthur E. Morgan, later of Antioch College and T.V.A. fame; Mr Eugene Randolph Smith, for years head of the Park School of Baltimore and later the director of the Beaver Country Day School, in Brookline, Mass.; Miss Anne E. George, chief proponent in the United States of Mme Montessori; Miss Gertrude Hartman, who soon after became editor of the group's magazine, *Progressive Education;* Mr Morton Snyder and Mr J. M. Dorey, each of whom served at various times as executive secretary of the association. Mr Charles W. Eliot and Mr John Dewey gave the new organization their blessing and successively accepted the title of honorary president. For the story of the formation of the Progressive Education Association see Stanwood Cobb's "Romance of Beginnings" in the January-March, 1929, issue of *Progressive Education.*

Within five years they were issuing their first magazine, called *Progressive Education*.[8]

Groping toward a New Idea: "Schools of Living"

For six to eight years after the Progressive Education Association was formed its leaders stood apart from both the public-school and college administrators and the "scientific" students; indeed, for three decades following the opening of the Deweys' school, each of these three groups went its own way. My own experience in education for thirty years, part of the time following one of these two main lines of development and part of the time another, leads me to differentiate the three this way: (1) the mass public schools as subject centered—with a leaning toward the society centered, the secondary divisions and the college preparatory institutions being addicted to classics, linguistics and the physical sciences; (2) the schools under the technological students of education as society centered, and (3) most of the progressive schools as child centered. I think the three groups stood apart from one another up to the early years of the Great Depression.

I became fairly active in the national work of the progressive schools about 1926–27. Several others with much the same study-of-society interests also began to take active part in the movement about that time.[9]

[8]First under the editorship of Miss Gertrude Hartman and then of Miss Ann Shumaker, formerly my assistant at Lincoln and my collaborator in writing *The Child-Centered School*.

[9]I think the most vigorous was Carleton Washburne, whose work at Winnetka, Ill., I have been close to from 1919 on, when he became superintendent there. I have watched him carry on two decades of important work in making Winnetka's public schools both society centered and child centered and in disseminating his message over America and abroad. I am confident that he has done both more successfully than any other superintendent in the history of American education. It is interesting to note the nature of his own home and school education. He, with Perry

Early Misconceptions of "Freedom"

Now for a further word about the much-discussed child-centered schools. One grave deficiency developed in them. Frequently in rebelling against the regimentation of children they went too far in the other direction, defining freedom as complete "absence of restraint." They took too literally the principle of Cizek and other artist-teachers: "Take off the lid!" In some cases liberty was extended to license. In their first years most of the new schools were too garrulous, noisy and not too clean. While they were active, alive and experimental, the fine balance of freedom and control which makes for child initiative, regard for order and for other personalities, were lacking in many of them.[10]

Smith, director of the North Shore Country Day School near Chicago, and Katherine Taylor, director of Shady Hill, Cambridge, Mass., was one of the first children to attend the original Francis W. Parker School. Later he became an associate of Frederick Burk, California pioneer and individualizer of subject curriculum. As I write he is the vigorous and efficient president of the Progressive Education Association. Thus Carleton's education and career have included both the society-centered and child-centered types.

Willard W. Beatty, president of the association for four years had much the same educational background. He was with Burk in California, later became assistant superintendent with Washburne and then served as superintendent of the progressive Bronxville (New York) schools; he is now director of Indian education. I think Willard Beatty did more than any other single person to make possible the distinctive achievements of the association's commissions since 1935. Others played a very important part in the commissions also—notably W. Carson Ryan, former president of the association; Frederick L. Redefer, executive secretary for the past decade; Wilford Aikin, chairman of the Commission on Relations between School and College; V. T. Thayer, director of the ethical-culture schools, and Caroline Zachry, a former colleague at Lincoln, educator, psychologist and psychiatrist, and active for years in the association's work.

[10]I shall never forget Billy Mearns's halfway serious proposal to my psychological department at a faculty meeting at Lincoln in 1924. Devise, he said, a scale for G.Q. to go along with those for I.Q., E.Q., A.Q., and the like. "Give us a 'garrulous quotient,' to measure the most dominant

I was in and out of a dozen of the child-centered schools after 1915; they did seem to me to have failed to reach the balance between discipline and initiative which we are seeking today for the true "modern school." Indeed, the original Dewey Laboratory School had such a reputation for disorderliness, it led to a thoroughgoing misinterpretation of Dewey's theories. From 1909, when I first went to Millikin, until 1920 at Lincoln I never heard the philosopher spoken of except with derision or scorn—and four of these years (1911–15) were spent with Bagley's group at Illinois and five years (1915–20) with Judd's at Chicago. Even as late as 1927 Miss Shumaker and I, in writing *The Child-Centered School*, devoted four chapters to criticism of the new schools[11]—admitting the "realness" or "lifelikeness" of the new activities but also pointing out the lack of systematic planning and the failure to pay sufficient attention to building ideas, thinking and skill.

The Problem of Motivation: How Make Education "Real"?

No problem has bedeviled parents, administrators and teachers—and the young people themselves—more than that of creating real "Schools of Living," school programs which are based upon real personal and social motivations,

trait of our youngsters." It was true that the children at Lincoln were active and sometimes even noisy and disorderly. Every year for a decade Abraham Flexner lectured to the staff, never failing to preach "order," "good form," "plan." At one long-to-be-remembered meeting, urging us against both regimentation and license, he coined the fine phrase "disciplined initiative."

[11]Chapters VII–X: "Enter Criticism," "More Criticism," "Still More Criticism" and "Criticism Continued." The adverse criticisms were emphatic, but in spite of them our book was attacked by the authoritarians in and out of schools, including the "scientific methodists," on the ground that it sponsored the ultrafree, unplanned atmosphere and program of the child-centered view.

springing from actual interests and values of young people and including, in terms of the maturity of the children, the actual problems of the adult community. The literature of the new schools is filled with discussion of this problem. Parent-teacher associations are becoming concerned about it. The task of finding real motivations for school-work is especially difficult in the large cities of our industrial civilization, although even in small towns and village communities the situation is becoming increasingly perplexing.

Many of the leaders of the newer schools recognized, I think, that the norm of reality was perhaps the premachine life of the American family—especially that on the frontier. Children and youth from the earliest years not only took part in every phase of the work and play of the community, but got their education from it in addition. Under such conditions there was no separate "school," isolated from the home; the home was the school and the actual work and play were the curriculum. Learning was "real," socially motivated. There were of course certain formal "educational" activities, such as those exercised by the church and especially those of wise parents who were interested in "educating" their children and guiding their growth. And there were also grave educational drawbacks, the chief one being that many parents did not regard themselves as obligated to teach the young people. But in a true sense what education there was came in large part from the daily living of the frontier family and community.

This example serves to remind us that for forty years the workers in the new schools have been groping toward creating real "Schools of Living," of sensitive, *guided* living, of *anticipated* as well as current living. To become such a program it is now recognized that education must be designed, certainly not left to the casual circumstances of

childlike whim or chance or to parental or teacher prejudice.

Designed, yes—but from what?

1. Reality from Child Interests

For twenty years I have watched enthusiastic teachers
struggling to answer this question. During the first years the
child-centered group tended to say: The program shall be
designed from the children's interests, from what they
want to do. Certain of the theorists committed themselves
straight out: "The chief task of the teacher is constantly to
build deeper, broader and more permanent interests." The
society-centered group said that it should be designed from
the actual problems and tasks of the children and the adult
community. Thus two quite different answers were given.

In the generation since the Deweys opened their school
the enthusiasts of child-centered education have made great
progress in working toward their goal. In hundreds of class-
rooms and laboratories teachers and scientific investigators
have documented children's activities and learning exercises
around them. De Croly in Europe built the whole program
of his school on the principle of "centers of interest," and
his ideas were spread over the Western world. The wide
reading of Mlle Hamaide's book,[12] which described De
Croly's school, the discussion of his plans at the world
meetings of the New Education Fellowship and of the
Progressive Education Association in America, led many
schools into the same practice. Emphasis on child interest
did bring many constructive changes in the programs of
the newer schools.

But it also tended toward a helter-skelter superficiality
and lack of design. The classics-minded and society-

[12]Hamaide, Amelie: *The De Croly Class*. E. P. Dutton and Company,
New York, 1924.

centered people frequently laughed at it as "lollipops" and scolded it as "sugar-coating" life. And under the recent trend toward orthodoxy in many aspects of American life and the consequent buttressing of the authoritarian outlook, such criticisms of progressive practices have greatly multiplied.[13]

Progressive Education Long in the Improvising Stage

Even by 1926 to 1928, as I have said, certain leaders began to sense the need for "balance" in the school's life and program, to see that the school should be designed *both* from child interest and from social problems, motivating the work around both interest and effort. I do not think that there are many administrators who have consciously designed the entire program of the school on the concepts of the social-esthetic frontiers as well as around personal interests and problems of youth. At least I have not found one in my visits to a dozen of the best schools during the past twenty years. As Lincoln and other schools developed there were men and women of enthusiastic loyalty to each of the two orientations. But there were no leaders who saw the total picture and set out to make a whole organized child-and-society-centered school.

The chief thwarting factor, I think, was the hectic rebellious and improvising nature of American culture during

[13]The most publicized recent one appeared in the *Saturday Evening Post*, written by A. L. Crockett. While admitting that the schools of yesterday were rigid, formal and dry, and that the progressivists did much to humanize the schools and adapt them to children's needs, nevertheless, she says, "The ideals of progressive education are being perverted by the excesses committed in its name." The children "can't spell"; they "can't write in good form"; they "can't stick to anything"; "many progressive educators are preparing their charges for the grim realities of modern life on a diet of lollipops." After a scorching indictment, which reveals very little knowledge of the half century of heroic effort to build really good educational programs, her final plea is for the very balance which is already being struck by the best of the new schools.

the first decade of the Long Armistice. We could not lift ourselves above the community climate of opinion. In only a very limited sense could the schools be truly experimental and given to "scientific research" on the original Dewey standard. The vagueness and fuzziness of thinking among educational leaders in the 1920s and 1930s (and in many places even today) merely reflected the same characteristic in other aspects of the culture—despite the sound educational theories, goals and standards voiced.[14]

2. Reality from Society's Problems

But the 1920s finally passed, and the shock of the Great Depression came. The cumulative effects of the work of socially oriented leaders and the cultural crash of the 1930s jolted many of the schools from the child-centered approach somewhat over toward the society-centered; Messrs Beatty, Washburne, Redefer, Ryan and a few others moved the Progressive Education Association very quickly in that direction. They designed plans for four important commissions,[15] secured many hundreds of thousands of dollars

[14]In a few schools, conspicuously in the Francis. Parker School of Chicago, the statement of philosophy was remarkably well balanced. As early as 1912 Miss Cooke and her faculty stated their principles thus: "Self-actuated work causes the greatest gain in the pupil; training in initiative is a child's great need; in his own interests we often find the educative spirit; freedom, with a balancing responsibility, is the best condition of moral and intellectual growth; real experience with actual material is an essential of learning; opportunity for varied expression is necessary for right education; for purposes of development children must be treated as individuals and not as a group; one of the most effective and wholesome motives of work is the social motive." ("The Social Motive in School Work." *The Yearbook of the Francis W. Parker School*, Vol. I, 1912.)

[15]Commission on the Relation of Secondary School and College, Wilford M. Aikin, Ohio State University, chairman; Commission on the Secondary-School Curriculum, Dr V. T. Thayer of the ethical-culture schools, New York City, chairman; Commission on Human Relations, Dr Alice V. Keliher, chairman; Commission on Educational Freedom, Dr Goodwin Watson, Teachers College, chairman. These commissions

of foundation support for them and turned out a long series of remarkably stimulating reports, studies and books. Meetings of the Progressive Education Association, the Child Study Association, the National Education Association and other organizations steadily reflected the more inclusive outlook.

All this, in turn, slowly changed school programs. One by one the new schools became quieter, more orderly, less garrulous. Correspondingly some of the subject-centered ones became freer. The program of the former became more carefully and systematically planned. They made use of the scientific studies of the social concepts and of the new psychology of learning. They profited greatly from co-operative experimentation and the interschool discussion which the regional meetings of the Progressive Education Association provided, and especially from the careful documentary work of its commissions after 1935.

"O, to Be Self-Balanced for Contingency."

Thus sang the poet—Walt Whitman—three quarters of a century ago. In a hostile world man must not only be balanced for contingency; he must be *self*-balanced. This is the sensitive artist's view of the problem: Order rather than disorder . . . form rather than chaos. Witness Frost's lines:

> Let chaos storm
> Let cloud shapes swarm
> I wait for form.

But the sensitive scientist agrees with the artist. Recall Walter Cannon's great concept, "homeostasis": that the delicate, differentiated living creature continually beset by

have already turned out such books as: *The Family Past and Present, Literature as Exploration, Life and Growth, Do Adolescents Need Parents?*

the danger of instability is equipped and uses sensitive means of *self*-regulation.

Thus from the three creative frontiers—those of the artist, the scientist and the artist-teacher—and from the thinking-feeling men of every century since the great Greeks and the great Chinese comes the affirmation of the need for the self-balanced personality. With it as the central concept we can sum up the concept of a school to implement democracy:

Education is conceived as living—the fullest living of which each individual is capable.

In a very real sense the school is a community. Young people, artist-teachers and parents work together to make its life and program.

The directing concepts of the school are: continuity and completeness of development; balance between interest and effort, freedom and discipline; harmonizing of rigorous thought and creative production; mastery of individual and social skills.

Through such planned individual and group living the school aims to produce persons of integrity and poise, of knowledge and insight, of initiative and resourcefulness. Such persons will be equipped to take their place in the world of which they will be a part.[16]

★　　　　★　　　　★

This is my brief preface to the volume that should be written on the question with which we started this chapter: Can education implement democracy? I am convinced that it cannot if we appease or drift. But I am equally convinced that it can—if we lift ourselves out of the lethargy either of indifference or of defeatism. But, as I said earlier, heroic measures will be required of us, for democracy confronts a battle.

And that takes us to our last problem in this book—the creative ordeal of our people.

[16]These are the words of the brochure of the Walt Whitman School, founded by Louise Krueger in 1937.

Chapter XV

THE CREATIVE ORDEAL

C AN THE AMERICAN PEOPLE create a design for an abundant life? Eventually they can and will. How soon? The immediate future is too uncertain for confident prevision. Certainly if there is a possibility for any people to succeed in our times we have the best chance. But the problem before us appears to be well-nigh overwhelming. I rephrase it in terms of our present national scene and the fragile interdependent world:

Can the Americans, scattered over a two-billion-acre continent, operate a technically efficient and sustained-yield economy and at the same time preserve the democratic principle?

Note carefully the conditions stated in this question:

One hundred and thirty-two million Americans, all individuals and individualists, varying widely in personality, interests, resources and wealth, scattered far apart over a dozen different geographic regions.

A technically efficient economy, one whose power-machine technology is already capable of producing enough "quantity" goods and services to supply every American with a fine way

of life, but at the same time exhibits difficult problems of unemployment.

Note the requirements imposed upon us to produce:

. . . an economic-social system which sustains the yield . . .
which conserves and replenishes natural and human resources
. . . which replants and fertilizes in proportion to its harvest . . . which keeps the technological machinery running
uninterruptedly and efficiently to provide security for all the
nation's workers.

. . . a design for living based upon the democratic principle,
that is, a society which truly operates as a confederation of
sovereign personalities.

The problem before us is clear; that much the depression
has shocked us into understanding. The question is then:
Can we create such a design?

The evidence accumulated by scientific students during
recent years shows that we have the natural resources
and technology, the democratic tradition and the creative
capacity to produce the good life. The American people
now stand on the verge of a possible Golden Day—an era
of physical and spiritual abundance. They are vigorous
and intelligent people, born out of Europe's most progressive stock. Ours is the fifth largest national territory on
earth, lying in the North Temperate Zone, where four
fifths of the earth's inhabitants live, and in the center of
the world's market. It is a magnificent land, with the natural makings of a great civilization—a climate for every need,
topography for every need, mineral resources for every
need. Its people have turned an almost untouched continent
into a giant industrial nation. It has been an astounding
physical achievement. And all of it has been done in a spirit
of democracy which is unique in the whole world. The
fame of our fathers will live on for having produced the
highest standard of living in human history.

Yet we must now confront the fact that we are not actually living in a Golden Day. We have merely come to the verge. We cannot blind ourselves to the fact that many of our natural resources have been savagely squandered, that our tradition of democracy is now being menaced, that our social-economic system is stalled and that our people are bewildered, uncertain which way to turn. Actually we are living in the twelfth year of the Great Depression, with millions of our workers, most of them able and willing, still unemployed—despite the stirring new activity in the production of armaments. Thus we stand at the threshold of the possible Golden Day, halted, challenged by dangerous forces.

I can only conclude that ours is, for the moment at least, a depressed society. This is not a concept uttered casually. By it I mean a society which reveals that the actual distribution of purchasing power to the people in general falls far short of the potential capacity of the system to produce—is, in fact, insufficient to buy the goods necessary to keep the system running at that capacity. It is a society with creative resources, many of which are not being discovered or developed. And, even more serious, its recent history gives little sign that the prolonged state of depression is being relieved.

But I am convinced that we can meet and face these problems and usher in the Golden Day of physical and spiritual abundance.

The Demand for Creative Power

Above all else we must gather all the courage and confidence there is in us and learn to work at the task of design with new concepts commensurate with the problems we face. We must marshal all our imagination to see life in

America clearly and to project against it the life that might be. New ideas must be forthcoming, new social invention, new forms of community design, new forms in the arts and in the crafts. Our central need is creative men and women, creative youth, creative children.

Do our people have the creative capacity demanded of them? For more than fifteen of the years of the Long Armistice I have been seeking the answer to that question. I believe now that both our contemporary life and the history of our culture prove that they have. They revealed it in their conquest and settlement of the continent, in their mechanical inventiveness, in their design and construction of power-machine factories and efficient business enterprises and in their development of new types of community government. In many of the arts of intellectual composition and esthetic design they revealed it—in the native architecture and community planning of the early days, in the brilliant state papers and passionate defenses of liberty at the time of the founding of our nation, in the writing of the literary men of the nineteenth century: Emerson, Whitman, Thoreau and Poe. And although there was an obvious lack of indigenous expression during the latter half of the nineteenth century, the creative trend has appeared again in our times. America's achievements reveal, therefore, that her people have creative capacity to meet the tasks of design.

Man as Master of Effective Methods of Inquiry and Work

The record of history discloses that man's achievements have advanced in two ways. On the one hand he has designed and built nations of communities, operated economic systems of complexity and power; on the other he has suc-

ceeded in stating a portrait of himself and his culture in a
wealth of materials and media—in community design, architecture, literature, music, painting, dance and theater. In
both of these he has fused technological efficiency with the
subtle principles of esthetics.

Man has worked, then, both as scientist-engineer and
as artist and, working thus, has brought into play two
methods of inquiry. For twenty-odd centuries philosophers
have explored these processes, stated them in various ways,
engaged in vigorous controversies over them. A few artists
and scientists also had their say about them. More recently
students of the psychology of the creative process have
gathered the statements together, analyzed and interpreted
them.

Each new adventure with ideas has added its bit of documentation and hence of clarification to the thesis that there
are two methods of inquiry and of work in the building of
industrial culture and in stating and appraising personal life
within it. The first is the method of science—of experimental inquiry, of that kind of thinking called problem
solving. The second is the method of organic awareness,
traditionally but inadequately named "intuition." This is
employed by man working either as scientist, as artist, as
speculative philosopher, as technologist or as man of religion. It is important to recognize that both of these methods of inquiry, while different and serving unique functions
in the creative process, are indispensable in solving our
present problems. A word now about the nature and role
of each of them.

1. The Scientific or Experimental Method of Inquiry

The scientific or experimental method of inquiry has absorbed the imagination of the students of thinking much
more deeply than has the intuitive method; it has been

studied for a longer time and has been phrased more explicitly. Granting that a large amount of spadework had been done in earlier centuries, we owe the clarification of the scientific approach largely to the workers on the philosophical and psychological frontiers during the past six or seven decades. And in this the Americans took a leading part. By 1910 the climate of opinion which had cleared the physical continent of North America had also stated itself in a philosophy called "pragmatism" or "experimentalism." Its originator was Charles Sanders Peirce—scientist, engineer and America's greatest logician; its chief phraser has been John Dewey. Especially through Dewey's efforts over a period of fifty years, the "experimental method of knowing" was described and a suggested outline of thinking as problem solving was sketched. The concept that meaning comes through active response was clarified; the unified character of experience was definitely and voluminously illustrated; the characteristics of a democratic society were stated; fundamental principles of educational reconstruction were phrased, and tentative movements for reconstruction were launched. For much of this intellectual groundwork for an American philosophy, a social program and an educational theory we are indebted to John Dewey.

The psychological heart of the pragmatic outlook and theory was the description of the experimental method of inquiry. The mechanics of the scientific method had long been clear: thinking out hypotheses from the best known data . . . observing accurately . . . experimenting to test the truth of the hypothesis . . . measuring as exactly as possible with scales of equal units . . . assembling a statistically sufficient number of measured facts . . . tabulating, classifying and otherwise treating the data statistically . . . drawing conclusions (new hypotheses), finding scientific "laws" and making predictions. These were the formal steps in the scientific method of working as built up in centuries of trial and error and success.

Central to it are the psychological concepts grasped first by Peirce and passed on to us best by Dewey, especially the concepts of: meaning as arising through active response . . . experience as making and doing . . . thinking defined as "response to the doubtful as such," that is, as solving problems by directly confronting alternatives . . . knowing as the result of tested consequences.

These are the central ideas embraced in the scientific, experimental outlook which came to grip most thinking Americans in our times. That they have made a significant contribution to the building of our civilization there can be no doubt. They created power-machine, straight-line factories, smashed the atom, analyzed the heavenly galaxy and rationalized the American climate of opinion. Motivated by the spirit of individualism, they produced the impressive structure of our present social system, brought into existence the world's highest standard of living. They doubled man's length of life, reduced pain and fatigue, hours of labor and physical slavery, provided a vast variety of leisure activities, ousted superstition from millions of young and alert minds.

It is the success of our thinking men in advancing the scientific method of thought and work that provides the chief conviction that we Americans can solve our baffling problems. But there is still another way of knowing and working which is indispensable to their solution.

More Adventures in Ideas: Other Ways of Knowing

Throughout modern history most thinking men accepted this "experimental" outlook and the definite steps in the process of scientific inquiry unqualifiedly. In recent years our educational institutions—particularly the teachers colleges under the guidance of the pragmatic view—have taught that all situations of life can be met successfully by that kind of thinking called problem solving via the direct confrontation of alternatives. Even the creative act was phrased in terms of this kind of thinking and this kind only. If we would only train people *to think*, said the pragmatists, they would solve all their social problems, straighten out their personal lives, design beautiful buildings, create poignant, powerful music, paint beautiful pictures, write profound and moving poems and energize depressed populations. The experimental method of inquiry, based upon the measured and classified data recorded by the five senses, would, they said, enable men to know all and be all.

★   ★   ★

As for my own attitude on this question, my years of work in engineering and statistical methods served merely to hasten and cement my acceptance of the philosophy of experimentalism, and up to 1923 or 1924 the design and preparation of the pamphlets at Lincoln absorbed so much of my energy and time that there was little left for critical study of the philosophical foundations, basic though they were. Thus I was quite satisfied with the experimental theory so far as I knew it.

But the vista-widening years came. The reading and study of Van Wyck Brooks's *America's Coming of Age* and his *Letters and Leadership* had ruffled my mental complacency a little in 1918. I had read Waldo Frank's *Our America*, most of the seventeen issues of *The Seven Arts* magazine and Randolph Bourne's essays, later gathered together in *The History of a Literary Radical*. In 1924 came the exciting meetings at Fred Howe's School of Opinion on Nantucket Island . . . the long walks and talks with Frank about *Our America* and about Brooks and Bourne . . . the days spent with Max Mertz and Gertrude Drueck, watching their Duncan dancers at work and discussing Isadora's principles, and with Max, listening to his endless talks on Spengler's *Decline of the West*, which had just been translated and set everybody buzzing. I listened to some of the new scientists—the biologist, Conklin, of Princeton and the astronomer, Shapley, of Harvard, for example. I met the psychologist, Everett Dean Martin, of the People's Institute, who was applying psychoanalysis to the behavior of crowds, and Horace Kallen, who lectured to us on individualism. There were long talks with the French publicist, André Siegfried, which led later to meetings at my New York house.

The ensuing winters in New York brought many new personalities and new ideas. I found Alfred Stieglitz' group and his Little Galleries—first "303" in the Anderson and then later, for many years, the "American Place." I met and talked with Stieglitz' painter wife, Georgia O'Keeffe, and John Marin, Marsden Hartley and others. I studied their paintings and Dove's and Stieglitz's photographs and listened to Stieglitz talk on and on. The library of all the frontiers expanded enormously as I was pushed out across the boundary of the social, economic, political regions into the exciting fields of social criticism and the arts—painting, poetry, architecture, the theater and the dance. It was a tremendous new orientation, this discovery of a whole new world of exciting personalities and new ideas.

Beginning in 1930, I made my home in Woodstock, N.Y., one of the oldest art communities in the country. Here contacts with Fagley and Billy Mearns, who had left us at Lincoln in 1925 to join the faculty of New York University, were re-established. Here also had settled several of the young artists who had been stimulated at the turn of the century by Robert Henri and by "The Eight." And here now were living an assembly of a hundred-odd painters, sculptors, writers, designers, illustrators, musicians, museum directors and educators. My years of living in their midst have contributed in an important way to the clarification of the creative process.[1]

Into my classes at Teachers College came artist-teachers from the child-centered schools and from a few creative groups in the public schools. From them I learned as much, I think, about the creative process as it takes place with children as they learned from me about other aspects of the changing civilization. Among these courageous mutants no one had a clearer view and was as articulate about it as Rosabell MacDonald (Mann). For years we have worked together. For three semesters she voluntarily gave her energy and imagination to our new integrative course at Teachers College, the Arts in Education and Life. I think I owe to her more than to any other single person my clarification of the steps in the creative process in the arts.

This is only a tiny glimpse of the personalities and contacts which opened the creative vista to me. Out of it came new ideas and a comprehensive orientation to the philosophy and pschology of man's way of working, especially the creative act.

Perhaps most important of all for me personally were the

---

[1] I cannot hope to mention them all, but among them were James T. Shotwell and his family, J. Donald Adams, Leon Whipple, Alfeo Faggi, Arnold Wiltz, Gene Speicher, Carl Walters, Dorothy Varian, Walter and Emmy Seaton, Georgina and Kaj Klitgaard, Arnold Blanch, Doris Lee, Russell Lee, Charlie Rosen, Edna and Herman More, Jane and Wendell Jones, Hannah and Gene Ludens, Wilna Hervey and Nan Mason, Jack Taylor and André Ruellen, Ned Thatcher, Felix Payant and many others.

discovery and exploration of the ideas of several free-lance social critics outside the universities. The leaders were Randolph Bourne, never known to me personally because of his death in 1919, Waldo Frank and Van Wyck Brooks. Although each gave me something new, Frank's influence through the years has been infinitely more profound. The reading of the poetry, essays and other material of *The Seven Arts*[2] magazine made me aware for the first time that there was ground for questioning the validity of experimentalism (or "pragmatism," to use Charles Peirce's original term) as an all-embracing approach, that it contained part of a fine psychology, but that it really did not provide an adequate foundation for a personal philosophy.

In adventure after adventure on the creative frontiers I discovered that there were those who were sure of other ways of knowing than the experimental or scientific. From Frank-Bourne-Brooks and company came pointed criticism of the pragmatic view. In *Twilight of Idols*[3] Bourne, reacting to Dewey's shift in position upon our entrance into the war, challenged the adequacy of the "pragmatist mind." He said it "gives the air of grappling . . . with a power too big for it." "What I come to," he went on,

[2]What a thrilling company of creative pioneers filled the pages of *The Seven Arts*, under the editor, James Oppenheim, and associate editor, Waldo Frank—critics and poets, painters and philosophers, economists, journalists and dramatists. In its short year-and-a-half life (1916–17) the magazine published the expressive materials of Amy Lowell, Robert Frost, Edgar Lee Masters, Carl Sandburg, Vachel Lindsay, Alfred Kreymborg, Babette Deutsch, Maxwell Bodenheim, Margaret Widdemer, Eugene O'Neill, Lee Simonson, Robert Edmond Jones, Kenneth Macgowan, Marsden Hartley, John Dewey, Bertrand Russell, Van Wyck Brooks, Randolph Bourne and Frank.

[3]Three sources, found in these years, stand out above all others as of philosophy-changing significance: Charles Peirce's articles on "How We Make Our Ideas Clear" in the *Popular Science Monthly* for 1879–80, my first contact with the pragmatic concept of "tested consequences"; Louis Sullivan's *Autobiography of an Idea*, which gave me my first criterion of "form" in the creative act, and Bourne's *Twilight of Idols*.

"is a sense of suddenly being left in the lurch, of suddenly finding that a philosophy upon which I had relied to carry us through no longer works." And:

One has a sense of having come to a sudden, short stop at the end of an intellectual era. In the crisis this philosophy of intelligent control just does not measure up to our needs. What is the root of this inadequacy that is felt so keenly by our restless minds? Van Wyck Brooks has pointed out searchingly the lack of poetic vision in our pragmatist "awakeners." Is there something in these realistic attitudes that works actually against poetic vision, against concern for the quality of life as above machinery of life? Apparently there is. The war has revealed a younger intelligentsia trained up in the pragmatic dispensation, immensely ready for the executive ordering of events, pitifully unprepared for the intellectual interpretation of the idealistic focusing of ends.

The young intellectuals, he said, showed very clearly they were not prepared for the vast task of formulating values; they had only "technical aptitudes." Dewey really meant to base his philosophy on values, but, said Bourne, there was that "unhappy ambiguity . . . as to just how values were created."[4] The American in living out this philosophy, Bourne went on,

has habitually confused results with product and been content with getting somewhere without asking too closely whether it was the desirable place to get. . . . It is now becoming plain that unless you start with the vividest kind of poetic vision, your instrumentalism is likely to land you just where it has landed this younger intelligentsia which is so happily and busily engaged in the national enterprise of war. You must have your vision and you must have your technique.

[4]This point has remained with me to the present day. Instrumentalism (pragmatism) is necessarily a psychology of method, not a statement of objects of allegiance. In generalized form this point served as the center of my critique in *Culture and Education in America.*

Here was confident support of my own questioning of the ultraconsumption of technique to which my colleagues and I in education had given ourselves.

★   ★   ★

Stimulated enormously by the new vision and orientation, I wrote *Culture and Education in America* and published it in 1931. The years since have constituted a decade-long search to get down to the foundations of the psychology of the creative act. To spur me on and to share the year-by-year product I organized a new course at Teachers College which dealt primarily with the problem.[5] The search led along several routes: the methods of children and grownups while they were engaged in various kinds of productive work; the discussion of the process with practicing scientists, poets, painters, designers, social engineers, architects and those working in other media; the endless discussion of it in educational conferences; a good deal of analysis and retrospection concerning my own methods of work, and the reading of "the books" on the creative process. As for the latter, I read everything I could get my hands on which gave promise of bringing clarification of the process. Sheldon Cheney's various books—especially his *Expressionism in Art*, which still seems to me to be the most incisive analysis of the modern expressionist trend—have been tremendously helpful, as have Parrington's three volumes[6] and most of the written words of Louis Sullivan, Walt Whitman, Isadora Duncan and Frank Lloyd Wright.

[5]In the middle 1930s I began to write what has become known in my laboratory as "the big book"; all the other writing is, in a sense, considered preparatory to my *Creative America*, the title of which has been and no doubt will continue to be changed until the manuscript reaches the press. I feel as I write today that this present record, *That Men May Understand*, is really the immediate preface to it.

[6]V. L. Parrington: *Main Currents in American Thought*, Harcourt Brace, New York, 1930.

I have studied the folk poets, Masters, Lindsay and Sand-burg, and what others said about them. I have sought the folk painters, Thomas Benton (and his *An Artist in America*), John Steuart Curry and Grant Wood and the little they had written. I found that Robinson Jeffers and such epic poems as his *Birth of an Age*, Edwin Arlington Robinson and his equally epic writings and the later work of such poets as Millay and MacLeish brought profound revelations of the depths of personal and social life in America and in world cultures. As the years have passed the description and analyses of the creative act steadily enlarged.

2. A Second Creative Method of Inquiry

I am now convinced that the creative human being employs two ways of working—not merely the single "experimental method." There are, I believe, certain situations in which one does not always respond with the direct problem-solving approach; to name one example, obviously one does not employ that attitude and method primarily in all acts of appreciation.

Digging back into the history of other cultures,[7] I have found that for centuries a heterogeneous company of scientists, philosophers, poets, artists and social engineers had also discovered other constituents of the creative process. One had to do with a kind of organic awareness in the human being, which precedes detailed analytic documentation of the scientific kind. It is the gathering together of the whole responding organism—as Waldo Frank put it, using exactly the terminology of the new biologists and psychologists, an awareness by the organism as a whole.

This method of inquiry has been badly named "intu-

[7]Especially while writing *Man at Work: His Arts and Crafts* with Louise Krueger Rugg.

ition"—"badly," I say, because it carries to most people a transcendental, supersensory, supernatural connotation.[8] It is not to be regarded as "mystic" in the supernatural sense. It assumes and is founded on a scientific, "naturalistic" outlook, as set forth in this book. The scientist-philosophers of ideas confirmed the findings of the artists and men of religion with regard to the intuitive approach. They insisted that it sometimes oriented and guided and sometimes supplemented the so-called experimental method. The experimental approach, they felt, depends too exclusively on the verbal and analytic description of the report of the five senses to be trusted alone. While agreeing that the world cannot be properly understood or controlled if the reports of the senses are neglected, they insisted that, used singly and alone, they are not sufficient even to permit the recognition of a problem. As Waldo Frank put it so well:

Reality must be apprehended before the reports of the senses can *make* sense . . . a prehension [to use Whitehead's term] must infuse *the entire process of experience,* qualitatively giving it life.[9]

Feeling as well as intellect enters into the picture; awareness—a *prehension*—arises through some, as yet partly unknown, process of relaxed organic approach. The too-tense concentration on direct confronting and analysis of alternatives appears to shut off needed meanings. Tangential, associational methods of thinking are called into play as the organism as a whole approaches the situation by a kind of emotional flank attack.

From many of my own personal experiences I have become convinced that this other, as yet unnamed, way of

[8]From the first exploration of this idea with the discussion group at Teachers College this connotation was insisted upon by Dr Kilpatrick.

[9]Waldo Frank in *The New Republic,* May 6, 1940, p. 605.

prehending—the "organismic" way—is the real method by which scientific hypotheses are originally drawn from a background of experience. From time to time I asked scientists to tell me *how* they work, to analyze their "creative" acts: "Do you make best headway by the direct head-on collision with your 'problem'?" The invariable response is "No," phrased, of course, in a variety of ways. Also in the drawing of hypotheses to meet complicated social problems the direct process of choosing between set alternatives has been found not to bring the best results.

Descriptions of what happens show the role of flashes of insight that come as from a tangent when one is relaxed. It is as if one is looking at the problem from the side. Sensitive people in the arts, analyzing how appreciation takes place, offer the same interpretation. The essence of the attitude seems to be a gathering together of the self, a mental and emotional synthesis. It is a unitary thing, a fusion of total physiology, emotion, intellect, the result of a consciously willed focusing of one's total energies. Two conditions exist—relaxed receptiveness and critical evaluation. On the one hand there is receptiveness to coming-in impressions, acceptance of the integral thing out there, but also a critical assimilation of it into one's organized experience.

The Creative Act: Man's Need to State Himself

I believe that the task of solving the social problems of the economic-political system, insistent though those are, should not monopolize the energy of the American people. I think that they should work equally hard at the job of creating a society in which each individual can live as a person, in which each can state himself for his own soul's sake, as completely and as well as he can.

Whether naïvely or in a consciously sophisticated way, I

believe that most men have the urge to express themselves
in some form. Throughout recorded history some have
felt the urge so strongly that they have chosen a definite
field of expression as the center of their lifework; they
have made it indeed their vocation. The pageant of history
is a glorious panorama because of men's portraits of themselves—in community design and organization, in government, in architecture, literature, drama, music, graphic and
plastic arts, what not. In every possible medium of expression man has found a way to record himself.

But he has done more than that; he has struggled to understand and describe the process through which the creative man works—"the creative act." In century after century of Western history, but most of all in our own dynamic era, increments of understanding of the process have
been added. Each of the frontiers of creative activity contributed its light, especially those in which the study of
human nature and behavior is the chief task, psychology
and philosophy and the esthetics of the arts.

What do we know about the "creative act"? Sheldon
Cheney described the whole process in six words: It is,
he said, "the formal expression of imagined conceptions."
Here are all the constituents, the foremost of which is
"expression."[10] Expression—man's best statement of his view
of the world. As Oskar Pfister phrases it, it is the portrayal
of "the intrinsic meaning of things . . . the only genuine
reality. . . . The Expressionist . . . creates out of the
depth of things because he knows himself to be in those
depths. To paint out of himself and to paint himself means
to reproduce the intrinsic nature of things." In another

[10]The central concept of the modern trend since the 1880s is Expressionism, in sharp contrast to the earlier Victorian Romantic Impression-
ism on the one hand and photographic Realism on the other.

place he says: "The Expressionist's world is the Expressionist himself as *the* world."

I like to describe the creative process in very homely
words; namely: "I say, competently in the most nearly perfect and complete form, what I see, my unique way." Thus
the first element "to say" means to express, to state—
whether it be to paint, speak, make, build, sing, what not.

But expression of what? It is not just any casual, un-
scrutinized utterance. It is the utterance of one's self, one's
feelings, thoughts, mood, one's view of life—with the best
possible form, with that organization of related elements
that states them most adequately. "The formal expression,"
says Cheney—the portrait of life with the acme of form.
Abbott speaks of each new creation as a "large or small
universe, self-centered in its own integrity and taking form
appropriate to express its inner life.[11] No criterion of the
creative act is more rigorous than that of form. Our articulate students of the psychology of the creative act discovered three good measures of form. My Los Angeles friend,
Louis Danz, in his recent book[12] says: "By form I mean an
expressive organic whole." . . . "Form denotes organization." . . . "*Form is that kind of organization to which
nothing can be added and from which nothing can be
taken.*"[13] The first principle of form, then, is *economy*.

Fifteen years ago in a great book I found a second prin-

[11]"A New Integration for Literature," *Teachers' College Record*,
Vol. XXVII.

[12]Louis Danz: *The Psychologist Looks at Art*, p. 77. Longmans Green,
New York.

[13]Danz goes on to say: "A mathematical definition has form. This is
the definition of a circle: 'A circle is the locus of all points in a plane at
equal distance from a point called the center.' This definition has form.
Nothing can be added to it, and nothing can be taken away. Just like
the circle itself, this definition is an organization which gives fullest expression to its content. Form and content are one indivisible, indissoluble
whole."

ciple—that of functionality. It was Louis Sullivan's *Autobiography of an Idea*.[14] Sullivan taught me to ask about any creative work of man—a building, a poem, a painting, a community, what not: What is it that determines the content and form? Is it the successful use of a classic content or style, the reproduction of the current mode, the employment of standard ornament or decoration? "No," said Sullivan, "it is the function, the product, that it is to serve." "Function determines form." Of every member of a building, of every word in a poem or prose page, of every gesture of the body, of every activity of the new school, the creative designer consciously designing the members of the structure asks: What is this thing to do? What is this beam or column to hold up? Exactly what shade of meaning is this phrase to convey? What mood is this gesture to evoke? What ideas and attitudes is this activity to develop? Of each one he tests: Does this have a function? Does it inevitably belong? Is it needed? Is it indispensable? Can I find something better?

The "idea" that form is determined by its function is, of course, directly related to the principle of economy, for in the truly functional thing there is nothing superfluous, nothing added on, nothing lacking. But there is also the principle of organization; that is, all the elements needed must be included and in their right relationships to give the appropriate expression. Which in turn leads to the principle of unity. All these measures taken together constitute "form," achieved by conscious design.

This is the heart of the creative process.

So much for the first element in the creative act, called "formal expression"; so much for the "I say, competently

[14]Press of the American Institute of Architects, Inc., New York, 1922.

in the most nearly perfect and complete form." But we must explore further into what it is the artist expresses. What does "my unique way" mean? Abbott says that the artist "creates a world that is in actuality his view"; according to Einstein, it is the person's own "simplified and intelligible picture of the world"; to Cheney it is man's "imagined conceptions," "the production of the *imagination* given form."

This phase of the creative act requires a determined effort to grasp *significant relationships*, not merely a docile adoption of insistent, familiar ones. It means getting hold of subtle meanings hidden from casual, superficial observation. To achieve it man as artist must give himself to prolonged concentration, weighing, observing, reflecting, scrutinizing —waiting always until the surface characteristics give way to awareness and comprehension of inner relationships. The thinker describes the ordeal as one of "thinking it through," seeing all the possible interconnections, variations and correlations of ideas; the painter says it is "looking until it burns into my head." The lesson in this for education is clear: we must *educate people to be clear, rather than to be "right."*

THE CREATIVE ORDEAL

Briefly phrased, these are the constituents of the creative process. We know this much about them today only because of the "creative ordeal" which man as expressive person has endured during modern times. And nowhere in the world and in no other period has the struggle of man as artist to express himself been more strikingly illustrated than in America during her short three-hundred-year history. The American has gone, indeed is still going, through the ordeal. Our cultural development seems clearly to have passed through one stage, is advancing steadily through a second and in certain areas seems to be already launched into a third.

Three Stages

The first was the two-century-long period, following the establishment of the original settlements,[15] during which our cultural norms were almost entirely imported from Europe and Britain. I have already made the point[16] that our Long Armistice is itself essentially a measure of the second one, namely, a confused transitional stage or period of rebellion against alien standards, with the slight emergence of partially indigenous improvisations of new forms of expression. The third, if we dare predict a trend from the growing company of creative mutants among us today, is to be one in which native forms of expression will come, steadily multiply in number and mature in truly creative quality—building a culture which will eventually reach a high level of creative production in all areas of life.

Three Questions

A word about each of these stages will throw light upon our present situation. As we review them briefly let us bear in mind three questions which will guide our appraisal of the creative development of our young and transplanted culture:

[15]It is most important to bear in mind that in the building of the first Eastern communities, even throughout the first century, there were many instances of thoroughly indigenous and truly creative expression of our people—nothing imported, nothing copied, nothing superfluous, nothing for the sake of classical tradition. Merely to illustrate, witness: the creative architecture and community planning throughout the entire Atlantic seaboard, the brilliant state papers of the Founding Fathers and the occasional great pronouncements of our early writing men.

[16]See Chapter VI.

First: Are our communities and other forms of social engineering, our architecture, books, music, theater, paintings and other expressions statements of what the men and women who made them have felt and seen of life? Or are they merely imitations of ancient or foreign modes?

Second: How deeply aware are our creative workers? Are their expressions reproductions merely of the surface contours clothed in photographic realism? Or do they pry down to the motivating depths of personal character? Or, still more profoundly, are their interpretations laid in cosmic and universal backgrounds?

Third: How competently executed are the expressions? Do they show signs of having been tested on the rigorous criteria of organic design? Or are the results merely initial and uncensored improvisations?

1 Imitation and Eclecticism of Ancient Classic Forms

Clear understanding and creative portraiture of life in infant America were greatly thwarted from the very beginning—largely because of pressing psychological forces at play upon the people. Of these forces three played especially important roles. The first was the raucous laissez-faire spirit of pre-emption and progress, the lure of comfort, the power and the glory—the din of construction—"Build bigger and better!" The second was the complete psychological devotion of our potentially creative men to the styles and standards of classical culture and to the mother-country norms. I have already made clear the third force, namely, the enslaving compression of an animistic theology and a mechanistic science upon the whole body of our thinking men.

Working against such forces, it is little wonder that for two centuries American expression in the arts was largely

domineered over by British and classical European styles
and standards. Most of the few persons of intelligence and
energy who did succeed in turning their backs on economic
invention, technology and business to devote themselves
to the more sensitive study and portraiture of life in America were unable to put down with integrity their own conceptions of life as it was actually lived here.[17] On the contrary, they recorded a prettified British-European version
of their romantic dreamworld for America. For two centuries almost every potential major creative American—
poet, novelist, architect, painter, "the artists" generally—
copied the ideas, standard styles and themes of Europe instead of creating their own. Almost nobody succeeded in
stating life as it was really lived in America by Americans.
As Emerson complained, our language, customs, letters,
the arts generally, all stemmed from England and Europe
and the classical cultures of the past. Expression, seen in the
whole, was sheer imitation of classic modes and their eclectic assembly into mosaics. The age was, as Sheldon Cheney
put it, one of "pickers and choosers" . . . "cultured re-
peaters of other men's styles."

America's first truly creative American master, Louis H.
Sullivan,[18] denounced the lack of courage and originality in
our architects as follows:

Thus we have now the abounding freedom of eclecticism,
the winning smile of taste, but no architecture. For architecture, be it known, is dead. . . . There is now a dazzling display of merchandise, all imported, excepting, to be sure, our
own cherished colonial, which maintains our Anglo-Saxon

[17]Here I am using two selected paragraphs from my Chapter V of
Democracy and the Curriculum: The Life and Program of the School,
Third Yearbook of the John Dewey Society, with the permission of the
publisher, D. Appleton-Century Company, N.Y.

[18]L. H. Sullivan, Autobiography of an Idea, pp. 325-26.

tradition in its purity. We have Tudor for colleges and residences, Roman for banks and railway stations and libraries—or Greek if you like—some customers prefer the Ionic to the Doric. We have French, English and Italian, Gothic, Classic and Renaissance for churches. In fact, we are prepared to satisfy in any manner of taste. Residences we offer in Italian or Louis Quinze. We make a small charge for alterations and adaptations. Our service we guarantee as exceptional and exclusive. Our importations are direct. We have our own agents abroad.

In every medium of expression the creative process was debased. A climate of imitation of foreign and ancient classic styles was spread over the land. In every field, I say—in architecture, in letters, in painting, in sculpture, in music, the dance, the theater, what not—until our own times. George Santayana, who grew up in it and lifted himself above it, gave it the name that it may never live down—the "Genteel Tradition."

II Our Times: Brilliant Improvisation of Original Forms of Expression

In the 1890s and early 1900s came the end of continental conquest. Steadily the din of expansion subsided. The grip of adoration of things British, European and classical loosened, and those Americans who had imaginative power were able to give themselves to creative thought and expression. The American at last began to stand up and walk alone. At first haltingly and stumbling, but—glory be!—alone. He began to *state himself*, to write, paint, dance, build, what he himself felt as he saw his people. He portrayed the world around him as he saw it his unique way. Thus he imposed on himself the criteria of the creative act: What do I myself feel about life? How deeply aware of it am I? What original forms can I create to express what I feel adequately? How competently can I do it in my chosen medium?

After 1900 a proud original expression began to emerge from an increasing number of creative Americans. Architects asked: How can I build an American house for the American life that is to be lived in it? Poets and novelists, musicians and dancers asked: How can we sound the true time beat and rhythm of our people living in their special habitat? Schoolmasters began to ask: How can I bring American life as it is actually lived into the school? Thus a new organic mood took hold of the imaginative Americans and a growing body of novel, original, indigenous American utterances began to appear.

The way had been prepared for it several decades before. The guns of the Civil War had barely been silenced when Walt Whitman, in *Democratic Vistas* (1870), stated the positive need of America:

Our fundamental want today in the United States . . . is of a class, and the clear idea of a class, of native authors, literatuses . . . permeating the whole mass of American mentality, taste, belief, breathing into it a new breath of life, giving it decision, affecting politics far more than the popular superficial suffrage . . . radiating, begetting appropriate teachers, schools, manners, and as its grandest result accomplishing . . . a religious and moral character.

For forty years Whitman himself was our first literatuse, the first to reconcile "I" and "We," chanting in his great cumulative volume, *Leaves of Grass*, both *The Song of Myself* and *The Song of These States*. Little wonder that Brooks in his first critical essay, *America's Coming of Age* (1915), called Whitman the precipitant of the American character.

On each of the frontiers of understanding—in architecture, in letters, in philosophy and psychology and on all the social frontiers—one or a few strong original personalities appeared to blaze new trails. Digging deep into the intellectual subsoil of American culture were Charles Peirce and Thorstein Veblen. Peirce was rationalizing the dynamic era of technology in a new active psychology of understanding and founding the pragmatic philosophy. Veblen and the new historians were laying bare hitherto unknown relationships on a half-dozen social frontiers.

In architecture, as early as the 1880s, Louis Henry Sullivan led the fight against both the feudal commercialism of the buccaneering period and the fearsome worship of classic styles. First among our builders, he saw that the Americans had reached the end of nomad wandering and hectic pre-emption and land clearance and were passing into a stage of cultural independence and advancing maturity. He could see that "shelter" from wind and weather was sufficient for nomads and that mere "habitation" met the "comfort" needs of a people in transition. But for the Americans, no longer nomads or frontier settlers but civilized creators of a potentially great culture, these forms, he believed, were not enough. Breaking new ground, he preached that America's designers must endure the creative ordeal and produce *organic architecture* appropriate to American life. A building must be indigenously *American*—from "the soil"—expressing the mood and rhythm of the culture; but especially it must be appropriate to the life to be lived in it. For thirty years, working as both technologist and artist, fusing science and art, reverence and knowledge, Sullivan struggled to find a principle on which organic architecture could be founded, one "so broad as to admit of no exception." And he found it—his original concept of functionality: "Form follows function." Simple, even obvious when stated, but profound and subtle. Forty years ago it was archheresy; today it is a platitude of the rank and file.

When Sullivan died, poverty-stricken, ignored, indeed derided by the big businessmen of his profession, he left not only the succinct statement of this concept in the theory of creative art, but more than a hundred buildings which exemplified its truth. Moreover, he left the seed of the creative spirit well nourished in the nucleus of a great school of modern young architects. Today true Americans, truly creative artists, are not only building America houses appropriate to the new life; they are leading the architects of the entire world in the creation of an organic architecture.

In this no one exceeds Frank Lloyd Wright in leadership. For six years Sullivan's admiring but contentious apprentice, he finally left his *Lieber Meister* after a series of stormy sessions. Wright opened an office of his own and began to build truly original American homes. Not a copy of older houses can be found among them. There are no Greek columns, no Roman or Byzantine domes or Gothic windows. There is no absurd overdecoration. Each house is made to fit its surrounding landscape. Each is made out of American materials and is designed to fit the needs of the life to be lived in it.

Under the influence of Sullivan and Wright a growing company of young American architects have been educated to understand that the new American industrial way of life demands new architecture. These men design every part of the buildings they put up—inside and out. And they and their company make it possible for Americans to boast today of having a truly American architecture.

★   ★   ★

With the new architecture has come in our own day the newest art of all—industrial design; more adequately stated —"design for industrialized ways of living." Man, art and the machine have combined to produce remarkable new materials and new art forms for everyday life—new designs of interiors, new furnishings and utensils for the home, factories, stores, and the like.

Two streams of creative influences have merged to bring it about—American engineering and abstract art. For the first time in modern history—under the financial support of owners of industries and retail stores—industrial engineers, architects, modern painters, sculptors and other artists have come together to design exteriors and interiors, appliances and furniture, show windows and costumes. Outstanding among those working in this field are Norman Bel Geddes, portrait painter and modern theater designer, who opened the first "industrial-design" laboratory as late as 1926, Kem Weber of California, Henry Dreyfuss, Raymond Loewy, Walter D. Teague, George Sakier, Otto Kuebler, Donald Deskey, William Lescaze and Eleanor Lemaire of New York, Harold van Doren of Toledo, Montgomery Ferar of Detroit. The result of the combined technical competence of the engineer, the creative abstract designer, the social psychologist of customs and mores, the manufacturer and the financier, is the economic mass production of useful articles of excellent design. Every physical thing, from ships and trains and automobiles to furnishings and articles of personal adornment around us, is being subjected to the most rigorous principles of creative design.

All materials are used honestly—steel, wood, glass or another material where each is appropriate. The principle of economy is followed: each object is made as simple and clear lined as engineering methods of mass production require. Function dictates form—the form dictated by the use to which the object is to be put. The machine itself is used as a craft tool.

One of the most astounding revelations of the creative spirit in America was the achievement of Isadora Duncan in creating a new conception of the use of the body in the dance. Practically without real antecedents in Europe or in America, she built the foundations for the "modern dance." Paraphrasing Walt Whitman's words "I hear America singing," Isadora imagined "the mighty song that Walt heard, from the surge of the Pacific, over the plains, the voices rising of the vast choral of children, youths, men and women singing democracy." As she said in her essay "I See America Dancing," she had a "vision of America dancing a dance that would be a worthy expression of the song Walt heard when he heard America singing."

So, like Sullivan, Isadora saw that multitudes of Americans must be awakened to the creative task of inventing forms, designs, which were appropriate personal interpretations of living *in* America. She broke completely with the standard imported patterns and to the best of the ability of a creative pioneer portrayed her feeling for herself and her culture. She threw off the cumbersome garments and shoes that the conventional dancers always wore and danced barefoot in loose flowing dresses. She insisted that dancers must not move in mechanical standardized ways, that they must express freely, but well, what they themselves see and feel of life.

Isadora's work aroused theater artists in the whole Western world, and in the past fifteen years her vision and her example have been consummated in the work of a score of young creative American dancers—Martha Graham,

Hanya Holm, Doris Humphrey, Charles Weidman, Tamiris, to name only a few of the most talented ones.

★   ★   ★

During the same years that Louis Sullivan and Isadora Duncan were blazing new trails a growing company of writers were throwing off the bonds of slavish imitation of Europe and were stating American life in story, essay and verse.

Hesitant bourgeois beginnings, though little more than surface photography, were made even in the post-bellum days of the 1870s and 1880s and in the midst of Lowell's and Aldrich's administration of the Genteel Tradition. There were Elizabeth Stuart Phelps's and Sara Orne Jewett's timorous novels about industrial New England. Mark Twain—"the authentic representative" of the American frontier, as Parrington described him—served America well as the outstanding transitional writer. In his *Gilded Age, Roughing It, Life on the Mississippi* and other writings he gave the world the authentic beginnings of a surface social description of our changing American life. Twain did state American life—honestly if not profoundly. So did his contemporaries, Howells and Garland. And there were of course the searches for Utopia described in Edward Bellamy's *Looking Backward* and Henry George's *Progress and Poverty*.

Near the turn of the century original American utterance revealed increased revolt and improvisation. Stephen Crane wrote *Maggie, a Girl of the Streets*. Theodore Dreiser wrote *Sister Carrie, Jennie Gerhardt* and other ground-breaking, realistic American portraits. With *The Jungle* Upton Sinclair began a half century of courageous and brilliant portraiture, via the documentary novel, of actual living and working conditions of industrial life. And there were other skillful and brave documents of photographic realism—Norris and London, for example, much of it lacking organic form but alive, sincere, original. It was all a far cry from the Genteel Tradition of the *Atlantic Monthly* group.

Then, especially after 1910, came new voices. In nearly every section of the country they appeared, writing poems and novels in an original style and taking American communities and American types as their subjects. Recall Carl Sandburg's creation of a new style in his *Chicago Poems* (1916), *Cornhuskers* (1918), *Smoke and Steel* (1920), *Slabs of the Sunburnt West* (1922), *Rootabaga Stories* (1922) and *The American Songbag* (1927). In these he painted thrilling word pictures of the bustling activity of the rising cities of the Middle West. A great poet, yes, but a skillful creative writer of prose as well—witness his recent several-volume biography of Abraham Lincoln.

Life in the small town—*Spoon River Anthology* (1915) —was similarly used as an American subject by the poet, Edgar Lee Masters. There followed more than a score of books, including his own autobiography, *Across Spoon River*, and a biography, *Whitman*, in prose. Robert Frost produced *A Boy's Will*, *North of Boston* and other collections, describing the daily happenings in the life of the common man who struggles to get a living from rocky soil. Among the poems of Edwin Arlington Robinson are several picturing life among the rank-and-file New Englanders. There came Joseph Auslander, singing of the industrial civilization of the great cities, and Stephen Vincent Benét, chanting songs of industrial America. A long list of others can be added—Vachel Lindsay, Robinson Jeffers, Archibald MacLeish, Edna St Vincent Millay, Alfred Kreymborg, Amy Lowell, Adelaide Cropsey—all new American

poets writing about our own American life and inventing
original ways of saying what they feel.

A new type of novel also began to appear, which por-
trayed the everyday lives of Americans in towns and
cities—Sinclair Lewis's *Main Street, Babbitt, Elmer Gantry,
Dodsworth* and others; Sherwood Anderson's *Poor White,
Winesburg, Ohio* and others. Deeply profound character
analyses and epic portraits of American life have appeared
more recently in the work of Waldo Frank, William
Faulkner, Erskine Caldwell, Willa Cather, Thornton
Wilder, John Dos Passos, Ernest Hemingway, William
Saroyan, Eugene O'Neill, Maxwell Anderson, Pearl Buck,
Thomas Wolfe, Robert Nathan and others.

Brilliant and virile creative social criticism appeared—
most of it outside the universities—led especially by the
group to which I have referred several times. A dozen
magazines of criticism were started, and in their pages
young essayists weighed American life honestly, balancing
the good against the questionable features. There were such
organs as Harriet Monroe's *Poetry* (1913), *The Little Review* (1914–29), *The Seven Arts* (1916–17), *The Dial*
(1920–25; 1925–29), and after 1938 Dorothy Norman's
Twice a Year, to name only a few. Among the imaginative
social critics writing their appraisals in these magazines and
in books were Frank, Brooks, Bourne, Herbert Croly,
Mencken, Lippmann, Mumford and others.

The whole body of these—poets, novelists and critics—
has actually laid the firm foundations for an *American*
literature. They have written for America and from the
American point of view.

Changes similar to those in architecture, the dance and
literature have come in the graphic and plastic arts. In

various centers talented men and women began to produce original American art. First in the 1880s and 1890s a few important forerunners stood out in painting. For example, there was Albert Ryder, Thomas Eakins and Winslow Homer. Then came the significant transition group—Robert Henri, the master teacher, who returned from study in Europe, determined to join with other young artists in freeing American painting from the imitative habits of the past. Around him developed an enthusiastic group, "The Eight"—Bellows, Sloan, Glackens, Luks, Lawson, Shinn and Prendergast. Although forced to earn their living as commercial illustrators, in their free moments they developed new ways of painting and used American themes—crowded city slums, children playing in the streets, boxing contests, and so on. The never-ending landscapes of the painters of the preceding half century held little interest for them.

After 1900 other centers of original painting developed. One was in Woodstock, N.Y., to which I have already referred. Another grew up around Alfred Stieglitz, internationally known creative photographer in 1900. His galleries have been a thrilling rendezvous of a profoundly creative group of artists—Marin, O'Keeffe, Dove, to name only three. The very name of his studio, "An American Place," emphasizes his lifelong leadership and interest in encouraging artists to portray what they feel about American life.

It was inevitable that in our times a score of able painters of social protest should develop. Typical of the best are Billings, Blanch, Soyer, Gropper, Biddle, Poor. A large number of competent folk painters made themselves sincere reporters of the social scene; again to name only three —of course the "Midwest Trinity"—Benton, Curry and Wood.

This is, of course, only a sketchy outline of the creative workers in painting. Many others could be named—Arthur Davies, William McFee, Henry Mattson, Alexander Brook, Eugene Speicher, John Carroll, Charles Rosen, Charles Sheeler, Emil Ganso, Yasuo Kunijoshi, Georgina Klitgaard, Doris Lee, Rockwell Kent and others. In sculpture a number of artists should be named—Alfeo Faggi, Jacob Epstein, Paul Manship, Carl Paul Jennewein, Leo Friedlander, Allan Clark, James Earl Frazer, Gaston Lachaise, Trygve Hammer and Ralph Stackpole. Certainly it can be said that in America today there is no lack of painters and sculptors who are showing vigorous styles, rugged strength and power in stating American life in the graphic and plastic arts.

The reader will not forget, of course, the great educational frontier about which so much has been said in this book. Artist-teachers, educational psychologists, technician-designers, parents and interested citizens are now working together to design school programs which will build true understanding of American life and implement our democratic way.

One of the most exciting discoveries of my searches for creativeness in America has been the revelation of the awakening in regional social engineering. Impoverished land is being treated and brought to vigorous life again. Progress is being made toward controlling the destructive floods of our rivers. Regional reconstruction and design are moving forward. This is not merely the work of creative engineers, agricultural experts and scientific students; millions of practical farmers, city people, businessmen and politicians as well are being brought to understand the need for a "regional" outlook and are co-operating in far-reaching programs of design and reconstruction. The work of the T.V.A. and the controversies it has raised have helped enormously in this awakening. So has the government's soil-conservation service under Hugh Bennett and its spectacular achievement in restoring millions of acres of the Dust Bowl to rich grass and grainfields. Programs of action in other parts of the country are likewise rousing the nation to attention. The leaders of the old Southeast are at the job of studying the exhaustion of the land and the people. The "promised land" of the Pacific Northwest builds the "biggest thing on earth"—Grand Coulee Dam—lifting a river up a great gorge to make possible the irrigation of a million acres of soil. In the Southwest garden plots are blooming in the Great American Desert.

So the story of "America Rebuilds" grows longer and more encouraging. Widespread health programs, housing projects, and the like, are making the lives of our people more secure. New and better industrial designs, processes and materials are being invented. America is waking up to rebuild its life. The sustained-yield principle at last?

III   *Is America Moving into the Third Culture Stage of Creative Maturity?*

From the vantage point of the 1940s then we can distinguish the characteristics of the expressive trends of the past fifty years. Certainly during the first thirty or forty years two developments stand out prominently—the widespread rebellion against the grip of alien and ancient forms of statement and the attempt to improvise new ones.

There is no doubt that we have fairly completely divorced ourselves from the parent cultures in every field of expression. The eclectic and imitative romanticism (and realism too!) of the Victorian era seems to be gone, and in every medium we see the American as artist experimenting, improvising—making up new word forms in poetry, essay, novel and playwriting and interpreting the literature in new ways with stage design, play production, lighting, what not, in the theaters; new gestures in the dance; new constructional materials and forms in architecture and industrial design.

Our social engineers are attacking the American problem directly, looking at the people, the continent, the resources, the social world, through creative American eyes. They are trying their best to state the problems of our people as they see them and to work out effective democratic solutions to build the new life.

All through the arts of life in America are revealed sincere, dynamic, original attempts to objectify life as it is being lived in America. That the new work is alive, experimental, native, indigenous, virile, cannot be doubted.

But it is likewise certain that most of it is still marked primarily by improvisation of new forms and concepts. American industrial society is still such a young culture that perhaps we should not expect more of our times than that we have weaned ourselves from the made-to-order sustenance of the mother cultures. We should not demand more, perhaps, than that we can answer *Yes!* to the first criterion of true creativeness, namely: Is the expression sincere, original and unimitative? That alone has been a conspicuous achievement.

But most encouraging of all is the cumulating evidence of expressive personalities now measuring themselves against the other two criteria as well: (1) Do they dig to the roots of the American character, seeing that character in cosmic and universal backgrounds? (2) Is the expression rigorously competent? Does it measure up to the demands of true form, that is, of organic design achieved by conscious effort?

Already a few contemporary creative workers are leading American expression into the third and more profound stage of development—a mature regime of indigenous and original design and competence of statement. That stage will have arrived for America when a large body of our people are truly living creative lives, when the climate of opinion is hospitable to creative effort and appreciation and when our creative workers on the social frontier will have succeeded in producing that abundant life for all which is now potentially possible.

Can Our People Solve the American Problem?

I restate the problem:

To bring forth on this continent that civilization of economic abundance, democratic behavior and integrity of expression which is now potentially available.

Or, putting it as we did at the beginning of this chapter:

To operate a technically efficient and sustained-yield economy and at the same time preserve the democratic principle of sovereign individual personalities.

Can our people do these things?

It is my confident judgment that they can. I am an optimist about the wonders that our people can still work, but an optimist by documentation and not by faith alone. I know our people have all the makings of a great civilization. They have the indispensable scientist-engineers to design it, the capable technicians to operate it, and the artists to guarantee its beauty. The creative ordeal ahead is to organize the makings into the fine way of life that is now possible.

We stand indeed at the crossroads to a new epoch; in various directions lie divers pathways to tomorrow. Some lead to social chaos and the possible destruction of interdependent ways of living. One leads, however, to the era of the Great Society. There is no way to short-circuit the building of this new epoch. There is only the way of education, and its great purpose is

THAT MEN MAY UNDERSTAND

INDEX

Abbott, Allan, 254
Ackerman, F. L., 145
Adult education, a program for, 148–56
Aikin, W. M., 305, 310
American Parents Committee on Education, 73, 243
American problem, 94, 348, 349
American spirit, 53–69
American system of free enterprise, 24, 94, 104
American way of progress, 15, 51, 94, 273
Americanism officers, 76, 79, 138
Angell, Norman, 196
Armstrong, O. K., 17, 39, 49, 72, 73, 86
Authoritarians within the schools, 23
Ayres, Leonard, 183

Bagley, William C., 180, 184, 306
Beard, C. A., 134, 147, 159, 164, 195, 198, 199, 200, 227, 241, 282
Beard, Miriam, 263
Beatty, W. W., 305, 310
Becker, Carl L., 165
Behaviorists, 287
Bellamy, Edward, 175, 263, 342
Billings, Neal, 219
Bingham, W. V., 183
Blaine, Mrs Emmons, 302
Boas, Franz, 282
Bode, Boyd, 277
Bourne, Randolph, 185, 320, 321, 323, 324, 344
Bradner, O., Rugg book burning, 3
Brooks, Van Wyck, 169–70, 185, 193, 320, 321, 323, 344

Buck, Pearl, 344
Buckingham, Burdette R., 36
Burk, Frederick L., 295

Caldwell, O. W., 123, 125, 126, 188, 190, 207
Cannon, Walter B., 311
Cattell, J. McKeen, 199
Censorship and social danger, 246–48
Chase, Stuart, 147
Cheney, Sheldon, 325, 329, 330
Child-centered schools, 111, 191, 300–03
Child Study Association, 311
Childs, John L., 155
Clark, Harold F., 155
Clark, John R., 192, 193, 203, 207, 228
Cobb, Stanwood, 303
Coffman, Lotus D., 180, 184
Commons, John R., 198
Comte, Auguste, 193, 210, 213
Consent, problem of, 224–35; psychology of, 227, 230; the stereotype, 230–35
Control, problem of, 262–73
Controversial issues in the school, 16, 244
Cooke, Flora, 302, 310
Coonley, Mrs Avery, 303
Coss, John, 169, 170, 193
Counts, George S., 87, 155, 162, 163, 164
Courtis, S. A., 181
Crane, Stephen, 175, 342
Creative act, 291, 328–33
Creative Americans, ten groups, 235